Colonial Rule in Africa

Colonial Rule in Africa

Readings from Primary Sources

Edited with an Introduction by
Bruce Fetter

The University of Wisconsin Press

Published 1979

The University of Wisconsin Press
114 North Murray Street
Madison, Wisconsin 53715

The University of Wisconsin Press, Ltd.
1 Gower Street
London WC1E 6HA, England

First printing

Printed in the United States of America

For LC CIP information see the colophon

ISBN 0-299-07780-2 cloth, 0-299-07784-5 paper

Acknowledgment is made for permission to quote from the following previously
published material.

Nnamdi Azikiwe, *Zik*, Cambridge University Press.
Simone de Beauvoir and Gisèle Halimi, *Djamila Boupacha*, with the permission of
Macmillan Publishing Co., Inc., André Deutsch Ltd., and Weidenfeld and
Nicolson © André Deutsch Limited 1962.
Raymond Betts, ed., *The "Scramble" for Africa*, D. C. Heath and Co.
R. L. Buell, *The Native Problem in Africa*, Cass & Co., 1928, 1965.
Theodore C. Caldwell, ed., *The Anglo-Boer War: Why Was It Fought? Who Was
Responsible?* D. C. Heath and Co.
Ronald H. Chilcote, ed. and trans., *Emerging Nationalism in Portuguese Africa:
Documents*, with the permission of the publishers, Hoover Institution Press,
copyright © 1972 by the Board of Trustees of the Leland Stanford Junior Uni-
versity.
Michael K. Clark, *Algeria in Turmoil*, copyright © 1959 by Frederick A. Praeger,
Inc., reprinted by permission of Holt, Rinehart and Winston.
Robert O. Collins, ed., *African History: Text and Readings*, Random House, Inc.

Hans W. Debrunner, *A Church between Colonial Powers*, World Council of Churches, Geneva, for the Lutterworth Press.

Khayr al-Din al-Tunisi, *The Surest Path: The Political Treatise of a Nineteenth-Century Muslim Statesman*, trans. by Leon Carl Brown from *The Surest Path to Knowledge concerning the Condition of Countries*, Harvard University Press, 1967.

Arthur Conan Doyle, *The Crime of the Congo*, Hutchinson Publishing Group Limited.

Frantz Fanon, *The Wretched of the Earth*, copyright © 1963 by *Présence Africaine*, reprinted by permission of Grove Press, Inc., and MacGibbon & Kee Ltd/ Granada Publishing Ltd.

'Allal al-Fasi, *The Independence Movements in Arab North Africa*, American Council of Learned Societies, 1954, Octagon Books, 1970.

Bruce Fetter, "Central Africa, 1914: German Schemes and British Designs," *Bulletin des Séances*, Académie royale des Sciences d'Outre-Mer.

R. Mugo Gatheru, *Child of Two Worlds: A Kikuyu's Story*, copyright © 1964 by R. Mugo Gatheru, reprinted by permission of Holt, Rinehart and Winston.

G. P. Gooch and H. W. V. Temperley, eds., *British Documents on the Origins of the War*, Vol. 10, H. M. Stationery Office.

David C. Gordon, *The Passing of French Algeria* © Oxford University Press 1966, by permission of the Oxford University Press.

Geoffrey Gorer, *Africa Dances: A Book about West African Negroes*, with the permission of W. W. Norton & Company, Inc., copyright © 1962 by Geoffrey Gorer, copyright 1935, 1949 by John Lehmann, Ltd.

William K. Hancock and Jean van der Poel, eds., *Selections from the Smuts Papers*, Vol. 1, Cambridge University Press.

John D. Hargreaves, ed., *France and West Africa*, by permission of Macmillan, London and Basingstoke, and St. Martin's Press, Inc.

Lyndon Harries, ed. and trans., *Swahili Prose Texts: A Selection from the Material Collected by Carl Velten from 1893 to 1896* © Oxford University Press 1965, by permission of the Oxford University Press.

Cecil Headlam, ed., *The Milner Papers*, Vol. 1, *South Africa, 1897-1899*, Cassell Ltd., 1931.

Albert Hourani, *Arabic Thought in the Liberal Age, 1798-1939*, Royal Institute of International Affairs.

J. C. Hurewitz, *Diplomacy in the Near and Middle East*, Vol. 2, D. Van Nostrand Company.

Josiah Mwangi Kariuki, *'Mau Mau' Detainee*, Oxford University Press, Eastern Africa.

D. W. Krüger, *South African Parties and Policies, 1910-1960: A Select Source Book*, published by Bowes & Bowes.

Robert G. Landen, *The Emergence of the Modern Middle East*, New York, D. Van Nostrand Company, 1970, by permission.

Norman Leys, *Kenya*, by permission of the author's literary estate and Hogarth Press Ltd.

F. D. Lugard, *The Dual Mandate in British Tropical Africa*, by permission of William Blackwood & Sons Ltd.

F. W. Maitland, *The Constitutional History of England*, ed. H. A. L. Fisher, Cambridge University Press.

P. G. Mockerie, *An African Speaks for His People*, Hogarth Press Ltd.

Anthony Nutting, *Nasser*, Constable Publishers.

T. O. Ranger, *The African Voice in Southern Rhodesia*, Northwestern University Press, Evanston, Ill., 1970, and Heinemann Educational Books Ltd.

Wulf Sachs, *Black Anger: The Mind of an African Revealed by Psychoanalysis*, Garnstone Press.

Martin Schlunk, "Das Schulwesen in den deutschen Schutzgebieten," in *Abhandlungen des Hamburgischen Kolonialinstituts*, Vol. 14, Firma Friedrichsen & Co., trans. by Wallace Morgan in *Traditions of African Education*, ed. D. G. Scanlon, Teachers College Press.

Léopold Sédar Senghor, "To the Senegalese Sharpshooters, Dead for France," trans. by Marie Collins, Charles Scribner's Sons.

Charles Wendell, *The Evolution of the Egyptian National Image*, University of California Press © 1972 by The Regents of the University of California.

Acknowledgment is also made for permission to quote from the following unpublished material.

F. L. Brown, "Legal proceedings including summaries of evidence in the Mwanaleza case, 1925," Rhodes House, Oxford University MSS Afr. S. 1066.

Njangu Canda-ciri, "La résistance Shi à la pénétration européenne (1900–1920)," M.A. thesis, National University of Zaire, 1973.

Yogolelo Tambwe ya Kasima, "Mission de recrutement des travailleurs de l'U.M.H.K. a Kivu-Maniema (1926–1928)," M.A. thesis, National University of Zaire, 1973.

Excerpts appear in the form given in the sources cited, with the following exceptions: American style for quotation marks has been used, minor spelling errors have been corrected, and footnotes have been renumbered as needed or, when not germane to the text, omitted.

To my students at Milwaukee and Lubumbashi

Acknowledgments

My thanks go to a number of individuals and institutions that helped me in the course of selecting documents and writing commentary. Most important, I am indebted to the library of the University of Wisconsin–Milwaukee, which provided almost all of the sources included in this volume. The Cartography Laboratory of the University of Wisconsin–Milwaukee drew all the maps.

The following individuals provided encouragement and suggestions for my work: David Healy, Abbas Hamdani, David Buck, and James Cronin of the University of Wisconsin–Milwaukee; David Gardinier of Marquette University; Jan Vansina and Gerald Noeske of the University of Wisconsin–Madison; John Cell of Duke University; and Peter Boyle of the University of Nottingham. The biases are all my own.

Contents

UNIT THREE
Toward Independence 163

Colonial Rule
in Africa

Africa Today

FOR TWENTY MILLION PEOPLE IN SOUTHERN AFRICA, COLONIAL RULE IS A HARSH reality, but for the rest of us, it is rapidly fading from memory. Injustice has by no means disappeared, but its forms have changed. No longer do foreigners who constitute a small minority of the population claim the right to rule the majority. Oppression, where it still exists, has passed into the hands of individuals who share a common language and culture with their subjects.

Colonialism is thus a disease that has largely run its course, a case history from oppressions past. But its defeat does not mean that it is no longer worthy of examination. On the contrary, by studying the mechanisms of diseases past, we can get a better idea of how to deal with those still raging out of control.

This collection of readings, then, is a case history of the imposition, implementation, and destruction of colonial rule in Africa. It is the first anthology to deal with both European rulers and their African subjects. It is continental in scope, bringing together the experience of such groups as Muslims in the north and Afrikaners in the south, who were more cosmopolitan, and animists in the center, who had not known of the outside world until they were conquered.

These primary sources cover the period from 1830 to 1962, a selection that some might well contest. Indeed, Europeans had conquered territory at the two ends of the continent many years earlier, and they continue to hold land in the south until the present day. To a certain extent this choice of time frame is arbitrary, dependent on the need to find a time period suited to a two-semester survey in African history. The initial and terminal dates nevertheless possess a rationality of their own. Before the conquest of Algeria, European holdings in Africa were by and large limited to the coast: Portuguese enclaves, slave-trading factories, and provisioning posts and their hinterlands. The French annexation of Algeria represented the first European claim to densely populated African lands.

Similarly, the French departure from Algeria in 1962 represented the end of classical colonialism, marking the last effort of a foreign elite to hold onto an African territory. Europeans left later in other colonies, Northern Rhodesia (Zambia), for example, but the decisions to leave had already been made when the French evacuated their last substantial settlement on the continent. Except for the Portuguese territories, the Europeans who re-

Introduction
and
Historical Summary

mained in power were locally based, having little regard for the lands of their ancestors. Thus, 1962 marked a watershed as important as 1830.

The history of colonial Africa has, of course, been the subject of a number of useful books by talented scholars. This collection differs from its predecessors because of its exclusive concern for primary sources. Rather than relying on testimony of contemporary experts, I have let the actors speak for themselves.

There are two advantages to this approach. First of all, the material is more dramatic when left in the words of the original participants. Instead of presenting the opinions of a single researcher or even a school of thought, the groups engaged in the colonial experience express themselves directly. In this way colonial lawmakers and administrators can be heard side by side with the people whose lives they controlled.

Second, by becoming acquainted with a wide variety of sources from the period, the reader is encouraged to weigh various testimonies concerning the process of colonization. The book becomes an exercise in historical criticism in which the reader is constantly confronted with the vital question so seldom posed directly—exactly how much of this can I believe? This is more than just a pedagogical device; it presents the reader with the historian's reality of conflicting versions of the truth.

The events described in the sources will be debated by historians for many years to come. Each will approach the material from a personal perspective. Already historians of colonial Africa are divided into a number of factions— Marxists, nationalists, liberals—and we can expect new schools to emerge in the future as different individuals acquire new insights about the region and the time period.

Undoubtedly other anthologies of source materials will also appear as the raw material of scholarship becomes available to the scholarly community. These new collections will reflect the biases of their authors in the same way that this anthology reflects my own. They may, in fact, seek to correct imbalances in the current presentation.

To many the present anthology may appear to overemphasize the European viewpoint. Indeed, more than half of the authors are Europeans rather than Africans, and one may well ask why a source book on the history of colonial Africa should contain so many passages written by foreigners. That is my central point: I firmly believe that most of the major events in the colonization of Africa were determined by the colonizers. This explains why Unit One in particular contains so many European authors. As time went on, Africans began to master their situation sufficiently to leave literary comments on it. Nonetheless, even after the Second World War, Europeans continued to make most of the decisions affecting the fundamental direction of African political development. Critics may well argue that the only evidence worth hearing is that of African resistance to European rule, but such a bias would exclude a substantial proportion of the existing primary source material. It would, moreover, make it impossible to determine what Europeans were trying to do in Africa and how they set about doing it.

My interest in the modalities of European power has led to a second bias in the selection of documents. The collection contains what to the uninitiated reader might seem an inordinate number of legal documents: treaties, laws, trial records. This selection is intentional. I believe that European law played a role which has been seriously underestimated in the colonization process. In order for readers to understand this role, they must have some notion of what the legal documents contained.

In addition to a general discussion of the criteria used to select the items included in the collection as a whole, most readers will need information concerning the individual documents. This is given in a variety of ways. Each document is identified according to its source and date of publication. The area referred to in each document is indicated on an outline map. And each selection is preceded by an introductory context, which describes the author or the historical context of the original document.

The collection is divided into three major parts. Unit One deals with the partition of Africa and the imposition of European rule on the continent. Unit Two covers what might be called the High Colonial Period of African history, the years between the two world wars. Unit Three treats the period between the Second World War and 1962, during which most African states obtained their independence.

At this point readers who are already familiar with the outlines of African colonial history may wish to proceed directly to the readings. For those who are less well grounded in the period, the following summary may be helpful in understanding its chronology and major trends.

European claims to Africa antedate the partition of the continent by over three hundred years. The oldest claims were based on tiny outposts on the coast, a form of settlement abandoned more often than not after a few years' occupation. Nonetheless, those outposts that did survive established the legal base for later claims to the interior. In the matter of ownership of African territory, as in so many other colonial questions, the law was in advance of the reality. Europeans, moreover, frequently claimed more land than they governed.

The earliest Europeans to assert title to black African territory were the Portuguese, who first explored the Atlantic Coast in the fifteenth century. Their first permanent settlements date from the sixteenth century, when they occupied the towns of Mozambique on the Indian Ocean and Luanda on the Atlantic. During the same period they settled coastal islands and established trading posts in the valleys of the Kwanza and Zambezi rivers. The towns, with their hinterlands, became the nuclei of the colonies of Angola and Mozambique.

From these bases the Portuguese established a profitable slave trade which attracted other Europeans to the African coast. During the seventeenth century the most successful European newcomers were the Dutch, the English, and the French. Between 1659 and 1677 the French established the towns of Saint Louis and Gorée, the nucleus of modern Senegal, and the British laid the foundations of the colony of Gambia. The Dutch, too, participated in the slave trade, but built their most lasting settlement, Cape Town, for another purpose: as a provisioning station on the sea route between Holland and the East Indies. From Cape Town settlers moved to the interior of South Africa.

The slave trade attracted Europeans to Africa in ever-increasing numbers during the eighteenth century, but they left no settlements from which colonies developed. Instead of trying to govern territory, they were content to buy slaves from Africans and to depart as quickly as possible to escape devastating mortality from tropical diseases.

The next colonies were intended for Africans rather than Europeans. In the late eighteenth century Europeans began to look on tropical Africa as a possible home for freed slaves. The most successful of these black colonies was Sierra Leone, settled under British asupices in 1787. Americans established Liberia for the same purpose in 1821, and the French followed suit at Gabon in 1843. None of these colonies extended more than a few miles beyond the coast.

With mid-nineteenth-century improvements in medicine that permitted Europeans to survive in tropical climates, the British and French founded a series of new colonies. During the 1840s the French established beachheads in what is today Guinea, the Ivory Coast, Benin, and the Malagasy Republic. Between 1854 and 1865 they also moved into the interior of West Africa under the leadership of General Louis Faidherbe, who extended French rule up the Senegal River. The British lagged somewhat behind the French in the establishment of colonial claims, but they too built new bases on the coast and moved inland. Their most important new coastal base was the town of Lagos, added to the empire in 1851, which became the keystone for their later conquest of Nigeria. Their most important inland domain was the Gold Coast Colony (southern Ghana), which they annexed in 1874.

Far more extensive than these relatively small annexations in West Africa were the European settlements in the temperate areas of northern and southern Africa. The region of deepest penetration was South Africa, which the British took from the Dutch in 1806. In the next three-quarters of a century, the British annexed the coastal areas of today's Cape Province and the province of Natal. In addition the Afrikaners, descendants of earlier Dutch and Huguenot settlers, established independent states in today's provinces of the Transvaal and the Orange Free State.

The conquest of North Africa began in 1830 with the French invasion of the former Turkish colony of Algeria. Beginning on the coastal plain, the Europeans pushed inland, crushing Algerian opponents in the mountains and on the northern edge of the Sahara. By 1879 the populated regions of Algeria had fallen under colonial rule.

In 1880, then, Europeans were poised for the conquest of Africa. They had penetrated the interior of Algeria and South Africa and had dotted the coast with a cluster of settlements that would serve as beachheads for later invasion. Possessing superior armaments, they were overwhelmingly stronger than any existing African state. Even the Ottoman Empire, which had ruled most of North Africa for 350 years, proved no match for them and yielded to each successive territorial demand.

Indeed, what has been called the "scramble for Africa" began with the occupation of the two richest territories in the Ottoman Empire, Egypt and Tunisia. The French, having obtained the consent of other European powers, declared a protectorate over Tunisia in 1881, the terms of which were tightened two years later. In 1882 the British invaded Egypt. From there the scramble spread to the mouth of the Congo River, where the French and the agents of King Leopold II of Belgium competed for control of the Congo Basin. The Germans entered the competition in 1884, establishing claims to coastal regions of South West Africa (Namibia), Togo, the Cameroons, and German East Africa (Tanzania).

By 1884 competition for the unclaimed territories of Africa had become so intense that the rulers of the colonizing nations concluded that it was necessary to regulate the process of annexation by international agreement. Germany's chancellor, Otto von Bismarck, invited the major Western powers to Berlin for a conference which met during the winter of 1884–85. As a result of their deliberations, the representatives of states deemed capable of colonization by the great powers of Europe agreed in 1885 to a legal document specifying rules for the colonization of the African coast. Five years later representatives of most of these same states met in Brussels and drew up a second agreement relating to the colonization of the interior. On the basis of these legal documents European states laid claim before the end of the century to all of sub-Saharan Africa.

The great African kingdoms faced a desperate situation. Some resisted European invasions outright and were vanquished by a single expedition. This was the fate of the centuries-old coastal kingdoms such as Dahomey, which fell to the French in 1892, and Benin, which the British sacked in 1897. Some kingdoms fought, sued for peace, then fought again until they were finally conquered. The Ashanti, for example, defeated European forces early in the century but were beaten in 1874, 1896, and again in 1901; and the Zulu, who had been the scourge of southern Africa, lost to the British in 1879 and again in 1906.

The inevitable conquest was delayed by those states that abandoned fixed combat in favor of guerrilla warfare. This tactic had been pioneered by the Algerian hero Abd el-Kadr, who resisted the French from 1831 until 1847. Later in the century Samory Touré was able to maintain a Muslim state in the West African savanna from 1884 until 1898, and the Sudanese adventurer Rabeh kept an army together from 1879 until 1900. Similarly, Kasongo Niembo of the Luba Katanga and the Mwami Nnabushi Kabare Rutaganda of the Shi people led resistance to the Belgians until the First World War. The Sanusiyya in southern Libya held out against their Italian colonizers from 1911 until 1932. The outcome in all of these cases was, nevertheless, the same: the Europeans prevailed and destroyed the old kingdoms.

Other African states fared somewhat better by avoiding direct military confrontation with the Europeans. This involved negotiating the terms under which the kingdom was to be colonized. Some rulers managed to get their domains incorporated as a whole into colonial systems. By this strategy Morocco, Tunisia, Lesotho, Swaziland, Rwanda, and Burundi have survived to the present day. Other monarchs lost their independence but managed to obtain special status within larger colonies, a strategy followed with varying degrees of success by the kabaka of Buganda in Uganda, Hausa emirs in northern Nigeria, and the Lozi king in Zambia.

At the outbreak of the First World War only two African states remained independent: Liberia, which enjoyed a certain privileged status because of the American origin of its black settlers, and the Christian kingdom of Ethiopia, whose soldiers had managed to withstand an Italian invasion in 1896. Even Ethiopia eventually fell to a renewed Italian invasion in 1935.

European expansionists, their appetites whetted by the partition, remained dissatisfied. Even before the last boundaries had been drawn, representatives of the larger European powers began to negotiate over how they might arrogate the colonies claimed by smaller powers. This process began in 1898 when the Germans and the British agreed on a tentative partition of Portuguese colonies in the event that the Portuguese should prove unable to govern them. In 1899 the British provoked a war with the Afrikaner republics, whose defeat and annexation further augmented British power in southern Africa. Beginning in 1904 humanitarians from Britain, France, and Germany launched a campaign of protest against abuses committed in King Leopold's Congo Free State. The concerted action of these colonial powers might have led to a dismemberment of the territory if the Belgian government had not, in 1908, assumed responsibility for administration of the state. The attacks of large colonizers against smaller ones continued in 1913 with a second Anglo-German agreement on the tentative partition of the Portuguese colonies.

The rivalry among colonizing powers reached its peak during the First World War, when the combat in Europe spread to Africa. The Allies invaded the four German colonies and divided the spoils at the peace conference in 1919. The German colonies officially took the status of League of Nations mandates; thereafter European officials recognized the futility of continued rivalry and subsequently refrained from serious efforts to steal their neighbors' colonies.

Once colonies had been acquired, the problem of administration became paramount. All of the colonizing powers were subject to a similar constraint, which considerably restricted their freedom of action. European governments could not spend money on colonial possessions without parliamentary appropriations, and parliamentarians who voted excessive expenditures risked the displeasure of the taxpayer.

As a result of this popular reluctance to finance colonial expansion, European administrators devised a series of schemes for annexing territory without immediately passing on the costs to metropolitan taxpayers. The earliest method was to write off the conquest of new colonies against the budgets of older ones. Thus the cost of conquering independent black kingdoms in South Africa was borne by the budgets of the British colonies of Natal and the Cape of Good Hope. The governments of Senegal and Dahomey (Benin) paid for at least part of the colonization of French West Africa, and Indian taxpayers subsidized the conquest of Kenya, Uganda, Nyasaland (Malawi), and the Sudan.

Another method developed in the 1880s was the attribution of governmental activities to private companies financed by metropolitan investors. The government of African colonies proved unprofitable and the companies soon gave up their political functions, but chartered companies played a vital role in the initial partition process: the Germans used chartered companies to rule South West Africa (1885-89) and German East Africa (1886-91). King Leopold and the Belgians used a similar device in Katanga (1891-1910), as did the British in Nigeria (1886-99), Kenya (1888-95) and the Rhodesias (1889-1924). Once initial claims had been made, the metropolitan governments were able to take over administration at lower cost and with little publicity.

The most common agency for coordinating colonial activities was the colonial ministry, headed by a member of the metropolitan cabinet and staffed by a metropolitan bureaucracy. Colonial ministries, however, were established rather late in the colonization process. In the early days, governments delegated colonial affairs to agencies created primarily for other purposes. The British Colonial Office was attached to the War Office when it was created in 1801 and was granted full cabinet status only in 1854. Other colonial ministries were created *after* European states had established their claims to African territory. The French were first, in 1894, followed by the Germans in 1906, the Belgians in 1908, and the Portuguese in 1911.

The desire to rationalize colonial administration at home was closely related to the call to reduce colonial expenditures overseas. French colonial expenses reached their peak in 1902, two years after the passage of a law requiring colonies to live within their means. In order to reduce expenditures, officials at the various ministries set about tightening up colonial administration. After the turn of the century, metropolitan officials consolidated a number of territories into federations on the grounds of efficiency and cost. The French were the best-known practitioners of this policy, creating a West African Federation in 1902 and one for Equatorial Africa in 1910. The British applied the policy by consolidating three territories into Nigeria (1906, 1914) and combining Northeastern and Northwestern Rhodesia (1911) into what would become Zambia.

Nonetheless, there were limits to the amounts that could be saved through administrative rationalization. The real aim of European administrators was to raise revenues in the colonies in order to eliminate metropolitan subsidies. This could be done only by imposing taxes on the local African populations. In those areas where Africans had already developed a substantial trade with the outside world, the colonizers raised money through tariffs on African consumer goods. This increased the cost of merchandise but did not substantially affect the lives of African consumers. Elsewhere the governments could not tap this source of revenue. In the Congo Basin, for example, the Berlin Agreement of 1885 restricted the tariffs which European powers could impose. Many Africans there, moreover, were not consumers of foreign goods.

Insufficient revenues forced certain regimes to adopt the hut tax, a measure which had been developed in South Africa in the 1840s. Under it able-bodied men were expected to pay a tax, levied in European money, on each nuclear family. Given the absence of export markets for African goods, the only way Africans could earn their tax money was by working for a European. Taxable Africans were therefore obliged to walk long distances in order to find the available jobs.

This involuntary labor migration caused great hardship and frequently precipitated revolts when the hut taxes were imposed. To this cause can be attributed two revolts in German East Africa (Tanzania), the Abushire revolt of 1886-87 and the Maji Maji rebellion of 1905-6; the Hut Tax War of 1898 in Sierra Leone; the Southern Rhodesian uprisings of 1896-97; and, to a certain extent, John Chilembwe's revolt in Nyasaland (Malawi) in 1915. As in the case of the early resistance to European conquest, these rebellions were put down by the European colonial powers.

Thousands of Africans thus accustomed themselves to the necessity of long absences from home in order to pay their colonial taxes. Many of these involuntary workers found jobs in the mines of Central and South Africa, where owners and managers were eager to obtain a supply of cheap labor. Africans constituted an essential element in a new mineral zone which extended from the diamond mines of Kimberley in South Africa, founded in 1869, to the gold mines of the Witwatersrand in South Africa (1886), and to the copper mines of the Belgian Congo (1911).

In these regions, the physical and social landscape was transformed by the mines. New cities grew up to house the mining industry and those dependent on it. People came from miles around to work in the mines. Very quickly, the southern African mineral zone became the most highly developed part of Africa from an economic viewpoint.

Elsewhere development was slower, following a less industrialized course. In North Africa and in parts of South Africa the major exports were farm crops grown by settlers. Even in these areas, of course, much of the labor essential for production came from the local African population. In many tropical portions of the continent Africans themselves were the major producers and sellers. In West Africa, African farmers directly controlled the production of such crops as peanuts, palm oil, and cacao. In these areas, however, European middlemen maintained a monopoly of the final export and so obtained a considerable portion of the profits.

In summary, Africans received certain economic benefits from the export industries developed at the onset of colonial rule, but much of the profit was siphoned off by European entrepreneurs and governments. Once taxes were paid, Africans were free to spend their remaining funds on consumer goods, but the cost to them cannot be measured exclusively in terms of money. In all too many cases, the productive capacity of rural African agriculture had been lowered by the forced conversion to export crops and the removal of able-bodied men from the rural work force. The harsh reality was that many Africans ate less as a result of European conquest.

Although the Europeans exploited their African subjects economically, they did provide certain services in return. Their governments put an end to the local wars which had ravaged the continent in precolonial times. New modes of transportation, notably the steamboat and the railroad, improved communications within the new colonies and between them and the outside world.

The most notable services were provided by European Protestant and Catholic missionaries. These individuals were attracted to the continent not by the prospects of conquest or profit but to win souls. This notion has a hollow ring to it for the postcolonial reader, who can scarcely envision devotion to such an otherworldly activity. Nonetheless, thousands of Europeans and Americans were attracted to it, and their efforts resulted in considerable benefits for Africans. One might even say that their greatest contributions were unintentional, because they discovered that they could only reach the souls of colonized Africans if they took care of their bodies and their minds.

To that end the missionaries constructed schools and hospitals which extended the lives of Africans and brought them into contact with European learning and technology. Before the First World War these facilities were often rudimentary, but missionaries were responsible for establishing the first good postprimary schools in Africa: Lovedale in South Africa (1820), Fourah Bay College in Sierra Leone (1824), Ngazobil in Senegal (1847), the Overtoun Institution (Livingstonia) in Malawi (1897), Gordon College in the Sudan (1903); and the Roman Catholic seminaries Saint Jean in Gabon (1856), Mayumba in the French Congo (1879), and Baudouinville in the Belgian Congo (Zaire, 1899). After the First World War the graduates of these educational institutions would constitute the nucleus of a colonial elite.

The High Colonial Period (1919-39), when compared with the scramble which preceded it and the decolonization which followed, was a time of political stability. Except for the Ethiopian monarchy, conquered by the Italians in 1935, no regimes fell and no territories changed hands. The League of Nations played a minimal role in its supervision of the former German colonies. In the region south of the Sahara, moreover, no black Africans possessed the political power or the organizational skills necessary to pose a serious challenge to European rule.

The political changes which took place between the two world wars were implemented either for the administrative convenience of the colonial bureaucracy or to satisfy various white settler groups. In the former category fall the replacement of the British South Africa Company by colonial regimes in Northern Rhodesia (Zambia) and Southern Rhodesia (Zimbabwe) in 1924, the detachment of Chad from Ubangi-Shari (Central African Empire) in 1920, and the temporary dissolution of Upper Volta (Voltaic Republic) during 1932–47. Settlers fought for powers similar to those obtained by Europeans in Algeria and by white South Africans, but did not always prevail. Thus, although settlers obtained virtual control of the Southern Rhodesian administration in 1924, the British government, after a protracted battle (1925–31), refused similar rights to the Kenya settlers.

Despite this political stability at the colonial level, administrators were constantly tinkering with local administration in order to tighten their governments' hold on the African population. For the British, one of the major efforts was to co-opt African chiefs into subordinate positions in the colonial hierarchy through the policy of Indirect Rule. Although justified to the outside world as a means of teaching Africans modern forms of government, Indirect Rule actually excluded educated Africans from practical politics. A more likely justification for Indirect Rule was its cheapness, since it was financed primarily by local taxes rather than allocation from central colonial treasuries. The doctrine became dogma among the British administrators trained between the wars and was adopted in a modified form by the Belgians between 1933 and 1940.

Needless to say, the colonizers never relinquished their political powers. Their reforms were for the most part fine-tuning to make their administrations more efficient. Many colonial governments created provinces as an intermediate level of government, just below that of the colony. The Belgians established their first set of provinces in the Congo in 1914 (modified in 1933), and the British initiated the same process in Nyasaland (1921) and Northern Rhodesia (1929). Several colonizers also designated new colonial capitals: Leopoldville (1926), now Kinshasa, in the Belgian Congo, Abidjan (1934) in the Ivory Coast, and Lusaka (1935) in Northern Rhodesia. In recognition of increased urbanization, colonizers granted limited representation to Africans in local affairs, sometimes creating special councils for Africans like that created for Elisabethville (Lubumbashi) in 1931.

Any discernible drift toward liberalization came to a grinding halt with the worldwide depression of the 1930s. From 1931 on, government receipts fell precipitously and the canons of administrative wisdom dictated immediate cutbacks in expenditures. This was no time for innovation; the only changes in government were retrenchments. Colonial budgets shrank considerably in the years 1931 to 1933, and services were reduced to the barest essentials. Although receipts rose again in the mid-thirties, frightened administrators remained conservative. The Northern Rhodesian government channeled revenues from the new copper industry into reserve accounts rather than spend them on social welfare. In French territories, administrators openly resisted the political reforms for Algeria and the economic reforms for black Africa proposed by the Popular Front government of 1936-38. No one wanted to rock the boat.

Although economic conditions affected colonial policy during the interwar period, the two phenomena were not always in phase. Political structures remained more or less stable in this period of European hegemony, but economic conditions were tied to the boom-bust cycle. Volatile markets for African products caused enormous fluctuations in the money Africans earned and the cost of consumer goods. After a brief postwar recession, prices for African goods and labor rose until about 1927, then declined until the mid-thirties. The prices of consumer goods remained high until 1931, after which they fell sharply until 1935. This disjuncture between the price of African exports and the cost of African imports created great problems for African workers in agriculture and in industry. Between 1927 and 1931, for example, Africans increased the production of export products in order to offset higher prices for consumer goods, doubling their efforts in order to buy the same amount. Between 1931 and 1935, the situation grew even worse—European goods became relatively cheaper, but there was little demand for Africa labor or goods. Africans could take little advantage of the bargains in the marketplace. Their main concern was to raise the money to pay the taxes which their colonial governments were still demanding.

The one long-term capital investment available to Africans was education. In black Africa, schools were still a scarce resource, controlled primarily by Christian missions, but the number and quality of educational institutions increased substantially after the First World War. Colonial administrations, recognizing that public education would drain their limited resources, avoided running schools everywhere but in French West Africa. In other regions officials asked various mission groups to take responsibility for education within their respective fields of evangelization. In exchange for small subsidies and uniform standards of performance, the missions received educational monopolies. Typical of these agreements were the de Jonghe Accords of 1925-26, reached between the Belgian colonial ministry and various Roman Catholic orders.

In exchange for these subsidies, the missionaries provided educational systems which usually served children from kindergarten to junior high school. Since the missionaries were interested primarily in the souls of their charges, they invested most of their effort and resources in younger children in an effort to provide everyone with a taste for Christianity and a smattering of literacy. Missionary systems therefore became pyramidal in population structure, containing fewer places for each succeeding grade. This meant that only the keenest of the African students could reach the top of the educational hierarchy.

Parents who were aware of the power of the colonizers were prepared to make enormous sacrifices in order for their children to rise in the educational system. Beyond primary school, most institutions were boarding schools, so children were separated from their families for all but a few weeks a year.

Schools frequently charged fees, which, though nominal in European terms, absorbed a large proportion of the family's available income. Nonetheless there were compensations at the end of the training period. Graduates of the mission schools could command the best jobs available to Africans—and the best salaries.

By the 1920s secondary schools were beginning to appear all over Africa. Muslims in North Africa, of course, had a centuries-long tradition of literacy and so adapted well to European-style facilities. In addition to the ancient Islamic universities, new high schools and universities developed in Egypt and the Maghreb. Since many officials objected to a mission-dominated educational network in West Africa, where a substantial part of the population was also Muslim, many of the best schools were run by the colonial governments. These included the Ecole Willem Ponty (1908) in Senegal and Achimota College (1926) in the Gold Coast (Ghana). South of the rain forest, the best schools were to be found in South Africa. Not only did many of the missionary organizations provide secondary schools, but the government financed an African university, Fort Hare (1916). Opportunities were not nearly so good in East and Central Africa, but a good secondary education was available at Makerere College, established in Uganda in 1924. In French-speaking countires, the best education available to Africans could be found in seminaries, which trained Africans for the priesthood. In the Belgian Congo, for example, the first major seminary was opened at Baudouinville in 1911 and the first priest was ordained six years later.

The graduates of these most advanced educational institutions found themselves in an uncomfortable position. Selected for their intelligence, they were nonetheless subordinated to the most humble whites in their work. Their salaries, too, were frequently a mere fraction of that of Europeans performing the same tasks. Thanks to their education, which moved them closer to their white masters, they frquently felt alienated from the mass of Africans. Thus they were rejected by the colonizers but felt little kinship to the majority of Africans from whose sort they had hoped to escape through education.

The marginal situation of educated Africans gave rise to a series of associations intended to improve African welfare. These associations usually appealed to a limited spectrum of Africans defined by their education. At the top were the Pan-African congresses held in Europe after the First World War, which attracted those few Africans who had been able to attend a European secondary school or university. In Africa itself, the most intellectual associations were the Native Welfare societies, national congresses, and trade unions, which expressed grievances of the elite to the colonial governments. As in other organizations, South African blacks led the way, founding the South African Native National Congress in 1912 and the Industrial and Commercial Union of Africa in 1919.

Less educated Africans who had suffered from colonization also joined associations based on a Western model. The most important vehicles for mass protest in the interwar period were religious in character—breakaway churches which rejected the authority of the missionaries, and African syn-cretistic cults which claimed to share the white man's power through in-corporating certain elements of his religion. The most spectacular of these sects were the offshoots of Jehovah's Witnesses, independent but know col-lectively as Watch Tower. From 1908 until the present, various forms of Watch Tower have attracted followings in much of South, Central, and East Africa. Although detested by European missionaries and administrators, these religious movements did not constitute a serious threat to colonial rule. The colonizers ran the governments and possessed weapons superior to those available to potential rebels.

At either end of the continent, however, educated Muslims and Afrikaners made political demands that were much harder to resist. Their leaders, familiar with the corpus of European constitutional law, began to demand the rights of nationhood then monopolized by the dominant nation-states of the world. Their argument was that local electoral majorities, par-ticularly when led by educated whites, had the right to run their own coun-tries. Backed by popular demonstrations and success at the polls, groups which could argue that they represented white majorities made substantial progress toward independence in the interwar period. Educated Egyptians, led by Sa'd Zaghlul and his Wafd party, succeeded in getting the British in 1923 to end their protectorate over Egypt. Between 1936 and 1939 the Egyptians even obtained the temporary removal of British troops from their country. Educated Afrikaners made similar progress. Their secret organiza-tion, the Broederbond, founded in 1918, became a leading political force in the late 1930s and took a leading role in the Nationalist party, which has ruled South Africa since 1948. In Tunisia the educated elite was frustrated in the short run but was ultimately successful. Beginning in 1934 a mass political party, the Neo-Destour, sought to promote Tunisian autonomy, a goal that was not achieved until 1956.

These "white" organizations had an influence beyond their own countries. Their success demonstrated to black Africans that political movements against the colonial regime could succeed. Their example was to provide an inspiration for postwar movements.

The Second World War stands with the Congress of Berlin as one of the notable milestones in the history of colonial Africa. Its effects were both im-mediate and long-term, resulting within twenty years in the decolonization of most of the continent.

At its very outset the war affected colonial politics. The prime minister of South Africa, General J. B. M. Hertzog, sought to keep his country neutral and resigned from office when his parliament voted by an exceedingly nar-row margin to enter the war. From that time onward, large numbers of Afri-kaners opposed the war effort, and some, including B. J. Vorster, prime minister from 1966 until 1978, went to jail for their activities. Although General J. C. Smuts remained head of the government, his opponents in the conspiratorial Broederbond became the spokesmen for a majority of Afrikaners after the national election of 1943.

Even graver problems faced the rulers of Belgian and French colonies after the fall of their mother countries in the spring of 1940. Colonial Belgians remained divided for five months over the question of whether or not to continue the war on the side of the Allies; ultimately they joined the British against the Germans. In French colonies the issue was decided by military might. Pro-Allied forces succeeded in overthrowing Vichy officials in French Equatorial Africa in the autumn of 1940, but in Madagascar, West Africa, and the Maghreb, pro-Vichy administrators held on to the reins of power.

The tide turned in favor of the Allies more quickly in Africa than it did in other theaters of the war. Late in 1941, the British and Belgians pushed the Italians out of Ethiopia and Somalia. A year later the Allies invaded North Africa. Pro-Vichy regimes fell soon thereafter to General De Gaulle's Free French, but the changes in French colonial government demonstrated its weakness to African nationalist leaders. Thus, in 1943, Habib Bourguiba demanded political reforms as the price for his cooperation against the Axis, and one year later, at the Brazzaville Conference, General De Gaulle promised improvements in the treatment of black Africans. Unfortunately the governments of the French Fourth Republic reneged on these promises and clamped down on colonial political activity. In 1945 the provisional government acted with considerable severity in its repression of Algerian demonstrations in and around the town of Sétif. A year later French voters turned down a constitution which would have made colonized people full citizens of the French Empire.

Despite these setbacks, some African countries advanced toward independence as a direct result of the war. The United Nations played a much more active role in the administration of former Italian territories than had the League of Nations in the supervision of former German colonies; and Ethiopia, Libya, and Somalia quickly obtained administrative autonomy. These developments, together with the independence of formerly colonized Asian territories, encouraged nationalists in many African countries to demand increased self-government.

When the colonizing powers resisted these demands, violence occurred in a number of countries: the Gold Coast (Ghana, 1948), Tunisia (1952-55), and Morocco (1953-55). Realizing the costs of trying to hold on to all colonies at once, the colonizers promised independence to selected colonies that seemed prepared for it in those cases where there was no substantial settler community to be protected. The British scheduled independence for the Sudan (1956) and for the West African colonies of Ghana (1957), Nigeria (1960), Sierra Leone (1961), and Gambia (1965), and the French grudgingly granted independence to Tunisia and Morocco in 1956.

Elsewhere the colonizers were more tenacious. The British, instead of promoting African rule in their three Central African territories (Northern

Rhodesia, Southern Rhodesia, and Nyasaland), amalgamated them into the Central African Federation under a white minority. Similarly, the French channeled their available resources into maintaining their hold on Algeria, where a war for independence broke out in November 1954.

The repression of anticolonial movements proved extremely costly to the colonizers. Less than ten thousand ill-armed and uneducated Kikuyu held at bay the entire colonial government of Kenya. Ten thousand Algerian insurgents required the presence of half a million French troops in Algeria and eventually caused the fall of the Fourth Republic. Between 1959 and 1962 small bands of Malawians and Zambians created disorders sufficient to convince the British government that the cost of supporting the Central African Federation would be prohibitive.

The insurgents' success has frequently been explained as a result of the passive support which they enjoyed from the colonized majorities in their respective countries. Indeed, as Mao Tse-tung has described it, the rebels were frequently fish swimming in a friendly sea, but they also enjoyed military advantages due to changes in the technology of warfare. During the Second World War, partisans discovered that lightly armed, highly mobile units could cause considerable damage to traditional fighting units by conducting lightning attacks against strategic locations. Another innovation was the Molotov cocktail, which enabled rebels to cause lethal explosions with nothing more complicated than gasoline. Thus the cost of maintaining colonial rule rose to unparalleled heights.

In a series of desperate gestures aimed at averting military expenditures, the colonizers offered independence to territories where serious movements for autonomy had not even developed: the French granted independence to its colonies in Madagascar, Equatorial Africa, and West Africa in 1960, and the British followed suit in East and Central Africa, according self-government to Kenya, Uganda, Tanganyika (Tanzania), Northern Rhodesia (Zambia), and Nyasaland (Malawi). Fearing similar consequences, the Belgians panicked after a relatively minor riot in 1959 and offered independence to the Congo (Zaire) a year later.

The only colonies that remained under European rule were those whose resources seemed valuable enough to the mother country to warrant a heavy military expense: the Portuguese colonies, Algeria, Southern Rhodesia, and South Africa. In the British colonies, the London government made it clear that it would no longer support minority rule, precipitating withdrawal by South Africa from the British Commonwealth in 1961 and a unilateral declaration of independence by the Rhodesian settlers in 1965. The French took similar measures. Charles De Gaulle, having become president after the government crisis of 1958, arranged for Algerian independence four years later.

The Portuguese and the white Rhodesians ultimately found that they could not afford colonial wars either. After thirteen years of colonial warfare, anticolonial forces overthrew the Portuguese government, and in 1974 the former colonies of Angola, Mozambique, and Guinea-Bissau became independent. Similarly, the white Rhodesians reached a settlement with their black African opposition in 1978. By the end of the 1970s only the white South Africans were willing to pay the cost of continued colonial rule, and they found themselves obliged to reach a settlement calling for the independence of the former German colony of South West Africa (Namibia).

Paradoxically, European financial aid to Africa was growing at just the time that the continent was being decolonized. Originally this aid was allocated in a colonial context, intended to help the various colonial empires recover from the Second World War. The British, for example, desperately short of vegetable oils, hastily devised schemes to grow peanuts in Nigeria and Tanganyika—schemes which failed utterly. The French, fearing that the franc would be as badly devalued after the Second World War as it had been after the First, sought to develop colonial supplies for all of the raw materials necessary for French industry.

Despite these transparent plans to enhance the national interest of the mother countries, a more humanitarian attitude developed in economic relations between the metropolitan powers and their colonies. Britain, France, and Belgium had been devastated by the war and were themselves relying on American aid to rebuild their economies. This transfer of aid from ally to ally encouraged a parallel, albeit considerably smaller, transfer of aid from mother country to colony. The British were the first colonial power to send modern economic aid to a colony without expecting repayment, voting funds for the West Indies through the Commonwealth Development and Welfare Act of 1940. Five years later they extended aid to African colonies, and the French followed their example in 1946. During the 1950s the French spent 2 percent of their national income on colonial aid. In 1952 the Belgians established a Ten Year Plan, whose costs were covered principally by loans rather than outright grants.

Even in the postwar period, however, European aid did not go directly to African officials or even to African entrepreneurs. European and American donors insisted that aid be channeled through political and economic institutions that were dominated by Europeans. As a result, Europeans played a proportionately greater role in African societies and economies than at any other time in the continent's history. Private companies invested as never before in the African infrastructure, and European settlers flocked to Africa to take jobs in government, industry, and agriculture. Between 1945 and 1960, the number of white settlers in Africa more than doubled. Thus, although European aid created large numbers of new jobs in the postwar period, it also attracted European settlers to fill them.

This postwar migration created a difficult situation for Africans who were beginning to emerge from the colonial education systems. Schools for Africans received substantial sums of postwar aid, and they expanded their facilities. Although most children could aspire only to a primary education—and that was far more easily obtainable in cities than in the villages—secondary and even university-level facilities were opening up to a limited elite. Between 1945 and 1949 the British created universities in Uganda, the Gold Coast (Ghana), the Sudan, and Nigeria and continued in the next decade with universities in Southern Rhodesia (Zimbabwe) and Sierra Leone. The Belgians were slower to respond, opening their first two universities in the Congo in 1954 and 1956. The French, who had created schools for teachers and medical assistants before the Second World War, sent promising Africans to France on scholarship rather than create local universities.

Most of these first African university graduates eventually found their way into politics. There is still substantial disagreement as to why this happened, but several considerations can be cited. The export sector of colonial economies was dominated by Europeans, and company managers preferred Europeans to Africans. After the Second World War, moreover, most colonial powers had liberalized their political regimes to allow African representation in various institutions: legislative councils in the British case, metropolitan political parties and trade unions in the French case. These institutions provided well-paying and highly prestigious jobs which attracted the small African elite. By the late 1950s, moreover, most colonial administrations had promised independence and many new jobs opened up in government. For these reasons the political sector provided better opportunities for jobs than did the economic sector.

University graduates, nevertheless, constituted only a minute proportion of the African population, and the political jobs open to them were frequently unavailable to the middle group of Africans who had completed a primary or secondary education. These individuals were relegated to subaltern positions in what was still a racist society. It was they who constituted the reservoir from which the pool of nationalist leaders was recruited. Increasing numbers of them lived in cities where they could personally witness the privileges granted to European settlers. They thus had constant reminders of their own poverty and subordinate status. It was from this group that the strongest demands for African independence emanated.

In many colonies the nationalists did not have to resort to open revolt to obtain satisfaction. Given the speed with which colonies acceded to independence after 1957, nationalists had only to attach themselves to elite leaders in order to obtain good jobs in the postcolonial governments. The presence of European settlers, however, brought out greater militance. Where European settlers resisted African demands for majority rule, African political leaders sought to mobilize their entire society against the colonizers. Needless to say, not everyone was willing to take arms against the Europeans. In fact, only a few Africans actually joined revolutionary movements aimed at ending European rule, but in appealing to the African masses elite leaders reached large numbers of uneducated Africans who were responsive to nationalist appeals even though few actually entered guerrilla units.

African nationalists fought settler regimes with varying degrees of success. In some places, such as Northern Rhodesia (Zambia) and Nyasaland

(Malawi), relatively little violence was necessary in order to obtain African rule. In Kenya, Mozambique, Algeria, and Angola, by contrast, African freedom fighters resisted colonial administrations for years. In South Africa, black revolutionaries did not succeed at all, although they gained considerable sympathy from the outside world.

Given the diverse means by which African states acceded to independence, a wide political spectrum developed in the politics of postcolonial Africa. Some regimes remained in the hands of the elite that had developed after the Second World War, others were ruled by revolutionaries, many fell to military elites drawn from the African ranks of colonial armies. Twenty years after independence, most were still unable to manage their own economies and were dependent on European cadres to make decisions and attract capital. Regimes may come and go, but their rulers cannot easily escape the heritage of a century and a half of colonization.

THE EUROPEAN PARTITION OF AFRICA HAS BEEN ONE OF THE MOST POPULAR topics in the history of the continent, but we still know relatively little about the period during which it occurred. Most scholarly attention has been focused on the diplomacy of partition rather than on its effect on the Africans who were being conquered. The reasons for this selection are easy to understand: the primary materials were readily available in European archives, and during the colonial period such scholarship tended to bolster the claims of the various imperial powers.

Chapter one approaches partition from a legal viewpoint, examining both general justifications for the process and particular arguments made by representatives of some of the major colonizing powers: the British, the Belgians, and the Portuguese. Other colonizers appear in other contexts in subsequent chapters.

Chapters two, three, and four are geographical in scope, each treating regions of Africa that had peculiar circumstances which set them off from the rest of the continent. Chapter two, for example, deals with Mediterranean Africa, which had long been in contact with the European world. All of the territories described in the documents in that chapter had in fact been part of the Turkish Empire before the Europeans took them.

Chapter three documents the history of southern Africa, which, like North Africa, had been subjected early to European influence. This region, moreover, was to have closer economic ties with Europe than any other part of the continent. For this reason I have begun with a set of documents on the mining industry there. This description leads to a section on the Boer War, whose issue decided the ownership of the region's mineral resources.

Unit One

The European Conquest of Africa

Chapter four provides a survey of the conquest and pacification of tropical Africa. Owing to considerations of space, I have chosen two topics which are more or less typical of the region: the French conquest of West Africa, and Belgian rule in the Congo. These topics are not merely regional but demonstrate important subjects in the history of imperialism: the former concentrates on the role of the military in African colonization, and the latter shows the consequences of colonization on a shoestring.

My one regret is that I have not been able to include more reactions to conquest from an African point of view. Such documents are still within the realm of specialists, although they deserve to come to the attention of a wide public.

THE SELECTIONS IN THIS CHAPTER ARE CONCERNED PRIMARILY WITH THE relationship of European law to colonization. In the thirty years before the First World War, the period covered by these documents, legislators, theorists, and diplomats shared certain assumptions about European law. Most believed it to be superior to the law of non-Western peoples, and, by virtue of that superiority, they believed that European states had the right to impose their laws—and government—upon the rest of the world.

European imperialists, however, were seldom conscious of the ramifications of imposing their law on the people they conquered. In their own countries, laws were a manifestation of the values of the ruling classes, often shared by other elements in the society. In colonized Africa, by contrast, laws were imposed from the outside by foreigners who had conquered the land. After conquest, moreover, laws became an agency for obliging colonized people to follow the dictates of their new rulers. This instrumental attitude toward law ultimately prevented colonized Africans from regarding law with the kind of respect shown by many members of the European working classes. Laws which could be quickly replaced by the colonizers were seen as just another tool of colonial manipulation. For colonized Africans, European law was merely a confirmation of the reality expressed in an American folk song ("Pretty Boy Floyd"): some men rob with a gun, others use a fountain pen.

No document in this chapter questions the propriety of European rule, but each lies along a spectrum of attitudes toward the relationship between European law and colonies. Paradoxically, the British constitutional scholar, Frederic W. Maitland, takes the broadest view of colonial law in the excerpt from his *Constitutional History of England* (Document 1). Maitland's book, which became required reading for colonial lawyers, clearly recognized a distinction between the laws of England and those of other parts of the British Empire.

The other texts cited below stress the superiority of the colonizing powers. The 1890 Foreign Jurisdiction Act (Document 2) was the last of a series of

---

Chapter One

The Background of European Colonization

British laws empowering agencies of the imperial government to extend British sovereignty over new territories. Emile Banning's defense in 1888 of the Congo Free State (Document 3) views nineteenth-century colonization as superior to earlier European practice because it was not characterized by wars between potential colonizers. Similarly, the signers of the 1885 Treaty of Berlin (Document 4) justified their partition of Africa in terms of the deity, civilization, and peaceful foreign relations.

Private pronouncements from the period indicate that European diplomats were not nearly as high-minded as they pretended. The internal correspondence between civil servants in the British Foreign Office at the outbreak of the First World War is a more accurate reflection of political thinking. Not only did the diplomats reject any obligation to keep Africa out of the European war, but they also denied the necessity of respecting the treaty rights of their European enemies (Document 5).

Representatives of the smaller states were acutely aware of the precariousness of their hold on their colonies. As the speech by the Portuguese Colonial Minister to the Portuguese Parliament in 1912 (Document 6) indicates, the smaller countries were willing to make considerable concessions to the more powerful European countries in order to retain their colonial possessions.

Needless to say, rigid statements of metropolitan aims seldom reflected the colonial reality. A more accurate description of colonial practice can be found in Selemani bin Mwenye Chande's account of his encounter with a German district officer (Document 7).

1

Frederic William Maitland, *The Constitutional History of England*

ed. H. A. L. Fisher (Cambridge, 1908), pp. 339–41

FREDERIC WILLIAM MAITLAND (1850-1906) was the leading British constitutional scholar at the time that the British were acquiring most of their African empire. Although of Scottish ancestry, Maitland's family had resided in England for three generations, where his grandfather had been a famous theologian and his father a civil servant. Maitland studied at Eton and Cambridge, going on to additional training in law. He became a lecturer at Cambridge in 1884, where he remained for the rest of his life. His lectures on the constitutional history of England, delivered in 1887 and 1888, have become a classic statement on the nature of British law.

As to the constitutions of the colonies. Subject to the general power of the British parliament there is considerable variety—for some the king can legislate, others have representative assemblies of their own. In these last the constitutional organization is modelled after that of the mother country—a royal governor represents the king, and the legislative assembly consists of two houses; but the upper house is not, like our House of Lords, a hereditary assembly. Their acts require the assent of the governor as representing the crown—this gives them a temporary validity—but they are liable to be disallowed by an order of the King in Council; not being sovereign, their legislative powers are limited: their statutes may be void. In this they differ from the statutes of the parliament of the United Kingdom, which cannot be void. However (at least in general) no attempt has been made to enumerate or specify the subjects about which a colonial legislature may legislate, or may not legislate. The general rule is laid down by an act of 1865 (28 and 29 Vic., c. 63): every law made by a colonial legislature is valid for the colony except in so far as it is repugnant to any *act of parliament* extending to the colony. This gives the colonial legislatures liberal powers, for the number of acts of parliament which extend to the colonies is not very great. Still a colonial judge or (on appeal) the Judicial Committee of the Privy Council may have to say "this colonial act is void, for it is repugnant to an act of parliament which extends to the colony."

As to the laws in force in the colonies, of course they vary greatly. In most of them the basis is English common law; but in some it is French law, in others Roman-Dutch law, that is to say, Roman law as expounded by the jurists of Holland. Past history decides this matter: territories acquired by conquest or cession from foreign states have generally been allowed to keep their old laws. Then on the top of this basis of common law, whatever it may be, come those acts of the British parliament which affect the colony, and the acts of the colonial legislature.

The Judicial Committee of the Privy Council (of the constitution of which hereafter) is the supreme court of appeal for all the king's lands outside the United Kingdom. The business that comes before it is of the most miscellaneous character; the world has never seen a tribunal with such worldwide powers. It has to administer Mohammedan law and Hindoo law, French law, Dutch law, English law; it has often to consider whether the legislative acts of colonial legislatures are valid or invalid, for instance, it may have to say that a statute of the Canadian parliament is invalid as repugnant to a statute which the parliament of the United Kingdom has made for Canada.

It is impossible in a few words to say much that is profitable about India, only let us remember this: that the parliament of the United Kingdom which we are about to describe is supreme over India, can, and in matters of the highest importance sometimes does, legislate for India.

In speaking then of king and parliament we are no longer speaking of what in strictness of language are merely English institutions; the parliament represents the United Kingdom, and king and parliament have supreme legislative power over territories which lie in every quarter of the globe. Of this parliament we must speak. Below it there are many institutions, some of which are specifically English, specifically Scottish, Irish, Canadian, Australian, Indian; for example, the judicial systems of England, Ireland and Scotland are distinct from each other, though at the supreme point they unite in the House of Lords. It is of great importance to distinguish those institutions which like the kingship and the parliament are (we can hardly avoid the term) imperial institutions, from those which like the High Court of Justice are specifically English, and I strongly advise you not to use the words England and English when you mean what is larger than England and more than English. When we have dealt with the institutions which have power over all the British dominions, we shall, being Englishmen in an English university, deal with some purely English institutions, as with the High Court of Justice, not with the Scottish Court of Sessions—but let us keep this distinction firmly in our minds; if we are Englishmen, we are also subjects of a sovereign whose power extends over millions and millions of men who are not English.

2

The Foreign Jurisdiction Act, 1890

53 and 54 Vic., c. 37, in Frederick Madden, *Imperial Constitutional Documents* (Oxford, 1953), pp. 88–90

THIS LEGISLATION, which is an act of the British Parliament, is one of a series of laws extending the right of the British government to rule foreign countries. Its provisions enabled the British government to establish subordinate colonial governments to rule over newly acquired territories in the non-European world.

Whereas by treaty, capitulation, grant, usage, sufferance and other lawful means, Her Majesty the Queen has jurisdiction within divers foreign countries, and it is expedient to consolidate the Acts relating to the exercise of Her Majesty's jurisdiction out of her dominions; Be it therefore enacted . . . .

I. It is and shall be lawful for Her Majesty the Queen to hold, exercise, and enjoy any jurisdiction which Her Majesty now has or may at time hereafter have within a foreign country in the same and as ample manner as if Her Majesty had acquired that jurisdiction by the cession or conquest of territory.

II. Where a foreign country is not subject to any Government from whom Her Majesty the Queen might obtain jurisdiction in the manner recited by this Act, Her Majesty shall by virtue of this Act have jurisdiction over Her Majesty's subjects for the time being resident in or resorting to that country, and that jurisdiction shall be jurisdiction of Her Majesty in a foreign country within the meaning of the other provisions of this Act.

III. Every act and thing done in pursuance of any jurisdiction of Her Majesty in a foreign country shall be as valid as if it had been done according to the local law then in force in that country. . . .

[Questions relating to the extent and existence of Her Majesty's jurisdiction in a foreign country would be referred to the Secretary of State for his decision.]

XI. Every Order in Council made in pursuance of this Act shall be laid before both Houses of Parliament forthwith after it is made . . . and shall have effect as if it were enacted in this Act. . . .

[Orders in Council would be void only to the extent of any repugnancy to an Act of Parliament, not on the ground of any repugnancy to the law of England.

Orders in Council might make provision for the government of Her Majesty's subjects up to one hundred miles from the coast of China or Japan as effectively as for those subjects within those countries.]

XVI. In this Act: the expression "foreign country" means any country or place out of Her Majesty's "dominions." The expression "British court in a foreign country" means any British court having jurisdiction out of Her Majesty's dominions in pursuance of an Order in Council whether made under any Act or otherwise. The expression "jurisdiction" includes power.

3

Emile Banning, *Le partage politique de l'Afrique d'après les transactions internationales les plus récentes, 1885 à 1888*

(Brussels, 1888), in The "Scramble" for Africa, ed. Raymond Betts (Boston, 1966), pp. 1–4. Translated by Irene and Raymond Betts

EMILE BANNING (1836-98) was one of the principal collaborators of King Leopold II of Belgium in the establishment of the Congo Free State. Born in Liège, he studied history before entering the permanent staff of the Ministry of Foreign Affairs. In 1876 he took an active part in the Brussels Conference, which resulted in the formation of the International African Association, and he became that organization's first secretary. He also attended the Berlin Conference of 1884-85 and the Brussels Conference of 1890 in his capacity of director general and chief archivist of the Ministry of Foreign Affairs. Although disagreeing with the king over the establishment of state monopolies in the Congo, he continued to serve in the ministry but became increasingly depressed. In the end, he took his own life.

Few epochs will hold a place in history comparable to that of the century which is ending. Despite some symptoms of lassitude which the contemporary generation revealed, despite the weaknesses and deceptions of which no period in the life of humanity is exempt, outstanding results and essential changes have been accumulated in all branches of activity and human thought, to the point that the mind is staggered by their weight and importance. The visible entry of Africa into the empire of civilization, the distribution of its vast territories among the nations of Europe, the initiation, under European guidance, of millions of Negroes into superior conditions of existence truly seems to be one of the most considerable revolutions of our time, one of the richest in economic and political consequences.

This activity began with the century and through three highly significant undertakings. At the head of the first figured that indefatigable mover of men and ideas who bore the name of Bonaparte. The expedition to Egypt was both a geographical and historical revelation. Since 1798 Egypt has become a European province, inseparably associated with the fortunes of the great Western States. At the same time that it was disclosing the secret of its monuments and its tombs, and while their testimony was renewing our knowledge of high antiquity, the valley of the Nile became the stage of completely modern activities. The point of departure or arrival of the first important discoveries directed toward Abyssinia, the West and Meridional Sudan, Egypt was equally to become, by means of the Suez Canal, the great route of maritime navigation to the Far East.

The definitive occupation of the Cape by England in 1815 produced analogous effects, but on a smaller scale, at the extreme south of the vast African continent. The site of the Cape, which up to that time had served only as a port of call and supply, became the embryo of a colony toward the development of which were applied the resources of a great commercial power. A new base of operations was organized, and little by little its activity was felt up to the banks of the Orange and Zambesi Rivers.

Beginning in 1830, the conquest of Algeria by French arms created a third center of attack, a new and powerful source of infiltration of civilizing influences. The task was bloody and laborious. Here it was not with the Negro and fetish-worshipping populations that the French clashed, but with the Arab and Moslem populations. Yet success was not long in doubt, and Africa, breached on three points of the triangle that it forms, became henceforth the object of a regularized, uninterrupted and almost always peaceful conquest.

It was toward the end of this first period of thirty years that the great voyages of exploration were organized. Begun at the end of the last century by Bruce and Mungo Park, they were continued without interruption from Rene Caillé and Clapperton up to Nachtigal and Stanley; and they included—only to mention the names of the most illustrious—explorations by H. Barth and Schweinfurth, Livingstone, Burton, Speke, Grant, Rohlfs and Cameron.

Up until the middle of this century, almost all of the African interior remained yet to be explored, but despite extreme difficulties and continued dangers, the exploration advanced with an extraordinary rapidity. To measure the effect of this forty-year accomplishment, contemporaries have only to recall the map of Africa that they studied in their youth.

Nevertheless, world public opinion hardly noticed this work of giants. Outside of the circle of geographic societies—and there was only a limited number of these—African questions awakened no response. The press ignored them; governments accorded them only a passing interest. But the remarkable initiative taken in 1876 by the King of the Belgians changed the entire outlook. The conference which was convened under his presidency in the month of September of that year, and the meeting at the palace of Brussels of seven of the most celebrated travellers who had just returned from the theatre of their discoveries, struck the imagination. Both what had been done in Africa and what remained to be done was now grasped. For several years, L'Association internationale africaine held public attention by the expeditions in which Belgian explorers brilliantly undertook their first campaigns.

The return of Stanley in 1877, after his remarkable crossing of Equatorial Africa, gave the signal for the foundation in the following year of the Congo enterprise. From the West coast as from the East coast, deep penetrations were directed toward the interior. The last obstacles gave way before this persistent effort. A dozen years ago the central core—of a size larger by one-third than Europe—was still an immense emptiness on our maps. Today it is the very heart of the Congo Free State, from which agents trek in all directions into the vast empire by means of one of the most admirable water systems which exist on earth.

This fact, which is the expression of colossal progress in geographical science, at the same time characterizes a revolution achieved in ideas. The persevering energy of the King of the Belgians had made the African question the first order of business in Europe and kept it there. The impetus given to the imagination was general. Governments could no longer abstain; rather, it was to be more feared that certain of them would hasten precipitously to make up for lost time. Each one felt, and some among them clearly saw, that a new continent and new races were going to collaborate in the civilization of the world and basically modify the balance of universal interests.

The convocation of a conference at Berlin in 1884 by the imperial government of Germany was the result and the sanction of this movement. The six great powers of Europe, the seven other maritime states, and the United States, all took part in it. This great assembly marks precisely the point where the scientific work found its complement in political action, where national enterprise came to cooperate with individual initiative.

The Berlin Conference fulfilled a double task: it endorsed the creation, in the very heart of Equatorial Africa, of a great interior state, commercially open to all nations, but politically shielded from their competition. It also set up the bases for economic legislation which was immediately applicable to the central zone of the continent but which virtually demanded more extensive application. These regulations, inspired by the most liberal ideas and discarding all whims of selfish exploration, will protect both the natives and the Europeans in their relations with the colonizing powers. The conference also upheld the principles—justly dear to our age—of religious and civil liberty, of loyal and peaceful competition, and it broke with the antiquated traditions of the former colonial system.

Three years have lapsed since the promulgation of the act of the Berlin Conference and already the political and economic thought which formed the bases of its clauses has been many times applied in Africa. Germany, England, France and Portugal have rivalled each other in activity in this area, while remaining faithful to the spirit of understanding and justice and to the reciprocal concessions which had dictated their common resolutions. The partition of Africa on both sides of the equator . . . was achieved peacefully, with neither trouble nor jolts, and without any of the onerous and bloody conflicts with accompanied and noticeably impeded the colonization of the two Americas. . . .

. . . The African enterprise rests on broad foundations. One can see with what vigor in action, scope in plans, and concern over their consequences all of Europe is involved. Never has the assault on a new continent been pursued by such a group nor has it been better organized in its details. Nothing of the sort happened in America or even in Australia. Where would the new world be today, what leaps forward would it have taken, if, at the end of the sixteenth century, an American conference could have done for it what the Berlin Conference has done for Africa? But the thought could never have risen. For it to have been possible and practical, the modern development of international law as well as the great progress of science and technology were necessary. The European nations had to become capable of collective action and able to place at the service of the common idea the enormous industrial and financial power of our age. From this ensued the grandiose evolution which we have witnessed and of which the glorious fruit will be the redemption of a continent and a race.

. . . The political situation which was produced in Africa by the cooperative action of the governments realized a thought which was already apparent since 1876 and which even then appeared to be the future solution of the problem. Each of the principal maritime peoples established itself in the area which best suited both its interests and its means of action. While engaging in this national activity, each of them fulfilled a social mission, spread abroad the germs of culture, created the sites for the spread of ideas, of which the rays converged on the common center. A similar plan, an identical tendency dominated the separate enterprises and subordinated them to a higher goal.

Thus the league of civilization was gradually organized in the conquest of virgin nature and heathen races. What was truly new in this conception, what has an original quality, was the role assigned to Belgium in this peaceful crusade. Belgium owes this role both to the generosity of its King and to the sympathy of the powers. If the Congo State is nowhere mentioned in the act of the Berlin Conference, it is understood in every article. It was in effect an essential idea in the general idea of which the regeneration of Africa was the object. The attack from the center is necessarily correlative to that which occurred from the diverse points of the circumference. The European states coordinated their activities with the action of the central power. Its foundation and development reveal the closest rapport with the others.

From this point of view the Congo State, in some respects, took on the aspect of an international institution: it served as the connecting link and the pivotal point for the establishments on both coasts. The efforts of the other powers were the guarantee of its success, in the same way that it cooperated in the activities of the others, endorsed their expansion, consolidated the results. All progress accomplished in the central state had its repercussions in all the colonial establishments which surrounded it, just as every conquest achieved in the maritime regions soon affected the interior. It is impossible to separate the two orders of activity without simultaneously compromising both. Whoever loses sight of the whole, whoever attempts to favor particular development to the detriment of general development hurts himself and condemns himself to emptiness. The theatre is too narrow for anyone to isolate himself with impunity. Never on any point of the globe has the joint action of peoples appeared to the same degree as the principle and guarantee of their success. Who harms one does injury to all; who facilitates the total plan comes to the aid of each one. The Congo State will prosper or fall reciprocally with all the colonial creations which envelop it.

This was a unanimous conviction at the Berlin Conference. Experience has confirmed it with each step and will contribute more and more to center on this point the sentiment of those men who are attracted to the study of this great problem. Here is strikingly revealed the immense superiority of the modern formula of colonization over those of previous centuries. Mercantile selfishness has been replaced by the impetus of a much higher order. National interests are reconciled with universal interests in a synthesis of which the final result will be to give to the world another continent; to production, the resources of a wealth and variety scarcely glimpsed; to militant humanity, a new family whose native faculties have already caused considerable surprises and which will reserve, after a century of culture, a goodly number more for future generations.

4

General Act of the Conference of Berlin (1885)

in Sir Edward Hertslet, *The Map of Africa by Treaty*, 3 vols. (3d ed., 1909; rpt. London, 1967), 2:468, 471–73, 474–75, 484–85

THIS TREATY was drawn up by the representatives of the major European powers and the United States in 1884-85. It became the major legal document which regulated the process by which European states claimed sovereignty over territory in black Africa.

In the Name of Almighty God.

Preamble

Her Majesty the Queen of the United Kingdom of Great Britain and Ireland, Empress of India; His Majesty the German Emperor, King of Prussia; His Majesty the Emperor of Austria, King of Bohemia, &c., and Apostolic King of Hungary; His Majesty the King of the Belgians; His Majesty the King of Denmark; His Majesty the King of Spain; the President of the United States of America; the President of the French Republic; His Majesty the King of Italy; His Majesty the King of the Netherlands, Grand Duke of Luxemburg, &c.; His Majesty the Emperor of all the Russias; His Majesty the King of Sweden and Norway, &c.; and His Majesty the Emperor of the Ottomans, wishing, in a spirit of good and mutual accord, to regulate the conditions in certain regions of Africa, and to assure to all nations the advantages of free navigation on the two chief rivers of Africa flowing into the Atlantic Ocean; being desirous, on the other hand, to obviate the misunderstanding and disputes which might in future arise from new acts of occupation ("prises de possession") on the coast of Africa; and concerned, at the same time, as to the means of furthering the moral and material well-being of the native populations, have resolved, on the invitation addressed to them by the Imperial Government of Germany, in agreement with the

Government of the French Republic, to meet for those purposes in Conference at Berlin, and have appointed as their Plenipotentiaries, to wit:—. . . .

CHAPTER 1.—DECLARATION RELATIVE TO FREEDOM OF TRADE IN THE BASIN OF THE CONGO. ITS MOUTHS AND CIRCUMJACENT REGIONS, WITH OTHER PROVISIONS CONNECTED THEREWITH.

Freedom of Trade to all Nations.

Art. I.—The trade of all nations shall enjoy complete freedom:. . . .

Free Trade Principles applied to Signatory Powers, and to such Independent States as may approve the same.

It is expressly recognized that in extending the principle of free trade to this eastern zone, the Conference Powers only undertake engagements for themselves, and that in the territories belonging to an independent Sovereign State this principle shall only be applicable in so far as it is approved by such State. But the Powers agree to use their good offices which the Governments established on the African shore of the Indian Ocean for the purpose of obtaining such approval, and in any case of securing the most favourable conditions to the transit (traffic) of all nations. . . .

No Taxes to be levied on Wares Imported (with slight exceptions).

Art. III.—Wares, of whatever origin, imported into these regions, under whatsoever flag, by sea or river, or overland, shall be subject to no other taxes than such as may be levied as fair compensation for expenditure in the interests of trade, and which for this reason must be equally borne by the subjects themselves and by foreigners of all nationalities.

Differential Duties forbidden.

All differential dues on vessels, as well as on merchandize are forbidden.

No Import or Transit Duties to be levied on Merchandize.

Art. IV.—Merchandize imported into these regions shall remain free from import and transit dues.

Question to be reconsidered after 20 years.

The Powers reserve to themselves to determine after the lapse of 20 years whether this freedom of import shall be retained or not.

No Monopolies or Favours to be granted.

Art. V.—No Power which exercises or shall exercise sovereign rights in the above-mentioned regions shall be allowed to grant therein a monopoly or favour of any kind in matters of trade.

Protection of Persons and Property, movable and immovable Possessions; Professions.

Foreigners, without distinction, shall enjoy therein with regard to the protection of their persons and effects, the acquisition and transmission of their movable and real property and with regard to the exercise of their professions, the same treatment and same rights as nationals.

Art. VI.—Provisions relative to Protection of the Natives, of Missionaries and Travellers, as well as relative to Religious Liberty:

Preservation and Improvement of Native Tribes; Slavery, and the Slave Trade.

All the Powers exercising sovereign rights or influence in the aforesaid territories bind themselves to watch over the preservation of the native tribes, and to care for the improvement of the conditions of their moral and material well-being, and to help in suppressing slavery, and especially the slave trade.

Religious and Other Institutions. Civilization of Natives.

They shall, without distinction of creed or nation, protect and favour all religious, scientific, or charitable institutions, and undertakings created and organized for the above ends, or which aim at instructing the natives and bringing home to them the blessings of civilization.

Protection of Missionaries, Scientists, and Explorers.

Christian missionaries, scientists and explorers, with their followers, property, and collections, shall likewise be the objects of especial protection.

Religious Toleration.

Freedom of conscience and religious toleration are expressly guaranteed to the natives, no less than to subjects and to foreigners.

Public Worship.

The free and public exercise of all forms of Divine worship, and the right to build edifices for religious purposes, and to organize religious missions belonging to all creeds, shall not be limited or fettered in any way whatsoever. . . .

CHAP. III.—DECLARATION RELATIVE TO THE NEUTRALITY OF THE TERRITORIES COMPRISED IN THE CONVENTIONAL BASIN OF THE CONGO.

Neutrality of Territories and Territorial Waters.

Art. X.—In order to give a new guarantee of security to trade and industry, and to encourage, by the maintenance of peace, the development of civilization in the countries mentioned in Article I, and placed under the free trade system, the High Signatory Parties to the present Act, and those who shall hereafter adopt it, bind themselves to respect the neutrality of the territories, or portions of territories, belonging to the said countries, comprising therein the territorial waters, so long as the Powers which exercise or shall exercise the rights of sovereignty or Protectorate over those territories, using their option of proclaiming themselves neutral, shall fulfill the duties which neutrality requires.

Hostilities not to extend to Neutralized States.

Art. XI.—In case a Power exercising rights of sovereignty or Protectorate in the countries mentioned in Article I, and placed under the free trade system, shall be involved in a war then the High Signatory Parties to the present Act, and those who shall hereafter adopt it, bind themselves to lend their good offices in order that the territories belonging to this Power and comprised in the Conventional free trade zone shall, by the common consent of this Power and of the other belligerent or belligerents, be placed during the war under the rule of neutrality, and considered as belonging to a non-belligerent State, the belligerents thenceforth abstaining from extending hostilities to the territories thus neutralized, and from using them as a base for warlike operations. . . .

CHAP. VI.—DECLARATION RELATIVE TO THE ESSENTIAL CONDITIONS TO BE OBSERVED IN ORDER THAT NEW OCCUPATIONS ON THE COASTS OF THE AFRICAN CONTINENT MAY BE HELD TO BE EFFECTIVE.

Notifications of Acquisitions and Protectorates on Coasts of African Continent.

Art. XXXIV.—Any Power which henceforth takes possession of a tract of land on the coasts of the African Continent outside of its present possessions, or which, being hitherto without such possessions, shall acquire them, as well as the Power which assumes a Protectorate there, shall accompany the respective act with a notification thereof, addressed to the other Signatory Powers of the present Act, in order to enable them, if need be, to make good any claims of their own.

Establishment of Authority in Territories occupied on Coasts. Protection of existing Rights. Freedom of Trade and Transit.

Art. XXXV.—The Signatory Powers of the present Act recognize the obligation to insure the establishment of authority in regions occupied by them on the coasts of the African Continent sufficient to protect existing rights, and, as the case may be, freedom of trade and of transit under the conditions agreed upon. . . .

5

Edwin Parkes, "Neutralisation of Conventional Basin of the Congo in the Event of War," August 10, 1914, with a Minute by Sir Eyre Crowe, August 11, 1914

in Bruce Fetter, "Central Africa, 1914: German Schemes and British Designs," Académie royale des Sciences d'Outre-mer, *Bulletin des Séances*, 18 (1972), pp. 547–48

Note: Parkes was a librarian at the British Foreign Office. His statement of policy is collected from earlier Foreign Office pronouncements.

EYRE ALEXANDER BARBY WICHART CROWE (1864-1925), whose memorandum is a part of this document, was one of the leading permanent officials in the British Foreign Office. The son of a diplomat, Crowe was educated in Germany before entering the Foreign Office at the age of twenty-one. He served on the British delegation to a number of international conferences, including the Second International Peace Conference at The Hague in 1907 and the Paris Peace Conference in 1919. Between 1920 and 1925, he served as permanent undersecretary of state for foreign affairs, the highest civil service post in the Foreign Office.

On November 15, 1898 the Colonial Defence Committee considered the desirability of neutralising the Basin (or the Free Trade Zone) from the point of view of a war with France. The Committee decided that "it seems clear to the Committee that the advantage of the observance of neutrality with respect to British and French Protectorates with the Free Trade Zone would lie with France and not with Great Britain."

[The question was renewed late in 1910 with regard to Zanzibar, opposite German East Africa. The advantage was again seen to lie with Britain's enemy. British legal advisors judged that the status of neutrality during a war required the consent of other belligerents.]

. . . the question of neutralization of territories in Africa has never been raised without being supported by the argument that war between European powers would endanger the whole civilizing process (not to speak of the prestige of the white races themselves) among the native populations. . . .

Major Wilson tells me this aspect of the case has already been considered recently by the Overseas Defence Committee but they have nevertheless decided to recommend the dispatch of an expedition to Dar-es-Salaam.

Minute by Sir Eyre Crowe, August 11, 1914:

I do not consider it practical politics to contemplate keeping the German possessions in Africa out of this war. I feel certain that any such attempt would meet with strong disapproval in the Union of South Africa, who may be assumed to be willing and eager to assume the burden of driving the Germans out of Africa bag and baggage.

It is also a well-recognized imperial interest to establish territorial connections between the British protectorate of East Africa and Uganda on the one hand and Rhodesia and the Union of South Africa on the other.

6

Augusto de Vasconcelos, address to the Portuguese Chamber of Deputies, March 15, 1912

in *British Documents on the Origins of the War,* ed. G. P. Gooch and H. W. V. Temperley, Vol. 10, Pt. II (London, 1938), p. 450. Translation by the British Embassy in Lisbon

AUGUSTO DE VASCONCELOS (1867-1951), a distinguished Portuguese diplomat, served as minister of colonies in the second cabinet after the establishment of the Portuguese republic. Born in Lisbon, he was trained as a surgeon and was head of surgery in two hospitals before he entered politics. In the last days of the monarchy he became a leading advocate of a change of regime and, once the republic has been installed, he served in a number of important posts, including that of minister of foreign affairs. In the 1920s he became active in the League of Nations and served as president of that body in 1935.

Finally reference has been made to the campaign which a certain press had for some time past conducted against the integrity of our colonial dominions. He* has already had occasion to refer in the Senate to the irritating echoes of that campaign which he always considered destitute of serious foundation. We need have no fear for our colonies: we are performing our duty as a colonial Power, contributing, with intelligent and honest efforts, sometimes at a great sacrifice, towards that colossal work of civilization in which both the great and small nations are expending their best energies. Let us show the world that the object of the Republic is not, and could not be, to keep her dominions closed to all foreign enterprize, to create only obstacles and impediments to all attempts at intelligent colonization. No, we can and must protect our trade and industry, but for this purpose we need not impede the progress of those who desire to penetrate our territories, to avail [themselves] of our excellent ports, to utilize our railways, to cultivate our lands, to explore our mines and to develop the wealth of the coun-

* The third person "He" here refers to Vasconcelos—B. F.

try. The example is shown to us by the Great Powers in throwing open the doors of their rich colonial lands to the boldest enter-prizes, in which capital from all purses is sewn [*sic*]. We cannot follow a different policy; should we refuse the intercourse and co-operation of those who dispose of capital, of the power of work and initiative. No, what we have to do is to accompany them and aid them wherever our duty towards civilization calls for our assistance and wherever our interests are at stake.

7

Selemani bin Mwenye Chande, "My Journey Up-Country in Africa"

in *Swahili Prose Texts: A Selection from the Material Collected by Carl Velten from 1893 to 1896*, ed. and trans. Lyndon Harries (London and Nairobi, 1965), pp. 243–44

SELEMANI BIN MWENYE CHANDE (fl. 1895) was a Swahili trader who served as an informant to the German scholar Carl Velten during Velten's term in German East Africa as translator to the colonial government. Selemani bin Mwenye Chande spent most of his life on the Indian Ocean coast but had, as had many of his generation, traveled to the interior on a trading mission. The particular expedition recounted here went all the way to the Bemba country in what is today Zambia. In this selection Selemani describes his appeal to the German district officer at Karema, on Lake Tanganyika, after the theft of his merchandise.

We consulted together, saying, "Brothers, hadn't we better get going? We talk, and this pagan does not hear. Perhaps he will change his mind and seek to kill us? Our property is lost, and shall not our souls be lost?" Some said, "Shall we not go to Karema and inform the European, because Chata has robbed us? Now when shall we get out of here? It is no good leaving in the daytime, for perhaps the tribesmen will follow us to get us on the way and kill us; we had better go to the Chief and tell him, We agree to what you say, keep our property safe, and we are going to look for Matumla."

We agreed and went to the Chief and told him what we intended, and he said, "Isn't that just what I wanted? Very well, take a hut and go to rest, do not be afraid; sleep until morning, let us take proper leave of one another, and I will give you food for the way (enough) until you arrive at your place (i.e. your destination)." And we sat disconsolately, being sorry for our property which was lost and for our brethren who were dead. It was without any proper reason, nor did we even know Matumla.

We went to bed, then at night we ran away, and went our way to Karema. When we reached the path one of our colleagues was taken by a lion. What could we do to the lion, there as we were with no guns? With what shall we shoot it? Shall we just make a din?

In the morning we reached Karema, and we found the European still in bed. We told his men, "Where is the Bwana?" And they said, "He is asleep, but he will wake up soon." So we sat down at the doorway. Between 8:30 and 9 a.m. the Bwana got up and asked, "Eh, boy, what's on out there?" And he said, "Some traders have come, they come from Tabora." The Bwana said, "Have they brought me a letter? Go and ask them." And we said, "We brought no letter, we have been attacked at Kafisa by this Chief Chata, it is he who attacked us, and he has robbed us of all our property, and he has killed our brethren; and so, we want the bwana, let us tell him what we have to say." The house-boy replied, "Bwana is in the dining-room now, you just stay a little while, wait for him, he will come very shortly."

So when the Bwana came, we told him, "Bwana, we have been attacked." And he asked, "Who has attacked you?" We replied, "Chata." And he said to us, "But haven't I said that all traders should first come to me! What did you go to do at the pagan's? But never mind, I will send soldiers to make enquiry why you traders have been robbed. And you provide one person from among you to go along with my soldier, so that he can listen to what my soldier says with Chata, and so that you yourselves may hear about it."

So they set off for Chata's place. The soldiers said to him, "You Chata, so now you have become a man who robs people of their property? Aren't you afraid of government rule?" And he said, "I did not attack them for nothing; I attacked them because of Matumla taking my property, twenty pieces of ivory." The soldiers told him, "Oh no, we don't agree, bring the traders' property, that is what the District Officer told us (you must do)." When he saw their superior strength he took out the stuff and gave it to the soldiers, and they brought it to Karema, all that was left of our goods.

When they reached Karema, the European called us (saying), "You traders, come here, come and look at your property, is this what Chata took?" We looked at it and told him, "Yes, Bwana, some more was lost in the fire." And he said, "Never mind, take this which is left."

OF ALL EUROPEAN EXPANSION IN THE NINETEENTH CENTURY, THE CONQUEST of Muslim North Africa was the hardest to justify. Europeans had long recognized the merits of Islamic civilization, more out of fear of Muslim military might than from an understanding of the culture. Throughout the nineteenth century, Turkey was recognized as a full though ailing member of the council of civilized nations. Nonetheless, Europeans shared the spoils resulting from the disintegration of the Ottoman Empire.

The disposition of formerly Turkish territories followed the racist lines which were solidifying in nineteenth-century European thought. In general, Turkish territories in Europe became independent while those in Africa became colonies, with no reference to previous status within the Ottoman Empire. Thus, Egypt and Tunisia, which had enjoyed considerable autonomy under the Turks, were attached to Britain and France respectively.

The documents relating to Egypt indicate the development of a British rationalization for conquest. Lady Duff-Gordon's letters from the 1860s (Document 8) helped convince the British public that the Turks were not fit to govern the country. This was quite misleading, since Egypt was actually ruled by a local dynasty which was only nominally subordinate to Istanbul. Lord Cromer, who ruled Egypt after the British invasion of 1882, admitted that the Egyptians did not like their conquerors but argued that his administration was more competent than the one it replaced (Document 9). That Cromer's administration was operating in British rather than Egyptian interests is clearly demonstrated by the Anglo-Egyptian treaty of 1899 (Document 10), which detached the Sudan from its former Egyptian masters. Behind the political rationale, of course, lay the prevailing racism. Egyptians were by no means oblivious to British self-interest, as Lutfi al-Sayyid's evaluation of Cromer's administration (Document 11) demonstrates.

The French had begun their conquest of Algeria a full half-century before the British invasion of Egypt, but their motives differed little from those of

---

Chapter Two

The Conquest of Islamic Africa

the British. As the ultimatum from the Count de Bourmont to the dey of Algiers indicates, the French felt that they could do a better job of ruling Algeria than could the Turks. Despite guarantees to the local Turks and Algerians alike (Document 12), few Muslims welcomed these European intruders. Most Algerians rallied to Abd el-Kadr, who promised to establish an independent Algerian state, which had never really existed before. Although he succeeded initially, bringing order to the interior (see his letter to the sultan of Morocco, Document 13), Abd el-Kadr ultimately fell to French military might. This conquest was ultimately recognized by other European powers—see Document 14, the letter from the British foreign secretary to the ambassador in Paris—without any reference to the opinions of the Algerian people.

In the 1880s the Tunisians also fell to the French juggernaut, but more than the Algerians or even the Egyptians, they seem to have understood some of the forces behind European conquest. Fourteen years before his country became a French protectorate, the Muslim scholar Khayr al-Din al-Tunisi published a keen analysis of European government (Document 15) in an effort to promote reform in his government which, like Egypt, was virtually autonomous in internal matters. Despite Tunisian efforts at reform, the French invaded, forcing an illegal treaty of protection on the bey of Tunis, which the other nations of Europe recognized, ignoring Turkish protests (Documents 16 and 17).

8

Lady Lucie Duff-Gordon, *Letters from Egypt, 1863–1865*
(London, 1865), pp. 369–70

LUCIE DUFF-GORDON (1821-69) was an aristocratic woman of letters who had broad geographic interests. At nineteen she married Sir Alexander Cornwall Duff-Gordon, and their house in London became a rendezvous for English and foreign celebrities. Her writings deal with almost the entire continent of Europe, including Greece, Germany, Austria, and Bulgaria. She moved to Egypt with her husband in 1862 and died there seven years later.

LETTER LV.

El-Uksur, Good Friday, 14 April 1865

The version of the massacre here, current at Alexandria, is quite curious to us.

I know well the Sheykh-el-Arab who helped to catch the poor people, and I know also a young Turk who stood by while Fadl Pasha had the men laid down by ten at a time, *chopped* with the pioneers' axes. He quite admired the affair (though a very good-natured young fellow), and expressed a desire to do likewise. The lowest computation of men, women, and children killed is sixteen hundred. M. M— reckons it at *above* two thousand.

I have seen *with my eyes* a second boat-load of prisoners. I wish fervently the Viceroy knew the deep exasperation which his subordinates are causing. I do not like to repeat all that I hear. What must it be, to force from all the most influential men and the most devout Muslims such a sentiment as this?—"We are Muslims, but we should thank God to send Europeans to govern us." The feeling is against the Turks, and not against Christians.

9

Evelyn Baring, the Earl of Cromer, *Modern Egypt*
2 vols. (New York, 1908), 1:4–6, 2:146–48

EVELYN BARING (1841-1917), first earl of Cromer, was one of the pillars of British imperialism. After attending Woolwich, a prestigious private school, he received an army commission at the age of seventeen. For the next eighteen years he served as aide-de-camp and private secretary to two leading figures. His first executive assignment came in 1877, when he was named British commissioner to the international commission appointed to enforce payment of the Egyptian khedive's debts. Upon his resignation, he spent three years in India where he had already served, then returned to Egypt as British consul-general after the invasion of 1882. Between 1883 and 1907, Cromer served as the virtual governor of Egypt. His major concerns were economic: first to pay off the Egyptian public debt, then to modernize the economy and the government. In 1884 he ordered the Egyptian government to withdraw from the Sudan during the Mahdi's revolt; in

1896-98 he championed that region's reconquest. The *Dictionary of National Biography* characterizes him as follows: "While not a genius, possessed powerful and versatile talents, whose full excercise was ensured by a strong character and vigorous constitution."

Egypt is not the only country which has been brought to the verge of ruin by a persistent neglect of economic laws and by a reckless administration of the finances of the State. Neither is it the only country in which undue privileges have been acquired by the influential classes to the detriment of the mass of the population. Nor is it the only country in whose administration the most elementary principles of law and justice have been ignored. Although the details may differ, there is a great similarity in the general character of the abuses which spring up under Eastern Governments wheresoever they may be situated. So also, although the remedies to be applied must vary according to local circumstances and according to the character, institutions, and habits of thought of the European nation under whose auspices reforms are initiated, the broad lines which those reforms must take are traced out by the commonplace requirements of European civilisation, and must of necessity present some identity of character, whether the scene of action be India, Algiers, Egypt, Tunis, or Bosnia.

The history of reform in Egypt, therefore, does not present any striking feature to which some analogy might not perhaps be found in other countries where European civilisation has, in a greater or less degree, been grafted on a backward Eastern Government and society.

But, so far as I am aware, no counterpart can be found to the special circumstances which have attended the work of Egyptian reform. Those circumstances have, in truth, been very peculiar.

In the first place, one alien race, the English, have had to control and guide a second alien race, the Turks, by whom they are disliked, in the government of a third race, the Egyptians. To these latter, both the paramount races are to a certain extent unsympathetic. In the case of the Turks, the want of sympathy has been mitigated by habit, by a common religion, and by the use of a common language. In the case of the English, it has been mitigated by the respect due to superior talents, and by the benefits which have accrued to the population from British interference.

In the second place, it is to be observed that for diplomatic and other reasons, on which it is unnecessary for the moment to dwell, the Egyptian administration had to be reformed without any organic changes being effected in the conditions under which the government had been conducted prior to the British occupation. . . .

Turn now to the mental and moral attributes of the two races. It will be found that the antitheses are striking.

Sir Alfred Lyall once said to me: "Accuracy is abhorrent to the Oriental mind. Every Anglo-Indian official should always remember that maxim." Want of accuracy, which easily degenerates into untruthfulness," is, in fact, the main characteristic of the Oriental mind.

The European is a close reasoner; his statements of fact are devoid of ambiguity; he is a natural logician, albeit he may not have studied logic; he loves symmetry in all things; he is by nature sceptical and requires proof before he can accept the truth of any proposition; his trained intelligence works like a piece of mechanism. The mind of the Oriental, on the other hand, like his picturesque streets, is eminently wanting in symmetry. His reasoning is of the most slipshod description. Although the ancient Arabs acquired in a somewhat high degree the science of dialectics, their descendants are singularly deficient in the logical faculty. They are often incapable of drawing the most obvious conclusions from any simple premises of which they may admit the truth. Endeavour to elicit a plain statement of facts from an ordinary Egyptian. His explanation will generally be lengthy, and wanting in lucidity. He will probably contradict himself half-a-dozen times before he has finished his story. He will often break down under the mildest process of cross-examination. The Egyptian is also eminently unsceptical. He readily becomes the dupe of the magician and the astrologer. Even highly educated Egyptians are prone to refer the common occurrences of life to the intervention of some supernatural agency. In political matters, as well as in the affairs of everyday life, the Egyptian will, without inquiry, accept as true the most absurd rumours. He will, indeed, do more than this. He will often accept or reject such rumours in the inverse ratio of their probability, for, true to his natural inconsistency and want of rational discrimination, he will occasionally develop a flash of hardy scepticism when he is asked to believe the truth.

Contrast again the talkative European, bursting with superfluous energy, active in mind, inquisitive about everything he sees and hears, chafing under delay, and impatient of suffering, with the grave and silent Eastern, devoid of energy and initiative, stagnant in mind, wanting in curiosity about matters which are new to him, careless of waste of time and patient under suffering.

Or, again, look at the fulsome flattery, which the Oriental will offer to his superior and expect to receive from his inferior, and compare the general approval of such practices with the European frame of mind, which spurns both the flatterer and the person who invites flattery. This contemptible flattery, "the nurse of crime," as it was called by the poet Gay, is, indeed, a thorn in the side of the Englishman in Egypt, for it prevents Khedives and Pashas from hearing the truth from their own countrymen.

10

Agreement between the British government and the government of the Khedive of Egypt, relative to the future administration of the Sudan, signed at Cairo, January 19, 1899

in Sir Edward Hertslet, *The Map of Africa by Treaty*, 3 vols. (3d ed., 1909; rpt. London, 1967), 2:620–21

THIS IS the legal agreement regarding the status of the Sudan forced on the Egyptians and the Sudanese by the British under Lord Cromer. The two territories were henceforth separately administered, and the Sudan was colonized even more directly than Egypt.

WHEREAS certain provinces in the Soudan which were in rebellion against the authority of His Highness the Khedive have now been reconquered by the joint military and financial efforts of Her Britannic Majesty's Government and the Government of His Highness the Khedive;

And whereas it has become necessary to decide upon a system for the administration of, and for the making of, laws for, the said reconquered provinces, under which due allowance may be made for the backward and unsettled condition of large portions thereof, and the varying requirements of different localities;

And whereas it is desired to give effect to the claims which have accrued to Her Britannic Majesty's Government, by right of conquest, to share in the present settlement and future working and development of the said system of administration and legislation; . . . .

Art. III.—The supreme military and civil command in the Soudan shall be vested in one officer, termed the "Governor-General of the Soudan." He shall be appointed by Khedivial Decree on the recommendation of Her Britannic Majesty's Government, and shall be removed only by Khedivial Decree, with the consent of Her Britannic Majesty's Government.

Art. IV.—Laws, as also Orders and Regulations, with the full force of law, for the good government of the Soudan, and for regulating the holding, disposal and devolution of property of every kind therein situate, may from time to time be made, altered, or abrogated by Proclamation of the Governor-General. Such Laws, Orders, and Regulations may apply to the whole or any named part of the Soudan, and may, either explicitly or by necessary implication, alter or abrogate any existing Law or Regulation.

All such Proclamations shall be forthwith notified to Her Britannic Majesty's Agent and Consul-General in Cairo, and to the President of the Council of Ministers of His Highness the Khedive.

Art. V.—No Egyptian Law, Decree, Ministerial Arrêté, or other enactment hereafter to be made or promulgated, shall apply to the Soudan or any part thereof, save in so far as the same shall be applied by Proclamation of the Governor-General in manner hereinbefore provided. . . .

(Signed) CROMER
BOUTROS GHALI

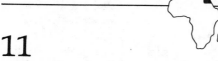

11

Ahmad Lutfi al-Sayyid, "Lord Cromer before History"

Al-Jarida, April 13, 1907, in Charles Wendell, *The Evolution of the Egyptian National Image* (Berkeley, 1972), pp. 300–301. Translated by Wendell

AHMAD LUTFI AL-SAYYID (1872–1963) was one of the founders of modern Egyptian nationalism. The son of a minor officeholder in the Nile Delta, he early showed great intellectual promise, obtaining the best available education at the Khedivial Secondary School and the School of Law in Cairo, from which he graduated in 1894. After eleven years in public service, he turned to private affairs and soon became editor of a new newspaper, *Al-Jarida* (The Journal), from which he expounded his nationalist convictions. After the outbreak of the First World War, he returned to government employment, serving in a number of capacities, including that of first chancellor of Cairo University and, for brief periods, in two cabinets. For the last twenty-two years of his life, he served as president of the Academy of the Arabic Language.

What is the total result of this policy? The result is that if we look at it through English eyes, we can only praise it. But if we look at it as any Egyptian must who seeks the welfare of his country, we cannot drum up the slightest praise for his political accomplishments in Egypt. He has deprived Egypt of the political life for which every living nation yearns. If we cannot but acknowledge that Lord Cromer extended the sphere of personal freedom we cannot deny that he did just the opposite with respect to the Egyptian officials in the government. He divested them of freedom, authority, and influence, and handed these over to the English officials, and therefore many gifted young Egyptians began to shun the government service. There is no greater proof of this than the current drastic need of the government for officials and employees. We do not think that the ineptitude that Lord Cromer mentions in his report is anything but the reflex of defective education and the poor treatment meted out to officials and employees in the government. Perhaps he thought that the abandonment of decent education was in accord with the best interests of Great Britain, for Lord Cromer seeks the interest of his country above all else in everything—which is the manner in which a zealous patriot will behave toward his fatherland. In the same vein are his pronouncements on Pan-Islamism and the existence of strong general support for it in Egypt, though there is absolutely no trace of such feeling in Egypt. But it is in the British interest to represent it as a frightening bugbear. And cut to the same pattern are every act, every agreement, every step, and every measure adopted by this great English statesman.

Perhaps it would have been within the power of Lord Cromer to obtain even more advantages for his country than he did, had he also put his mind to winning the affection of the Egyptians as whose friend he described himself, to establishing the foundations of a kind of public education that would be productive and serviceable to the nation, and to expelling those who opposed this from the educational system. And if he had relied on competent Egyptians to effect his reforms, and had trained them for good administration by allowing them freedom of action; and if he had refrained from simply eliminating true Eyptian nationality by his remarks about creating an "internationalist" nationality for Egypt, there is no doubt that he would have won the friendship of the Egyptian nation for his country, and for himself praise from the Egyptians equaling their praise for his work in enlarging the domain of personal freedom, and inculcating respect for justice and equality among all classes of the nation.

12

Count de Bourmont to the Dey of Algiers, July 4, 1830

in Perceval, Barton Lord, *Algiers, with Notices of the Neighbouring States of Barbary*, 2 vols. (London, 1835), 1:119–20

COUNT LOUIS DE BOURMONT (1773-1846) led the French invasion of the Algerian coast. More a professional soldier than an ideologue, he fought with Napoleon until 1814 and then joined Louis XVIII. Under the restored monarchy he became a marshal of France.

Ultimatum to the Dey of Algiers:

1. The fort of the Kassaubah, with all the other forts dependent on Algiers, and the harbour, shall be placed in the hands of the French troops the 5th of July, at 10 o'clock, a.m.

2. The general-in-chief of the French army ensures the Dey of Algiers personal liberty, and all his private property.

3. The Dey shall be free to retire with his family and wealth wherever he pleases. While he remains at Algiers he and his family shall be under the protection of the commander-in-chief. A guard shall insure his safety, and that of his family.

4. The same advantages, and same protection are assured to all the soldiers of the militia.

5. The exercise of the Mohammedan religion shall remain free; the liberty of the inhabitants of all classes, their religion, property, commerce, and industry shall receive no injury; their women shall be respected: the general takes this on his own responsibility.

6. The ratification of this convention to be made before 10 a.m., on the 5th of July, and the French troops immediately after to take possession of the Kassaubah, and other forts.

13

Abd el-Kadr to the Sultan of Morocco, October 1838

in Colonel Charles Henry Spencer Churchill, *The Life of Abdel Kader, Ex-Sultan of the Arabs of Algeria* (London, 1867), pp. 150–52

ABD EL-KADR (1808–83) rallied the Algerian people against the French invasion of 1830. Born to a prominent family he was at both a sharif (a descendant of the Prophet's tribe in Arabia) and the son of a marabout (the leader of a North African Sufi order). Although the Turkish garrisons which had formerly ruled Algeria submitted quickly to the French, Abd el-Kadr refused to recognize European conquest, declaring himself sultan of Algeria. Between 1832 and 1843 he kept the French at bay, necessitating the importation of 100,000 French troops. Time finally caught up with him, and after a series of defeats he surrendered in 1847. Six years later, he announced his approval of the French regime.

The people of Algeria are now united. The standard of the Djehad is furled. The roads are secure and practicable. The usages of barbarism have been abandoned and obliterated. A girl can traverse the land alone, by night and by day, from east to west, without fearing obstruction. A man even meeting the murderer of his brother dares not retaliate, but appeals for justice to the authorities.

We have been ever on the alert, night and day, moving through the length and breadth of the land, in mountains and in plains; sometimes leading forth to battle, and at other times regulating affairs. We now beg your highness to send one of your sons, grandsons, or servants, to assume the reins of government; for now there is neither trouble nor opposition from any quarter. I will be the first to serve under him, and to exert my poor abilities to the utmost, to counsel and advise him.

I trust to that consideration and indulgence which distinguishes you, to accept this my prayer to be relieved from the charge which is weighing on me.

I send your Highness some presents which have been sent me by the King of the French, from which I have only retained a pair of pistols. Also some of the best mules in Algeria. Their number, together with that of the other articles, are detailed in the account enclosed in this letter.

14

The Earl of Aberdeen, British Foreign Secretary, to Lord Cowley, British Ambassador in Paris, January 28, 1841

in Sir Edward Hertslet, *The Map of Africa by Treaty*, 3 vols. (3d ed., 1909; rpt. London, 1967), 2:644–45

GEORGE HAMILTON-GORDON, fourth earl of Aberdeen (1784–1860), was one of the leaders of British government during the early years of Queen Victoria's reign. Although a Scot, he was educated in England at Harrow and Cambridge. After sitting in the House of Lords and serving on a number of diplomatic missions, in 1828 he entered the British cabinet, where he served in numerous capacities over the next twenty-six years. Between

1841 and 1846 he was foreign secretary, and in 1852 he became prime minister, serving until 1855, when he was forced to resign over his conduct of the Crimean War.

Foreign Office, January 28, 1841.

MY LORD,

My attention has been directed to the report in the "Moniteur," of a speech delivered in the Chamber of Deputies by M. Guizot, on the 20th instant. On that occasion his Excellency read in the "Tribune" an account of a conversation between the Count de St. Aulaire and myself, which has reference to the French possessions in Africa, and which had been transmitted by the Ambassador to the French Minister.

In this relation, the Count de St. Aulaire observes, "I began by asserting that the security of our African possessions was for us an interest of the highest importance, which he could not allow to give way before any consideration; and Lord Aberdeen, after having listened to me attentively, said, I am very glad to be able to explain myself distinctly to you upon this point. I was Minister in 1830. If I were to go back to that time, I should have much to say; but I take affairs as they are in 1841, and in the state in which they have been left by preceding Cabinets; I therefore look upon your position in Africa as a *fait accompli*, against which I have no further objection to make."

Now, I readily subscribe to the accuracy of this statement, with the exception of the last sentence. I never said that I had now no objection to make to the establishment of the French in Algiers; but that I had no observation to make on the subject, and that it was my intention to be silent. The context shows that such was my meaning; and, in fact, this decision was the result of mature reflection. I felt that, after 10 years of acquiescence, any objections at the present moment would have been misplaced, and that the course which it would have been impossible for me formerly to have adopted had now become entirely consistent with propriety and duty. It does not follow, however, that objections, although not expressed, may not be entertained.

I have explained to the French Ambassador the misapprehension into which he had fallen, and the erroneous statement which, in consequence, he had made to his Government.

With the same object in view, your Excellency will have the goodness to read this despatch to M. Guizot.

I am, &c.,

ABERDEEN

H. E. Lord Cowley

15

Khayr al-Din al-Tunisi, *The Surest Path to Knowledge concerning the Condition of Countries*

in Leon Carl Brown, *The Surest Path: The Political Treatise of a Nineteenth-Century Muslim Statesman* (Cambridge, Mass., 1967), pp. 160–61, 163–64. Translated by Brown

KHAYR AL-DIN AL-TUNISI (1810–90) was one of the leading figures in the government of the bey of Tunis. Although Tunisia was legally a part of the Ottoman Empire, Khayr al-Din consistently advocated greater autonomy for the territory, which was already nearly self-governing. He was also concerned with the challenge of European powers, which had already annexed considerable portions of the Ottoman Empire, and his book *The Surest Path*, published in 1867 in Arabic and later translated into French, is devoted to the problem of dealing with the Europeans. He served as vizier to the bey from 1873 to 1877. When the French invaded Tunisia in 1881, Khayr al-Din moved to Istanbul rather than live under colonial rule.

Since what we have been presenting on this subject indicates that liberty is the basis of the great development of knowledge and civilization in the European kingdoms, we believe it imperative to demonstrate the meaning of liberty in actual practice in order to avert any possible ambiguity.

The expression "liberty" is used by Europeans in two senses. One is called "personal liberty." This is the individual's complete freedom of action over himself and his property, and the protection of his person, his honor and his wealth. . . .

The second sense of liberty is political liberty which is the demand of the subjects to participate in the politics of the kingdom and to discuss the best course of action. . . .

Among the most important things the Europeans have gathered from the lofty tree of liberty are the improvements in communications by means of railroads, support for commercial societies, and the attention given to technical training. By means of the railroads products can be imported from distant lands quickly enough to be useful, whereas their importation was formerly impossible. They would have spoiled en route or the freight costs would have been several times the value of the goods.

With these societies the circulation of capital is expanded, profits increase accordingly, and wealth is put into the hands of the most proficient who can cause it to increase.

Through technical training wealth gains the necessary means of productive activity from among the ranks of those without capital.

16

Treaty of peace between France and Tunis, May 12, 1881

in Sir Edward Hertslet, *The Map of Africa by Treaty*, 3 vols. (3d ed., 1909; rpt. London, 1967), 3:1185–87. Translation by the British Foreign Office

THE VALIDITY of this treaty depends on an extremely loose interpretation of international law. According to the Turks, Tunisia was a subordinate part of the Ottoman Empire and could not enter treaties without Turkish permission. The French rather disingenuously argued that the Tunisians were independent, in order to bring them into the French Empire.

The Government of the French Republic and that of His Highness the Bey of Tunis, wishing to prevent for ever the renewal of the disturbances which have recently occurred on the frontiers of the two States and on the Tunisian coast, and being desirous of drawing closer their ancient relations of friendship and good neighbourhood, have determined to conclude a Convention to this effect, in the interest of the two High Contracting Parties.

In consequence, the President of the French Republic has named as his Plenipotentiary M. le Général Bréard, who has agreed with his Highness the Bey upon the following stipulations:—

Confirmation of existing Treaties between France and Tunis.

Art. I.—The Treaties of Peace, Friendship, and Commerce, and all other Conventions actually existing between the French Republic and His Highness the Bey of Tunis, are expressly confirmed and renewed.

Temporary Occupation by French Troops
of certain points in Tunis.

Art. II.—With a view of facilitating the accomplishment by the French Republic of the measures which it will have to take in order to attain the end proposed by the High Contracting Parties, His Highness the Bey of Tunis consents that the French military authorities should occupy the points which they may deem necessary to ensure the re-establishment of order and the security of the frontiers and of the coast.

French Occupation to cease on re-establishment of Order.

This occupation shall cease when the French and Tunisian military authorities shall have recognized by common consent that the Local Administration is capable of guaranteeing the maintenance of order.

French assistance to be afforded to the Bey.

Art. III.—The Government of the French Republic undertakes to give constant support to His Highness the Bey of Tunis against any danger which may menace the person or dynasty of His Highness, or which may compromise the tranquility of his States.

Guarantee of existing Treaties between
Tunis and Foreign Powers.

Art. IV.—The Government of the French Republic guarantees the execution of the Treaties at present existing between the Government of the Regency and the different European Powers.

Appointment of a French Minister-Resident in Tunis.

Art. V.—The Government of the French Republic shall be represented near His Highness the Bey of Tunis by a Minister-Resident who will watch over the execution of the present instrument, and who will be the medium of communication between the

French Government and the Tunisian authorities for all affairs common to the two countries.

French Diplomatic and Consular Agents to protect Tunisian Interests Abroad.

Art. VI.—The Diplomatic and Consular Agents of France in foreign countries will be charged with the protection of Tunisian interests and of the nationals of the Regency.

No International Act to be conducted by the Bey without French authority.

In return, His Highness the Bey undertakes to conclude no act having an international character without having communicated it to the Government of the French Republic, and without having previously come to an understanding with them.

Tunisian Finances and Creditors of Tunis.

Art. VII.—The Government of the French Republic and the Government of His Highness the Bey of Tunis reserve to themselves the right to fix, by a common agreement, the bases of a financial organization of the Regency, which shall be of a nature to assure the creditors of Tunis.

17

Protest of the Turks against the French treaty, May 16, 1881

in Sir Edward Hertslet, *Map of Africa by Treaty*, 3 vols. (3d ed., 1909; rpt. London, 1967), 3:1187–88. Translation by the British Foreign Office

Assim Pasha to Musurus Pasha.

(Telegraphic.) *Constantinople*, May 16, 1881.

We did not fail, when the events which have just taken place at Tunis occurred, repeatedly to bring to the notice of the Signatories of the Berlin Treaty the full and entire sovereign rights of the

Sublime Porte over that province, an integral portion of the Ottoman Empire. Those rights, established *ab antiquo,* have been exercised by the Turkish Government without interruption up to the present day, and have obtained recognition from the Powers in general.

Nor did we fail, both before and after the entry of French troops into Tunis, to propose that a friendly understanding should be come to between the Sublime Porte and the Government of the French Republic with the view of reconciling our rights with the interests of French, and of thus removing all grounds for the complaints made by the latter country of the raids of certain Berber tribes, which raids the authorities of Tunis had declared themselves ready to repress without delay from the first commencement of the quarrel.

The Pasha of Tunis and the people entrusted to his government by Imperial Firman, on their side, appealed, as was their duty, to the Suzerain Court for the purpose of laying before it the critical situation in which they found themselves placed by the advance of French troops into their country, and of urgently requesting us, as their legitimate rulers, to come to their assistance.

No attention was paid to our markedly conciliatory proposals, nor to the irrefutable proofs which we adduced in support of our rights; nay, more, the Government of the French Republic thought fit to deny the existence of the immemorial ties of vassalage which bind Tunis to the Ottoman Empire, by asserting the alleged independence of that country, and thus to run counter to all our remonstrances, and in spite of the protests of the Governor-General and people, by gradually occupying the greater the greater part of the territory of Tunis, and, finally, by forbidding us, in a peremptory and threatening manner, to send a single ship to the spot. . . .

I request you to communicate this protest, officially and without the slightest delay, to His Excellence Her Britannic Majesty's Minister for Foreign Affairs.

THE MOTIVATIONS IMPELLING EUROPEANS TO COLONIZE SOUTHERN AFRICA were quite different from those leading them to the northern part of the continent. Beginning with a strategic interest in the Cape of Good Hope, whose commanding position on the route to India had been recognized in the fifteenth century, different European powers had established successive colonies there. At first the major question was the degree of control over the hinterland necessary to protect the base at the Cape. White settlers, the ancestors of the Afrikaners, soon expanded beyond the first narrow boundaries, demanding protection for their colonial interests. By the late nineteenth century, these settlers and a new wave of British settlers had conquered most of what is today the Republic of South Africa.

Despite these military successes, which deprived the local Africans of most of their land, the conquering Europeans could not agree on a single government appropriate to the new territory. Many Afrikaners—Boers, as they were called in those days—had left the British Cape Colony to establish new states in the interior—on lands vacated as a result of African wars. These Afrikaners were extremely reluctant to accept British rule. The British government in London also resisted suggestions to annex the Afrikaner republics on grounds of cost until unanticipated economic opportunities changed the situation.

After the discovery of diamonds at Kimberley, British partisans in South Africa and in London renewed their call to extend the British flag over these new sources of wealth. Over the objections of the Afrikaners living in the Orange Free State, the British government of the Cape Colony annexed the diamond fields, and if one is to believe the promotional book quoted in Document 18, all concerned prospered. Astute businessmen, led by Cecil Rhodes (Document 19), amassed great wealth and began to call for the annexation of additional territories, which would bring even greater wealth and glory to the British Empire. As Document 20 shows, Rhodes' agents were as unscrupulous as European diplomats, using legal documents to gain rights over African land. By the late 1880s the scramble for Africa had progressed

---

Chapter Three

South Africa:
The Clash of Liberalisms

to the point that the British government stood firmly behind Rhodes and his methods (see Documents 21 and 22).

No European power was willing to expend the time and energy necessary to challenge the British in southern Africa, but the tiny Afrikaner republics constituted an unexpected obstacle. The Transvaal (known for a time as the South African Republic) stood on deposits of gold which were more valuable than the diamonds at Kimberley. By the late 1890s Rhodes and other British South African settlers had convinced high officials of the British government that it was unwise to allow the Afrikaner republics to remain independent. Playing on fears of the Germans, who gave the Afrikaners at least verbal support, and on alleged abuses to English-speakers in Johannesburg, the settlers demanded a war against the Afrikaners. The British high commissioner for South Africa, Lord Milner, adopted this position in the memorandum reproduced as Document 23. Although elements of the British Left, led by John Hobson, opposed the war (Document 24), the British sent out their full military might against the Boers. These latter proved unexpectedly difficult to defeat, resorting to guerrilla war in the face of losses in more traditional engagements (Document 25). After two and a half years of fighting, however, the Afrikaners realized that they could not survive indefinitely against British arms and concentration camps and surrendered. Responding to the situation, one of the Boer generals, J. C. Smuts, eloquently made the case for surrender (Document 26), and the Boer republics became part of the British Empire.

18

Theodore Reunert, "Diamond Mining at the Cape"

in John Noble, *Official Handbook: History, Production, and Resources of the Cape of Good Hope*, 2d ed. (Cape Town, 1886) pp. 180–81, 194–95

JOHN NOBLE was clerk of the Cape Colony House of Assembly. He also compiled the first edition of the handbook, which appeared in 1875.

Hardly a more dreary existence can be imagined than that of the early days on the Diamond Fields. Comforts there were absolutely none. Not a single substantial dwelling afforded shelter from the burning sun: men lived under canvas, and the owner of an iron or wooden shanty was looked upon as a lord. If you crossed the street you trod ankle deep in sand, and probably before reaching the other side a small dust storm in embryo had choked and blinded you. The dust and the flies, and worse, pervaded everywhere; they sat down with you to meals and escorted you to bed. The want of good food and pure water brought on disease, and many a poor fellow who had expected to find an Eldorado on the Fields succumbed to the fever which threatened to become endemic. Yet the men who had subjected themselves to this sort of life were mostly fresh from the comforts of civilization. There was an entire absence of the rowdy uncouth class such as peopled the "Roaring Camps" of the far West. The expense and difficulty of reaching the Diamond Fields, even from the nearest towns of the Cape Colony, kept rogues and loafers out of the place. Though distant only 650 miles from Cape Town, and 500 from Port Elizabeth, the journey from the latter port occupied a month and six weeks from the former. It had to be performed in a springless transport-wagon, drawn by ten to sixteen bullocks, over roads that no description could convey the vileness of, and the cost per passenger was not less than fifty pounds.

To-day all this is changed. The railway, which has placed the Diamond Fields within 30 hours' journey of the coast, now brings a daily supply of all the luxuries the Colony can produce, whilst the establishment of the Kimberley waterworks provides a constant store of good and cheap water, which not only removes the greatest hardship of the early days, but gives an impetus to gardening, so that thousands of trees have been planted, and nearly every house now boasts its flower-plot. In the last five years large sums have been spent in building and other permanent improvements. The town has been drained, paved, and lighted, and the public health has so greatly improved that "camp fever" is said to be dying out, and seldom now proves fatal. . . .

Kaffir* labour is mainly employed in all the less responsible operations of the mines: in drilling holes for the dynamite cartridges, in picking and breaking up the ground in the claims and *trucking* it away from the depositing boxes and the margin on the mine and tipping it on the depositing floors, where it undergoes a variety of processes before it is ready for washing, and is again filled into trucks and driven to the machines. For every three truck-

* Kaffir, a term borrowed from the Arabic term for pagan, was an extremely insulting term used by whites to describe blacks in South Africa.— B.F.

loads of ground daily hauled out of the mine there is on an average one Kaffir labourer employed, and to every five Kaffirs there is one white overseer or artizan. In 1882 the number of native labourers in Kimberley Mine was 4,000; but in 1884, owing to the serious stoppage of works, they had sunk to 1,500. These labourers are recruited from 16 or 20 different native tribes from various parts of the Colony and the Interior, the proportion of the several tribes at any time on the Fields varying greatly according to the internal state, whether of peace or war, of the district whence they hail. Out of 20,000 natives arriving in search of work in the first half of 1882, 8,000 were Secocoeni's Basutos, 6,000 Shangaans, 1,500 British Basutos, and 1,000 Zulus, the balance consisting of representatives of no less than 16 other different tribes and races. The market afforded for the employment of native labour and the consequent development of native trade is not the least of the incidental benefits conferred on South Africa by the discovery of the Diamond Fields. . . .

19

Sir Lewis Michell, *The Life of the Right Honourable Cecil John Rhodes*

2 vols. (London, 1910), 1:180–81, 2:311–12

LEWIS LOYD MICHELL (1842-1928), one of Cecil Rhodes' most successful associates, wrote an official biography of the empire builder in 1910, eight years after Rhodes' death. Like his mentor, Michell was born and educated in Britain but spent most of his active life in South Africa. Sent out to Port Elizabeth by a British bank in 1864, he became manager of the local branch of the recently created Standard Bank of South Africa in 1872. He moved to Cape Town in 1885, where he quickly became involved in Rhodes' enterprises, serving as sole general manager of the Standard Bank, chairman of De Beers Consolidated Mines, as a director of the British South Africa Company, and as a member of the Cape House of Assembly.

The first excerpt describes Rhodes at the peak of his powers, when he was creating the diamond trust in 1887-88. The second excerpt contains Michell's evaluation of the place of Rhodes in history.

It will be seen that the position of Rhodes was not an easy one. He had his full share of monetary troubles. Financially he was far less strong than Barnato, and the claims he had acquired in the De Beers Mine were poorer, claim for claim, than those held by his competitor in the Kimberley Mine. He had none of Barnato's light-hearted geniality or, as some called it, irresponsible frivolity. He possessed few intimate friends, and not even to all of them did he disclose his hand. Mere acquaintances disliked his moody silences, varied with fits of rather boisterous fun. They considered him ex-clusive, morose, rough and overbearing. And it must be admitted that he was a good hater, violent when thwarted, and at times blunt to the point of rudeness. It is difficult to be sufficiently un-conventional to shock a mining camp, but he shocked it. In dress he was almost disreputable. He seldom took pains to ingratiate himself with any one, and a man who too openly scorns his fellows must expect to suffer social ostracism and to have his character traduced. It would be idle to deny that for a time there were un-favourable rumours in circulation regarding him, or that he was, in many circles, unpopular. But like Gallio he "cared for none of those things." Behind a mask of indifference, he strove strenuously for wealth, because wealth was power, and he coveted power in order to gain supremacy over rival interests, and because he aimed at making Kimberley a force to be reckoned with and a help to his ripening policy of Northern expansion. To superficial observers he was a cynical, surly dreamer. Only Jameson knew, and Beit and Rudd, and a very few others. To the rest of his little world he was an unknown quantity, and his manners were misliked, but few im-portant transactions were mooted without his being approached for assistance or advice. . . .

It will be more to the purpose to say that he still lives in the hearts and imagination of colonists: that almost all our high and fruitful thoughts and acts of late years are traceable to his com-pelling example. South African mining, agriculture, and education, all owe their new life to his tenacity of purpose and his resourceful energy. His Scholarship Foundation, still in its infancy, may in time move the world, though as yet its potentialities are hardly realised beyond a narrow circle. Above all we have to thank Rhodes for his preservation of that immense territory called after his name—a ter-ritory which in alien hands would have barred our further expan-sion northward, seriously shaken the prestige of Great Britain and rendered nugatory all prospect of friendly union under the flag of England. We have also to thank him that throughout his career he preached in season and out of season the salutary doctrine of equal rights—a doctrine the negation of which drenched South Africa for nearly three years in the blood of its noblest sons.

Regard him as we may, with critical or uncritical eyes, we must all admit that he was a great Englishman and one of the few who have left a permanent mark on the Empire. For my own part I confidently leave his fame to the verdict of posterity.

20
The Rudd Concession, 1888

in Sir Lewis Michell, *The Life of the Right Honourable Cecil John Rhodes*, 2 vols. (London, 1910), 1:244–45

THE RUDD CONCESSION is typical of the piously self-serving legal documents used to deprive African chiefs of their lands. Although it does not call for incorporation of Ndebele territory into the British Empire, it makes such incorporation possible by a clause granting full powers to the concession holders, who were agents of Cecil Rhodes.

Know all men by these presents, that whereas Charles Dunell Rudd, of Kimberley; Rochfort Maguire, of London; and Francis Robert Thompson, of Kimberley, hereinafter called the grantees, have covenanted and agreed, and do hereby covenant and agree, to pay to me, my heirs and successors, the sum of one hundred pounds sterling, British currency, on the first day of every lunar month; and, further, to deliver at my royal kraal one thousand Martini-Henry breech-loading rifles, together with one hundred thousand rounds of suitable ball cartridge, five hundred of the said rifles and fifty thousand of the said cartridges to be ordered from England forthwith and delivered with reasonable despatch, and the remainder of the said rifles and cartridges to be delivered as soon as the said grantees shall have commenced to work mining machinery within my territory; and further, to deliver on the

Zambesi River a steamboat with guns suitable for defensive purposes upon the said river, or in lieu of the said steamboat, should I
so elect to pay to me the sum of five hundred pounds sterling,
British currency. On the execution of these presents, I, Lo Bengula,
King of Matabeleland, Mashonaland, and other adjoining territories, in exercise of my council of indunas, do hereby grant and
assign unto the said grantees, their heirs, representatives, and
assigns, jointly and severally, the complete and exclusive charge
over all metals and minerals situated and contained in my
kingdoms, principalities, and dominions, together with full power
to do all things that they may deem necessary to win and procure
the same, and to hold, collect, and enjoy the profits and revenues,
if any, derivable from the said metals and minerals, subject to the
aforesaid payment; and whereas I have been much molested to late
by diverse persons seeking and desiring to obtain grants and concessions of land and mining rights in my territories, I do hereby
authorise the said grantees, their heirs, representatives, and
assigns, to take all necessary and lawful steps to exclude from my
kingdom, principalities, and dominions all persons seeking land,
metals, minerals, or mining rights therein, and I do hereby undertake to render them all such needful assistance as they may from
time to time require for the exclusion of such persons, and to grant
no concessions of land or mining rights from and after this date
without their consent and concurrence; provided that, if at any
time the said monthly payment of one hundred pounds shall cease
and determine from the date of the last-made payment; and, further, provided, that nothing contained in these presents shall extend to or affect a grant made by me of certain mining rights in a
portion of my territory south of the Ramaquaban River, which
grant is common known as the Tati Concession.

This, given under my hand this thirtieth day of October, in the
year of our Lord 1888, at my royal kraal.

LO BENGULA X his mark.

Witnesses: CHAS. D. HELM   C. D. RUDD.
ROCHFORT MAGUIRE.
F. R. THOMPSON.

21

Charter of Incorporation of the British South Africa Company, October 29, 1889

in Sir Lewis Michell, *The Life of the Right Honourable Cecil John Rhodes*, 2 vols. (London, 1910), 1:331–36

THE BRITISH SOUTH AFRICA COMPANY'S charter is yet another kind of legal document which played an important role in the colonization of Africa. The company received a royal charter based directly on the authority of Queen Victoria, rather than the simple incorporation statute normally obtained by joint-stock companies. Needless to say, this charter was authorized by Lord Salisbury's government before it appeared in the Queen's name.

In effect the charter authorized Rhodes' company to govern lands in Central Africa on behalf of the British government. By allotting this responsibility to a private company rather than a colonial government, the British government at home counted on saving the cost of military subventions normally allocated to new colonies.

VICTORIA by the Grace of God, of the United Kingdom of Great Britain and Ireland, Queen, Defender of the Faith.

To all to whom these presents shall come, Greetings:

WHEREAS a Humble Petition has been presented to Us in Our Council by THE MOST NOBLE JAMES DUKE OF ABERCORN Companion of the Most Honourable Order of the Bath; THE MOST NOBLE ALEXANDER WILLIAM GEORGE DUKE OF FIFE Knight of the Most Ancient and Most Noble Order of the Thistle, Privy Councillor; THE RIGHT HONOURABLE EDRIC FREDICK Lord GIFFORD, V.C.; CECIL JOHN RHODES, of Kimberley, in the Cape Colony, Member of the Executive Council and of the House of Assembly of the Colony of the Cape of Good Hope; ALFRED BEIT, of 29, Holborn Viaduct, London, Merchant; ALBERT HENRY GEORGE GREY, of Howick, Northumberland, ESQUIRE; and GEORGE CASTON, of 18, Lennox Gardens, London, Esquire, Barrister-at-Law. . . .

1. The principal field of the operations of the British South Africa Company (in this Our Charter referred to as "the Company") shall be the region of South Africa lying immediately to the

north of British Bechuanaland, and to the north and west of the South African Republic, and to the west of the Portuguese Dominions. . . .

6. The Company shall always be and remain British in character and domicile, and shall have its principal office in Great Britain, and the Company's principal representative in South Africa, and the Directors shall always be natural born British subjects or persons who have been naturalized as British subjects by or under an Act of Parliament of Our United Kingdom; but this Article shall not disqualify any person nominated a Director by this Our Charter, or any person whose election as a Director shall have been approved by Our Secretary of State, from acting in that capacity. . . .

10. The Company shall to the best of its ability preserve peace and order in such ways and manners as it shall consider necessary, and may with that object make ordinances (to be approved by Our Secretary of State) and may establish and maintain a force of police. . . .

13. The Company as such, or its officers as such, shall not in any way interfere with the religion of any class or tribe of the peoples of the territories aforesaid or of any of the inhabitants thereof, except so far as may be necessary in the interest of humanity and all forms of religious worship or religious ordinances may be exercised within the said territories and no hindrance shall be offered thereto except as aforesaid. . . .

14. In the administration of justice to the said peoples or inhabitants, careful regard shall always be had to the customs and laws of the class or tribe or nation to which the parties respectively belong, especially with respect to the holding, possession, transfer and disposition of lands and goods and testate or intestate succession thereto, and marriage, divorce and legitimacy and other rights of property and personal rights, but subject to any British laws which may be in force in any of the territories aforesaid, and applicable to the peoples or inhabitants thereof. . . .

22

Colonial Office to Foreign Office, May 16, 1889: the British interpretation of the Charter's significance

in Sir Lewis Michell, *The Life of the Right Honourable Cecil John Rhodes,* 2 vols. (London, 1910), 1:266

In consenting to consider this scheme in more detail, Lord Knutsford has been influenced by the consideration that if such a company is incorporated by Royal Charter, its constitution, objects and operations will become more directly subject to control by Her Majesty's Government than if it were left to these gentlemen to incorporate themselves under the Joint Stock Companies Acts, as they are entitled to do. The example of the Imperial East Africa Company shows that such a body may, to some considerable extent, relieve Her Majesty's Government from diplomatic difficulties and heavy expenditure.

23

Lord Alfred Milner, High Commissioner for South Africa, to Joseph Chamberlain, Secretary of State for the Colonies, May 4, 1899

in *The Milner Papers,* Cecil Headlam, ed., Vol. 1: *South Africa, 1897-1899* (London, 1931), pp. 351-53

LORD ALFRED MILNER (1854-1925), like Lord Cromer, under whom he served early in his career, was a pillar of British imperialism. The son of a physician, he was born in Germany and began school there, completing his education in Britain, where he obtained highest honors from Oxford in classics and philosophy. After three years—from 1882 to 1885—as a journalist, he joined the British administration in Egypt, where he worked in financial affairs from 1884 to 1892. He then returned to England for five years, serving in a similar capacity. In 1897 he received his first job as an administrator, high commissioner for South Africa, where he served until 1905.

Milner is best known because of his role in South Africa, where he is frequently seen as being the individual most nearly responsible for the Second Anglo-Boer War (1899-1902). In his prosecution of the civil side of the war and the reconstruction of the conquered Afrikaner republics, Milner proved himself an authoritarian whose major concern was the welfare of the British Empire rather than the rights of populations within it.

After his departure from South Africa, in 1905, he temporarily retired from politics and devoted himself to finances, through which he was closely connected with South African interests. In 1918 he returned to political life, joining Lloyd George's cabinet first as secretary for war and then, from 1918 to 1921, as secretary of state for the colonies.

A busy industrial community is not naturally prone to political unrest. But they bear the chief burden of taxation; they constantly feel in their business and daily lives the effects of chaotic legislation and of incompetent and unsympathetic administration; they have many grievances, but they believe all this could be gradually removed if they had only a fair share of political power. This is the meaning of their vehement demand for enfranchisement. Moreover, they are mostly British subjects, accustomed to a free system and equal rights; they feel deeply the personal indignity involved in position of permanent subjection to the ruling caste which owes its wealth and power to their exertion. The political turmoil in the Transvaal Republic will never end till the permanent Uitlander population is admitted to a share in the Government, and while that turmoil lasts there will be no tranquillity or adequate progress in Her Majesty's South African dominions. . . .

The case for intervention is overwhelming. The only attempted answer is that things will right themselves if left alone. But, in fact, the policy of leaving things alone has been tried for years, and it had led to their going from bad to worse. It is not true that this is owing to the Raid. They were going from bad to worse before the Raid. We were on the verge of war before the Raid, and the Transvaal was on the verge of revolution. The effect of the Raid has been to give the policy of leaving things alone a new lease of life, and with the old consequences. . . .

The spectacle of thousands of British subjects kept permanently in the position of helots, constantly chafing under undoubted grievances, and calling vainly to Her Majesty's Government for redress, does steadily undermine the influence and reputation of Great Britain and the respect for the British Government within its own dominions. . .

24

J. A. Hobson, *The War in South Africa: Its Causes and Effects*

2d ed. (London, 1900), in *The Anglo-Boer War: Why Was It Fought? Who Was Responsible?* ed. Theodore C. Caldwell (Boston, 1965), pp. 18–19, 21–22

JOHN ATKINSON HOBSON (1858-1940) was perhaps the best-known critic of British imperialism. Hobson came from a more modest background than Lord Cromer or Lord Milner, attending Derby School before studying at Oxford. Hobson spent most of his life as a journalist, writing first for the *Manchester Guardian* and then for the American magazine *The Nation*. In 1899, while employed by the *Guardian*, he visited South Africa, where he came away with the impression that the impending war with the Boers would be fought on behalf of British capitalists rather than the British empire. He put together his thoughts in their best-known form in his book *Imperialism*, which appeared in 1902.

THE HELOTS IN JOHANNESBURG

I take it that the motive which has led the majority of English people to approve, so far as they have approved, the policy of their Government, is not their convictions on the merits of the franchise or the suzerainty issues, but a deep and genuine belief that British subjects were grievously oppressed by the Boer Government, and were without security of life, liberty, and property. A recent issue of the *Nineteenth Century* contains a statement from Sir Sidney Sheppard that "neither their persons nor their property can be held safe during the present regime." Those who are responsible for working public opinion have been wisely aware that the most effective means of rousing British anger against the Transvaal was to reiterate the statement that English people in Johannesburg were subject to brutal ill-treatment and went about in fear of their lives. I found it very difficult to persuade people upon the spot of the prevalence of this English view of their grievances; and no wonder, for the audacity of the misrepresentation is almost incredible. . . .

During the weeks I spent there, public feeling ran high, and then, if at any time, it would seem reasonable to expect scenes of disorder and even riot. But never have I seen a large English town more quiet or more orderly at night than Johannesburg. Though a great deal of drinking goes on at the bars, where the company (Outlanders almost to a man) has often a most disreputable aspect, there was scarcely any of the street-brawling which I saw in Cape Town. Where occasionally a noisy tippler staggered by, the neighbouring "Zarp," with orthodox official delicacy, generally looked the other way, though the delinquent was in most instances one of the Britishers who wanted his country. I have no desire to whitewash Johannesburg or its administration; there is much reason to suppose its police to be more bribable than those of London, and more ignorant and incapable; but I saw literally no indication of the prevailing terrorism and oppression, the insecurity of person and property, charged against it, nor did my cross-examination of many Outlanders elicit any material support for such accusations.

That the machinery for the detection and punishment of crime has reached any high standard of excellence may certainly be doubted. When the rapid growth of this huge cosmopolitan city, with its environment of gold mines, peopled by ten thousand white and nearly a hundred thousand black miners, is taken into consideration, it will be recognised as most unfair to compare the order and government of Johannesburg with those of Manchester or Glasgow. . . .

FOR WHAT ARE WE FIGHTING?

In former chapters I have shown who the persons are that have brought about this war and the methods they have employed—a small confederacy of international financiers working through a kept press. It remains to describe the nature and the size of the gain which is their object.

There is no secret about the matter. This war is a terrible disaster for every one else in England and South Africa, but for the mine owners it means a large increase of profits from a more economical working of the mines, and from speculative operations. Mr. Fitz-patrick puts into the mouth of "leading men of the Rand" the following statement of grievances in 1896. "If you want the chief economic grievances they are: The Netherlands Railway Conces-sion, the dynamite monopoly, the liquor constitute an unwar-rantable burden of indirect taxation on the industry of over two and a half million sterling annually." In other words, the mining capitalists stood to gain an income of two millions and a half by a successful political or military coup. . . .

The only all-important object is to secure a full, cheap, regular, submissive supply of Kaffir and white labour. Wages form about 55 per cent. of the working expenses of the mines, and of the 6s. per ton in which Mr. Hammond expresses the advantages of "good government." . . .

The attitude of the mining industry towards the Transvaal Gov-ernment in respect of the labour question is instructive. Witnesses before the Industrial Commission at Johannesburg were unanimous in maintaining that it was the duty of the Government to procure a steady and sufficient supply of Kaffirs for the mines. The Govern-ment was called upon to accredit and assist agents of the mining in-dustry to obtain native labour, to "pay premiums to Kaffir chiefs," to furnish extra pay to native Commissioners for the same object, to convey this labour "under supervision" to the mines, erecting "compounds" along the road, reducing railway fares to one-third of the existing rate, and in a dozen other ways spending public money to serve the private interests of the mines. Why "politics and economics are so closely connected" that the public purse should be used to keep down the wages-bill of the mines is not intelligible to English people. But it is perfectly clear that under a "reformed" Government the mine owners will take every care to press these claims.

Put in a concise form, it may be said that this war is being waged in order to secure for the mines a cheap adequate supply of labour.

25

Annexation of the Orange Free State by Great Britain, May 24, 1900

in Sir Edward Hertslet, *The Map of Africa by Treaty,* 3 vols. (3d ed., 1909; rpt. London, 1967), 1:216–17

THIS PROCLAMATION is yet another legal document used in British imperial expansion. In it, the commander of British forces in South Africa, Lord Roberts, proclaims the conquest of the Orange Free State and the consequent creation of a British colony. The Boers, who still had armies in the field, did not recognize British conquest until their surrender two years later, but the British nonetheless used the annexation as the basis for establishing a military administration in the territory under their control.

Proclamation.

Whereas, certain territories in South Africa, heretofore known as the Orange Free State, have been conquered by Her Majesty's Forces, and it has seemed expedient to Her Majesty that the said territories should be annexed to, and should henceforth form part of Her Majesty's dominions, and that I should provisionally, and until Her Majesty's pleasure is more fully known, be appointed Administrator of the said territories with power to take all such measures and to make and enforce such laws as I may deem necessary for the peace, order and good government of the said territories.

Now, therefore, I, Frederick Sleigh, Baron Roberts of Kandahar, K.P., G.C.B., G.C.S.I., G.C.I.E., V.C., Field-Marshal and Commanding in Chief the British Forces in South Africa, by Her Majesty's command, and in virtue of the power and authority conferred upon me in that behalf by Her Majesty's Royal Commission, dated the 21st day of May, 1900, and in accordance with Her Majesty's instructions thereby and otherwise signified to me, do proclaim and make known that, from and after the publication hereof, the territories known as the Orange Free State are annexed to and form part of Her Majesty's dominions, and that provisionally, and until Her Majesty's pleasure is fully declared, the said territories will be administered by me with such powers as aforesaid.

Her Majesty is pleased to direct that the new territories shall henceforth be known as the *Orange River Colony*.

God Save the Queen.

Given under my hand and seal at the Head-quarters of the Army in South Africa, Camp south of the Vaal River, in the said territories, this *24th day of May, in the year of our Lord 1900.*

ROBERTS, Field-Marshal
Commanding in Chief
Her Majesty's Forces in South Africa.

26

General J. C. Smuts' speech to the representatives of the Boer republics, May 30, 1902

in *Selections from the Smuts Papers,* vols. 1–4 ed. William K. Hancock and Jean van der Poel (Cambridge, 1966), 1:529–31. Translated by J. D. Kestell

JAN CHRISTIAAN SMUTS (1870–1950) is the prototype of the person who was first defeated by the British, then became part of their regime. After completing his university years in South Africa, Smuts went to Cambridge for a law degree, which he received with the highest honors. After a few years of farming and law practice, he joined the government of the South African Republic (Transvaal) as state attorney, a position in which he served from 1898 until the republic's surrender in 1902. In the last year of the war he was general of a guerrilla army which harassed British forces.

After former officials of the Afrikaner republics were allowed in 1905 to return to political life, he made politics his main activity. He was responsible for the founding of an Afrikaner party and soon became a member of the Transvaal legislative assembly. Together with his former comrade-in-arms, General Louis Botha, he created the South African party, which appealed to English-speakers as well as to Afrikaners.

Smuts held ministries in the South African government for all but nine years during the period 1910–48. During the First World War he commanded British expeditionary forces in the German colonies of South West

Africa and East Africa (Namibia and Tanzania) and served in the British war cabinet. Upon Botha's death in 1919, he became South Africa's prime minister, an office which he held from 1919 to 1924 and from 1939 to 1948. After his defeat by Daniel Malan in 1948, he became chancellor of Cambridge University, an office normally reserved for British royalty.

We have arrived at a dark stage in the development of the war, and our cause is all the darker and more painful to me because I, as a member of the Government of the South African Republic, was one of the persons who entered into the war with England. A man may, however, not shrink from the consequences of his acts, and on an occasion like this, we must restrain all private feelings and decide only and exclusively with a view to the permanent interests of the Afrikaner people. These are great moments for us, perhaps the last time when we meet as a free people, and a free Government. Let us thus rise to the magnitude of the opportunity and arrive at a decision for which the future Afrikaner generation will bless and not curse us. The great danger before this meeting is, that it will come to a decision from a purely military point of view. Almost all the representatives here are officers who do not know fear, who have never been afraid, nor will ever become afraid of the overwhelming strength of the enemy, and who are prepared to give their last drop of blood for their country and their people. Now, if we view the matter merely from a military standpoint, if we consider it only as a military matter, then I must admit that we can still go on with the struggle. We are still an unvanquished military force. We have still 18,000 men in the field, veterans, with whom you can do almost any work. We can thus push our cause, from a military point of view, still further. But we are not here as an army, but as a people; we have not only a military question, but also a national matter to deal with. No one here represents his own commando. Everyone here represents the Afrikaner people, and not only that portion which is still in the field, but also those who are already under the sod and those who will live after we have gone. We represent, not only ourselves, but also the thousands who are dead, and have made the last sacrifice for their people, the prisoners of war scattered all over the world, and the women and children who are dying out by thousands in the concentration camps of the enemy; we represent the blood and the tears of an entire nation. . . .

What reasonable chance is there still to retain our independence? We have now fought for almost three years without a break. Without deceiving ourselves we can say that we have exerted all our powers and employed every means to further our cause. We have given thousands of lives, we have sacrificed all our earthly goods; our cherished country is one continuous desert; more than 20,000 women and children have already died in the concentration camps of the enemy. Has all this brought us nearer to our independence? On the contrary, we are getting ever further from it, and the longer we continue, the greater will be the gap between us and the object for which we have fought. The manner in which the enemy has carried on this war and still carries it on has reduced us to a condition of exhaustion which will ultimately make the continuance of the war a physical impossibility.

WHEN CONTRASTED WITH THE ANNEXATIONS OF NORTHERN AND SOUTHERN Africa, the conquest of tropical Africa is a relatively pure example of late nineteenth-century imperialism. Triumphant French and Belgian colonizers found neither Turks nor Afrikaners barring the way to expansion—only the sporadic competition of other European powers and the fruitless efforts of valiant Africans who lacked the technological means to resist the weapons developed during the Industrial Revolution.

The main opposition to Franco-Belgian expansion was internal. The elected representatives of the newly enfranchised bourgeoisie were highly suspicious of colonial adventures, opposing the allocation of taxpayers' money to projects which did not directly benefit the nation. Reflecting this concern, the documents contained in this chapter all relate in one way or another to the expenditure of government money.

The quotations from French military officers in West Africa justify imperial expansion in terms of money earned or money saved. General Louis Faidherbe, who initiated the first substantial French conquest in black Africa during the 1850s and 1860s, justified his expeditions in the Senegal Valley (Document 27) as protecting French trade. Thirty years later, when General Louis Archinard was extending Faidherbe's conquests at the height of the scramble, officials no longer had to demonstrate profitability. They were, however, obliged to show that their territorial acquisitions were cheap to administer, which was Archinard's rationale, in Document 28, for using African allies to rule new territories. After the turn of the century, Governor-General L.-G. Angoulvant used this same argument of economy (Document 29) to justify ruling the Ivory Coast through French officials rather than African ones!

On the surface, economic arguments played a less important role in the documents concerning Belgian rule in the Congo than they did in the French Empire. This is only because the Belgian Parliament took a clear stand in the 1880s opposing any allocation of public monies to King Leopold's Congo Free State. During most of that entity's existence, from

---

Chapter Four

The French and Belgian Conquests in Africa

1885 to 1908, the main economic question in the Free State was not how to get money from the mother country but how to extract it from the local population.

Although the Belgian Parliament took over direct responsibility for the government of the Congo in 1908, atrocities did not entirely cease. During the First World War, as Document 31 shows, Belgian officials were still capable of employing great brutality against Africans who resisted their authority. Thus, colonial force remained in reserve after the completion of the initial conquest.

27

General Louis Faidherbe to Chasseloup-Labat, May 1864

in *France and West Africa*, ed. John Hargreaves (London, 1969), pp. 145–47. Translated by Hargreaves

LOUIS FAIDHERBE (1818-89) was one of the principal exponents of French territorial expansion in Africa during the Second Empire, when such ideas were by no means popular. The son of a small merchant in the northern French city of Lille, Faidherbe received a partial scholarship to the Ecole polytechnique, which, like West Point, trained engineers for the army. After two missions in Algeria, one in the West Indies, and one in France itself, he was stationed in 1852 at Saint Louis, at the mouth of the Senegal River. For the next thirteen years he set about to expand French influence up the river, a task which he accomplished by dint of careful study of the region and by his military genius. After his departure from Senegal, he spent two more terms in Algeria and then organized resistance in the north of France during the Franco-Prussian War. Later, he organized an archaeological expedition to Egypt and served from 1879 to 1888 as senator from the Nord department.

The position may be summarised thus. French trade with the West Coast of Africa may be estimated at an annual value of 40 million francs, namely 24,000,000 francs of imports into France and 15,600,000 francs of exports. Of this sum Senegal (Saint-Louis and Gorée) accounts for a value of 19 millions (8 millions of imports into France, 11 millions of exports); Gabon accounts for

500,000 francs only. At Grand Bassam and Assinie trade is almost
nil. Thus the trade which we carry out in competition with other
European powers, either on parts of the coast which are open to all
comers or in actual foreign establishments, accounts for *more than
half* of the general movement of French shipping to the West Coast
of Africa. The creation of our *comptoirs* has had almost no discernible influence on this state of things, and although our trade
has found for the most part a regime concerned to give it exclusive
protection, it has successively abandoned these points, where for
twenty years, at an annual cost of 470,000 francs to the government, and of regrettable casualties caused by fever in the ranks of
the administrative and naval personnel, we have maintained our
occupation without serious results for our shipping or our influence. The moment seems come to draw clear conclusions from
this situation. Two principal facts emerge from our experience. The
first is the *stable* character of our interests in the Senegal district
[*cercle*], the second the essentially *inconstant* nature of our relations on other parts of the coast. Our commerce, which seems to
have found at Saint-Louis, under effective and progressive supervision, a centre from which to spread out, inland by the river and
southwards through our coastal establishments, is leaving Gabon
and our posts on the Gold Coast and resolutely facing in other
districts—often with marked success—the hazards of a trade exposed to arbitrary acts of the natives and to the difficulties of com-
petion.

It appears that we would be responding to these present tendencies of our traders, in the first place by consolidating the territorial
base so well established around Saint-Louis, and then by guaranteeing them on the rest of the coast, instead of a limited and
costly armed protection about which they seem to care very little,
active general supervision in their relations with the natives, and
favourable treatment from European nations. To achieve this
double purpose it would be appropriate to enter into an arrangement with England, the only power which today competes seriously with us in these waters. . . . In exchange for the Gambia, the
English might be offered Gabon, Assinie . . . , Grand Bassam and
Dabou, together with the rights conferred on us by the Protectorate
of Porto Novo, which is considerably impeding British designs
upon Dahomey. . . . (If this compensation were judged insufficient,

one might go so far as to grant access for their flag to our colony of Saint-Louis.) We would further stipulate for equality of customs, shipping and port duties in all places thus exchanged.

After such a transaction, our Senegalese colony would form a compact and homogeneous territory, bounded by its natural frontiers; all the sources from which the trade of these coasts is drawn would be completely in our hands. Those who are resisting our plans for colonisation and development would receive no more supplies with which to do so, and caravans from the interior would henceforth follow the routes we saw fit to indicate. The great projects which might be conceived for extending our influence towards Timbuktu and the upper Niger would henceforth have a large and solid base. . . .

(This negotiation would in my view be the starting point for a system on which I believe the commercial future of the West Coast of Africa depends, and which might be the culmination of European policies in these waters; I mean the neutralisation of the coast, and the admission of all countries and nations to trade in its rich products, under the guarantee of an agreement concluded among the great powers, and under the protection of all the navies of Europe.)

28

General Louis Archinard to the chiefs of Segu, April 11, 1890

in *France and West Africa*, ed. John Hargreaves (London, 1969), pp. 198–99. Translated by Hargreaves

LOUIS ARCHINARD (1850–1932), following Faidherbe's example, pursued the conquest of the Senegal and Niger valleys in the 1880s and 1890s during the high point of the scramble for Africa. Born in the northern port city of Le Havre, Archinard graduated from the Ecole polytechnique in 1870, the year of the outbreak of the Franco-Prussian War, in which he fought. He obtained his first West African post in 1880 and within eight years rose to the position of commander-in-chief of French forces on the upper Senegal River. Between 1892 and 1893 he served as lieutenant governor of the

French Sudan (now Mali). He showed little mercy toward Africans who stood in his way.

I have had you brought here to explain to you the French way of doing things. The French have not come to Ségou to take the country and govern it themselves, but with the intention of restoring it to the Bambaras, from whom it was stolen by the Tukolors. . . .

I am going to give Ségou to the son of your ancient kings. As from today your *Fama* will be Mari-Diara; but on certain conditions which will provide us with guarantees that the welfare of the country will be assured, that trade will be free, and that the Bambaras of the right bank will not be pillaged as were those of the left bank, where Mari-Diara was recently living.

To ensure this, the Commandant Supérieur will firstly station a white officer here, with troops. This Resident will reside in the *dionfoutou* of Ahmadu. Part of the fort will be demolished so that the Resident can have a private gate leading out of the village, and a view over the Niger.

The French Resident will not concern himself with administrative problems between the *Fama* and his villages. The *Fama* will exercise all his rights, will appoint or change chiefs as he thinks fit, but the Resident will have the right to be kept fully informed on all matters and to know everything that takes place.

He may help the *Fama* maintain order in the country by giving him military support, with his troops. . . . But the *Fama* will not have the right to make war or undertake negotiations in neighbouring countries without authorisation from the Resident. If such actions should be undertaken without the Resident's approval, the *Fama* would have to meet all the costs, and accept all the consequences. The Resident would not help him, but would report to the Commandant Supérieur, who is to decide whether the *Fama* has acted wisely or must be reprimanded. . . .

The Tukolors must leave the country within three days after the departure of the Commandant Supérieur; Major Colonna de Giovellina will protect their convoy. After that date the Bambaras may massacre those who remain behind.

29

Governor-General Louis-Gabriel Angoulvant, general instructions to civilian administrators of the Ivory Coast, November 26, 1908

in *France and West Africa,* ed. John Hargreaves (London, 1969), pp. 205–6. Translated by Hargreaves

LOUIS-GABRIEL ANGOULVANT (1872-1935?) was one of the French colonial executives most closely associated with the policy of pacification. Born near Paris, he studied at the Ecole coloniale before entering military service. After twelve years in Vietnam, China, French Somaliland, the French Congo, and Martinique, he obtained his first executive position as governor of French India, where he served from 1906 to 1908. Following his departure from India, he became governor of the Ivory Coast, where he distinguished himself through the development of the colony's cash economy. The methods he used to obtain African labor, however, were far from distinguished. He did not shrink from the use of terror to enforce labor recruitment and tax collection. He then became governor of French Equatorial Africa and served for a brief period as governor-general of both the French West African and French Equatorial African federations. Upon his retirement in 1919, he served on the boards of directors of a number of colonial companies which operated in territories formerly under his jurisdiction.

Not that I have the slightest notion of attempting here any experiment in indirect administration. Except in a few northern districts the Ivory Coast does not have, among its own natives, any subjects capable of even roughly discharging the role of native officials, of holding even the slightest fragment of public authority. Long years will be needed before we can find individuals who are at once relatively well educated, energetic, active, honest, loyal, ready to face the dangers involved for a native in exercising of power in his own country, and sufficiently disinterested to serve us as administrative auxiliaries, even at the price of close and continuing control.

We must thus confine ourselves to practising direct administration, which is in any case the most moral system in Negro countries, for it involves far fewer of those excesses which are the undeniable consequence of any participation by natives in public affairs. . . .

Some will doubtless think that innovations of the sort which I have outlined and will enlarge on later would gravely jeopardise an existing social order for which they do not believe we can safely substitute an organisation made out of nothing.

On the contrary, I believe that we are in this country precisely in order to change the social order of the people now submitted to our laws. What this social order amounts to, among the forest-dwellers and the Baoule, is permanent and general anarchy, resulting from the absence of any authority and obstructing the realisation of any useful reform. . . . It is our mission to bring civilisation, moral and social progress, economic prosperity. We shall never succeed in this if we think ourselves obliged to preserve a deplorable situation where the weight of the past prevents any reform; or if we do succeed it will be at a speed out of keeping with the importance of the sacrifices we have made and the interests which are involved.

In colonial politics nothing is more dangerous than a conservative policy. Why make firm resolutions if they are to weaken in face of a situation which it was their very purpose to bring to an end? Why make such efforts if we doom them to failure in advance, condemning them to remain platonic on the pretext of respecting the customs and instincts of the natives?

30

Decree of Leopold II, King of the Belgians, regarding settlements for African children, July 21, 1890

in H. W. Wack, *The Story of the Congo Free State* (New York, 1905), pp. 561–62. Translation by the British Embassy in Brussels

UNDER THE peculiar constitutional arrangement which prevailed in the Congo Free State, all laws emanated from the king, Leopold II of the Belgians. Thus, although Leopold II was a constitutional monarch in Europe, his word was supreme in his African possessions, which he never visited. The legislation quoted below seems as much concerned with the creation of a cheap labor force as with the plight of African orphans.

SETTLEMENTS FOR NATIVE CHILDREN

Leopold II, King of the Belgians, Sovereign of the Independent State of the Congo.

To all present and to come, greeting:

Whereas it is expedient to make provision for the protection of those children who have been victims of the Slave Trade; and

Whereas it is the general duty of the State to assume the guardianship of abandoned children, or of those whose parents do not fulfil their duties;

Now, therefore, on the proposal of our Administrator-General of the Foreign Department, we have decreed and do hereby decree:—

Article I. The State shall assume the guardianship of children liberated in consequence of the arrest and dispersal of a convoy of slaves; of fugitive slaves who demand such protection, of children forsaken, abandoned, or orphans, and of those whose parents do not fulfil their duty with regard to maintaining and educating them.

They shall be provided with the means of livelihood and a practical education, and established in life.

Art. II. With this object agricultural and professional settlements shall be established, which shall admit not only such children as come under the definitions of Article I, but, as far as may be, those children who shall ask to be admitted.

Art. III. From the day of their admission the children shall be placed exclusively under the guardianship of the State, to which they shall remain subject, and shall be liable to work, at the discretion of the Governor-General, up to the expiration of their twenty-fifth year in return for maintenance, food, lodging, and free medical attendance.

31

Sir Arthur Conan Doyle, *The Crime of the Congo*

(New York, 1909), pp. iii–v

Arthur Conan Doyle (1859–1930), although better known today as the creator of Sherlock Holmes, was an outspoken defender of British imperialism. Born to an artistic family in Edinburgh, he took a medical degree from the University of Edinburgh but also embarked on a second career as a writer. His first Sherlock Holmes story appeared in 1887. In 1899 he volunteered as a physician for the troops in the South African War and was knighted for his services in 1902. In that same year he published a defense of the British cause. He was not so tolerant of other colonial powers, and in 1909 he published an indictment of the Congo Free State. He devoted most of his later years to spiritualism.

There are many of us in England who consider the crime which has been wrought in the Congo lands by King Leopold of Belgium and his followers to be the greatest which has even been known in human annals. Personally I am strongly of that opinion. There have been great expropriations like that of the Normans in England or of the English in Ireland. There have been massacres of populations like that of the South Americans by the Spaniards or of subject nations by the Turks. But never before has there been such a mixture of wholesale expropriation and wholesale massacre all done under an odious guise of philanthropy and with the lowest commercial motives as a reason. It is this sordid cause and the unctuous hypocrisy which makes this crime unparalleled in its horror.

Attempts will be made in America (for the Congo has its paid apologists everywhere) to pretend that England wants to oust Belgium from her colony and take it herself. Such accusations are folly. To run a tropical colony honestly without enslaving the natives is an expensive process. For example Nigeria, the nearest English colony, has to be subsidized to the extent of $2,000,000 a year. Whoever takes over the Congo will, considering its present demoralized condition, have a certain expense of $10,000,000 a year for twenty years. Belgium has not run the colony. It has simply sacked it, forcing the inhabitants without pay to ship everything of value to Antwerp. No decent European Power could do this. For many years to come the Congo will be a heavy expense and it will truly be a philanthropic call upon the next owner. I trust it will not fall to England.

Attempts have been made too (for there is considerable ingenuity and unlimited money on the other side) to pretend that it is a question of Protestant missions against Catholic. Any one who thinks this should read the book, "La Question Kongolaise," of the eloquent and holy Jesuit, Father Vermeersch. He lived in the country and, as he says, it was the sight of the "immeasurable misery," which drove him to write.

We English who are earnest over this matter look eagerly to the westward to see some sign of moral support of material leading. It would be a grand sight to see the banner of humanity and civilization carried forward in such a cause by the two great English-speaking nations.

32

Report of the Official Commission of Inquiry appointed to investigate allegations concerning the Congo Free State

(Brussels, 1905), in Sir Arthur Conan Doyle, *The Crime of the Congo* (New York, 1909), pp. 68–69, 78

LEOPOLD II appointed the Official Commission of Inquiry when he could no longer deny the atrocities that were taking place within his African empire. The members included a Belgian, an Italian, a Swiss, and a Briton, who came up with a remarkably honest report, which condemned many current practices. The king tried to brush aside the commission's findings and indeed blocked the publication of the commission's evidence. Three years later the Belgian Parliament took matters into its own hands, forcing the king to cede the Congo to Belgium.

As the greater portion of the land in the Congo is not under cultivation, this interpretation concedes to the State a right of absolute and exclusive ownership over virtually the whole of the land, with this consequence: that it can dispose—itself and solely—of all the products of the soil; prosecute as a poacher any one who takes from that land the least of its fruits, or as a receiver of stolen goods any one who receives such fruit: forbid any one to establish himself on the greater part of the territory. The activity of the natives is thus limited to very restricted areas, and their economic condition is immobilized. Thus abusively applied, such legislation would prevent any development of native life. In this manner, not only has the native been often forbidden to shift his village, but he has even been forbidden to visit, even temporarily, a neighbouring village without special permit. A native displacing himself without being the bearer of such an authorization, would leave himself open to arrest, to be taken back and even punished.

This circumstance [exhaustion of the rubber] explains the repugnance of the native for rubber work, which in itself is not particularly painful. In the majority of cases the native must go one or two days' march every fortnight, until he arrives at that part of the forest where the rubber vines can be met with in a certain degree of abundance. There the collector passes a number of days in a miserable existence. He has to build himself an improvised shelter, which cannot, obviously, replace his hut. He has not the food to which he is accustomed. He is deprived of his wife, exposed to the inclemencies of the weather and the attacks of wild beasts. When once he has collected the rubber he must bring it to the State station or to that of the Company, and only then can he return to his village, where he can sojourn for barely more than two or three days, because the next demand is upon him. . . . It is hardly necessary to add that this state of affairs is a flagrant violation of the forty hours' law. . . .

This system of native supervisors (*surveillants*) has given rise to numerous criticisms, even on the part of State officials. The Protestant missionaries heard at Bolobo, Ikoko (Lake Mantumba), Lulonga, Bonginda, Ikau, Baringa and Bongandange, drew up formidable accusations against the acts of these intermediaries. They brought before the Commission a multitude of native witnesses, who revealed a large number of crimes and excesses alleged to have been committed by the sentinels. According to the witnesses these auxiliaries, especially those stationed in the villages, abuse the authority conferred upon them, convert themselves into despots, claiming the women and the food, not only for themselves but for the body of parasites and creatures without any calling which a love of rapine causes to become associated with them, and with whom they surround themselves as with a veritable bodyguard; they kill without pity all those who attempt to resist their exigencies and whims. The Commission was obviously unable in all cases to verify the exactitude of the allegations made before it, the more so that the facts were often several years old. However, truth of the charges is borne out by a mass of evidence and official report.

33

Notes from the Diary of the (White Fathers') Mission at Katana

in Njangu Canda-ciri, "La résistance Shi à la pénétration européenne (1900–1920)," M.A. thesis, National University of Zaire, Lubumbashi Campus, App. IV, pp. 1–2. Translated by Bruce Fetter

THE ATROCITIES that accompanied Belgian conquest did not end with the termination of the Congo Free State. As long as African rulers refused to accept colonial dictates, the colonizers were prepared to use extremely cruel means to bring them to heel. This was particularly true in the eastern Congo during the First World War, when the Belgians were preparing their invasion of German East Africa.

The following excerpt was collected by the Zairian historian Njangu Canda-ciri as part of a thesis on the resistance of the Shi people to European rule. It came from a diary kept by the White Fathers in the Kivu region. The narrative describes an abortive revolt on the part of a group of Africans conscripted to serve as porters for the colonial army. Except for the officers, the soldiers described in the quotation were Africans.

April 4, 1916.

Arrival of Lieutenant Philippin, who has just replaced Captain Duckers. He has taken command of [Katana].

Messrs. Ketele, Hurlet, and Brass, who had gone on an expedition to Kabi and Bihogo in search of porters, have returned today. They have brought 150 men taken by force and as many heads of cattle.

April 6, 1916.

Beginning at nine at night, I heard from my room confused shouts which persisted and kept me more or less awake. About eleven o'clock shots resounded. I could tell that they came from the camp behind Shokola, about ten meters from here. The noise soon ceased and I fell asleep. About midnight Captain Duckers had me summoned to his tent to look after a mortally wounded soldier. I learned then that the natives who had been taken at Bihogo and

Kabi had revolted; that they had struck the Captain (who indeed had a wound on his hand) and Mr. Brass; that they had knocked over Mr. Ketele and kicked him. Several of these porters had been caught and whipped, on the assumption that this example would have calmed the mob. Then one of the rioters was shot. After that, they summoned Chief Kabi to speak to his men in order to quiet them. Kabi harangued his men, but the shouts grew louder than ever after he had finished speaking. Someone had thrown some burning branches from the fire on Mr. Brass. Then (in retaliation) someone set the porters' house on fire; a certain number of them had been trapped in the flames. The soldiers, despite orders to the contrary, had fired on those running away, who had retaliated, killing one soldier and wounding four others who had been standing guard behind the burning house.

April 7, 1916.

In the morning I went to the site of the massacre. It was a horrible spectacle. In the burned house there was a pile of charred corpses (twenty to twenty-five of them); in front of the house there were the dying, totally naked, wounded and burned. Squads of soldiers were preparing the dead for burial. Other soldiers were standing guard around the camp. I entered the house where the survivors were kept; there were 24 of them. I asked them, "What insanity possessed you last night?" They answered: "We had not drunk any beer, but we were mad with hunger."

Captain Duckers arrived just then and I asked him to send the wounded survivors to the Mission. He said that he would do it at once. About noon they sent us 16 wounded (from shots, bayonets, and burns). They also brought the wounded soldiers. . . .

April 28, 1916.

Every day, Auditor General Dellicour has been working on the Duckers Affair and the misdeeds committed by the soldiers of this company. Already Major Müller has given 110 cows to (Chief) Kabi, in compensation for the lives of the men slain. The Auditor General has given 4 cows to some women from Bihogo's village and Chinyabalange Island in compensation for the children that the soldiers killed.

THE YEARS BETWEEN THE COMPLETION OF THE PEACE TREATIES IN 1919 AND THE German invasion of Western Europe in 1940 might well be called the High Colonial Period. Serious competition between colonial powers had come to an end, and effective colonial demands for independence had not yet begun. In the absence of these political pressures, colonial officials acted with a security almost unparalleled in administrative history, pursuing their goals with a minimum of interference.

Their foremost goal was political: the installation of an effective administration over their entire colonial domain. Before the First World War, when other European nations were still seen as rivals, administrations spent more time establishing their territorial claims than governing their changes. Freed from these considerations after the war, the civil servants of each colonial regime attempted to impose their national stamp on the people under their jurisdiction. As chapter five demonstrates, the British, French, and Portuguese all had national styles but also shared common colonial goals.

In order to pay for the administrations which they were imposing on colonized Africans, the European officials had to find means of raising local revenues. In economic terms this involved the accumulation of surpluses in the local balance of payments: each colony was to export more than it imported, so that the excess could be spent on local government. This obliged administrators to subordinate all local economic activities to those which stimulated exports. As chapter six shows, the colonies of Africa fell into three broad economic categories: peasant colonies where African farmers produced the export crop; mining colonies where large European corpora-

Unit Two

The High Colonial Period

tions organized operations; and settlement colonies where European settlers attempted to grow the export crops. Even though Europeans directed production in the last two instances, badly paid Africans did the actual labor.

Education was originally a lower priority on the European agenda, having at first been assigned primarily to privately funded missionaries. By the 1920s, however, colonial officials had realized the importance of schools in training colonial intermediaries and were willing to give the missionaries a larger share of colonial resources. As a result of this upgrading of the priority of education, the administration took a more active role in the educational process, demanding uniform standards of instruction.

Africans, who had long been attracted to mission schools as a means of advancement in colonial society, competed vigorously for the available places, for there were seldom enough classes to satisfy local demand. As chapter seven demonstrates, some Africans accepted the values of the mission schools, while others rejected them. In the interwar period, Africans who rejected the missions were seen by administrators as the greatest threat to colonial stability. In later years, however, it was the mission-school graduates who became the leaders of colonial nationalism.

The two African groups that developed nationalist movements before the Second World War paradoxically had little to do with the missions. The Muslims of Egypt and Tunisia had little use for Christian schools; their leaders were formed in secular Western institutions or in the Koranic schools. Similarly, the Afrikaners of South Africa were not attending mission schools; they were actually sending their own missionaries to black Africa. Like the North African Muslims, the leaders of the South African nationalist movement described in chapter eight were the product of universities built on the European model. Such people were a far greater threat to colonial rule than the mass of mission-educated, primary-school scholars.

DURING THE HIGH COLONIAL PERIOD, EUROPEANS WERE MORE CONCERNED with administration than with any other aspect of African affairs. The accords reached after the First World War put an end to competition between colonizing powers, allowing them to establish administrations which they considered more or less permanent.

The high priest of colonialism in this period was Lord Frederick Lugard. By this time Lugard had already retired from active administration, but he nonetheless wielded enormous influence through his *Dual Mandate in British Tropical Africa* (Document 34) and his commanding role on the Permanent Mandates Commission of the League of Nations. Although Lugard's name was most often associated with his policy of indirect rule, by which certain administrative functions devolved to African chiefs, he was by no means a proponent of African self-government. In Document 34 he makes clear his belief that real power should remain in the hands of the European executive.

The Gold Coast constitution, as summarized in the *Gold Coast Handbook* of 1937 (Document 35), demonstrates the real limits of African representation in the Lugardian scheme. Of the twenty-nine members on the Legislative Council, only nine were Africans—six chiefs and three elected members from the coastal towns. Real power lay in the hands of European appointed officials, who constituted an absolute majority of the council.

The twin themes of executive authority and indirect rule also dominated French administration in the High Colonial Period. Theoretically, the French administration was more autocratic than that of the British, depending (as R. L. Buell's description shows in Document 36) on a single chain of command to the Colonial Ministry in Paris. In fact, individuals with strong personalities could leave their mark on local policy as much as their British counterparts. Such was the case with Félix Eboué, the black man from French Guiana who became governor-general of French Equatorial Africa during the Second World War. Despite the predisposition of many of his colleagues to override the local chiefs, Eboué, in Document

Chapter Five

Colonial
Administrations

37, adopts a line of thinking not far removed from that of Lord Lugard.

The Portuguese, by contrast to the British and French in black Africa, did not legally recognize the chiefs at all. As the constitutional legislation cited in Document 38 demonstrates, the Portuguese called their colonies "overseas provinces," admitting no fundamental distinction between the people of Portugal and those of Portuguese Africa. The French also employed this legal fiction, but only in Algeria.

34

Lord F. D. Lugard, *The Dual Mandate in British Tropical Africa*

(Edinburgh, 1922), pp. 94–95, 97, 103–4

FREDERICK JOHN DEALTRY LUGARD (1858-1945), best known for his advocacy of "indirect rule," was the leading British colonial expert during the interwar period. Born in India, where his father was serving as chaplain to a British regiment, Lugard attended a British public school and then went on to Sandhurst, the British military academy. He returned to India in 1878, and later served in nearly every trouble spot in the British Empire: the Sudan, Burma, Nyasaland (Malawi), Uganda, Nigeria, and Bechuanaland (Botswana). He then settled down in Nigeria, where he spent all but five of the years between 1897 and 1919. It was there that he acquired the unique title of governor-general and a reputation for knowing how to incorporate Africans into the colonial hierarchy. His most famous book, *The Dual Mandate in British Tropical Africa*, contains Lugard's conclusions about colonial administration. Between 1922 and his death he served on a number of international bodies, of which the most important was the League of Nations Permanent Mandates Commission, which he dominated from 1922 until 1936.

The British Empire, as General Smuts has well said, has only one mission—for liberty and self-development on no standardised lines, so that all may feel that their interests and religion are safe under the British flag. Such liberty and self-development can be best secured to the native population by leaving them free to manage their own affairs through their own rulers, proportionately to their degree of advancement, under the guidance of the British staff, and subject to the laws and policy of the administration.

But apart from the administration of native affairs the local Government has to preserve law and order, to develop the trade and communications of the country, and to protect the interests of the merchants and others who are engaged in the development of its commercial and mineral resources. What, then, are the functions of the British staff, and how can the machinery of Government be most efficiently constituted from the discharge of its duties in those countries in Africa which fall under British control?

The staff must necessarily be limited in numbers, for if the best class of men are to be attracted to a service which often involves separation from family and a strain on health, they must be offered adequate salaries and inducements in the way of leave, housing, medical aid—or their equivalents in money—for their maintenance in health and comfort while serving abroad, and this forms a heavy charge on the revenues. Policy and economy alike demand restriction in numbers, but the best that England can supply. . . .

The Governor, by delegating work to others, would seem to lighten his own task, but in point of fact the more he delgates the more he will find to do in co-ordinating the progress of the whole. Moreover, in order to have a right appreciation of the abilities, and of the personal character of each principal administrative officer and head of department, he must be the directing brain, and leave the execution to others. The task he undertakes is no light one, and if he should be called on to create an administration *ab ovo*, or to lay down new lines of policy in an old one, the work may become more than the time at his command suffices for, and the personal touch with his officers may temporarily suffer from the insistent demands of his office, until he is able gradually to delegate to those in whom he has confidence.

In applying the principle of decentralisation it is very essential to maintain a strong central co-ordinating authority, in order to avoid centrifugal tendencies, and the multiplication of units without a sufficiently cohesive bond. . . .

It is especially important that the decisions of the Governor should be fully recorded in writing, and not merely by an initial of acquiescence or a verbal order. This involves heavy office work, but it is work which cannot be neglected if misunderstandings are to be avoided and continuity preserved. The very detailed instructions regarding the duties of each newly-created department which were issued when the administration of Northern Nigeria was first inaugurated, served a very useful purpose in maintaining continuity of policy, till superseded on amalgamation by briefer general orders.

In the sphere of administration there are obviously many subjects—education, taxation, slavery and labour, native courts, land tenure, &c.—in which uniformity and continuity of policy is impossible in so large a country, unless explicit instructions are issued for guidance. By a perusal of the periodical reports of Residents, the Governor could inform himself of the difficulties which presented themselves in the varying circumstances of each province, and think out the best way in which they could be met, and could note where misunderstandings or mistakes had been made. By these means a series of Memoranda were compiled, and constantly revised as new problems came to light, and as progress rendered the earlier instructions obsolete. They formed the reference book and authority of the Resident and his staff.

35

The Gold Coast Handbook, 1937
(London, 1937), pp. 29–31

THE COLONIAL HANDBOOKS, much like the state blue books in the United States, were the official guides to colonial government. In addition to serving as reference books, they were also used to promote the various colonies which they described.

GOVERNMENT

The Gold Coast Colony is administered by the Governor, assisted by an Executive Council constituted by Letters Patent and Royal Instructions dated the 23rd May, 1925, and composed of the Colonial Secretary, the Attorney-General, the Treasurer, the Director of Medical Services and the Secretary for Native Affairs, who are ex-officio members, and such other persons as may be appointed under Royal Instructions, or by the Governor in pursuance of instructions through the Secretary of State. The Governor may summon any person as an extraordinary member of the Executive Council for any special occasion, and he also has the power to appoint provisional members to fill casual vacancies amongst members other than the ex-officio members.

The laws of the Colony are made by the Governor, with the advice and consent of a Legislative Council constituted by the Gold Coast Colony (Legislative Council) Order-in-Council, 1925, and consisting of the Governor, fifteen official members and fourteen unofficial members. It contains an elective element, provision being made for the election of six head chiefs as provincial members, three municipal members to represent the towns of Accra, Cape Coast and Sekondi respectively, a mercantile member and a mining member.

The official members are:—

(1) The five members for the time being of the Executive Council;
(2) The officers for the time being acted in the under-mentioned offices:—
  (a) Comptroller of Customs;
  (b) Director of Public Works;
  (c) General Manager of the Railways;
  (d) Commissioner of the Eastern Province;
  (e) Commissioner of the Central Province;
  (f) Commissioner of the Western Province;
  (g) Director of Agriculture;
  (h) Director of Education; and
(3) Such other Government officers, not exceeding two in number, as the Governor may from time to time appoint under the Public Seal of the Colony.

The persons referred to in clauses (1) and (2) above are styled "ex-officio members," and those referred to in clause (3) are styled "nominated official members." The latter are appointed for four years, but may be re-appointed for a further term.

The unofficial members are the following:—

(1) Six provincial members: viz., three for the Eastern Province, two for the Central and one for the Western.
(2) Three municipal members, viz., one each for the towns of Accra, Cape Coast, and Sekondi.
(3) Five European unofficial members, viz.,
  (a) One "mercantile member," representing commerce;
  (b) One "mining member," representing the mining industry; and
  (c) Three European unofficial members appointed by the Governor under the Public Seal of the Colony.

Provision is made for the establishment of three Provincial Councils, each consisting of the Head Chiefs of each of the three provinces in the Colony respectively.

The Provincial Councils of the Central and Western Provinces form (when constituted) one undivided body; that of the Eastern Province is divided into three sections: —

(a) The Ga Adangme Section;
(b) The Ewe Section;
(c) The Akan Section.

It is the duty of the Provincial Councils to elect a representative or representatives to serve as a provincial member or as provincial members of the Legislative Council. The Provincial Councils of the Central and Western Provinces and each section of the Provincial Council of the Eastern Provinces each elect one such member. Each member of a Provincial Council has one vote for every unit of ten thousand inhabitants (or part of such unit, not being less than five thousand inhabitants) in his division. In certain circumstances the Governor may nominate a head chief as provincial member of Council, in order to make up the necessary number.

The municipal members are elected, the electorate for this purpose coinciding with the electorate for the purpose of election of a member of the Town Council.

The mercantile member is elected by a committee, which is nominated by the "recognized Chambers of Commerce" declared as such from time to time by an instrument under the hand of the Governor.

The Governor may provisionally appoint additional official and unofficial members. Unofficial members, except those appointed provisionally, hold their seats for four years, but they are eligible for election or appointment for one further term, if not otherwise disqualified.

The Governor may also appoint particular persons to be extraordinary members for a specific occasion.

The Governor presides over meetings of the Legislative Council, and all questions are decided by a majority of votes, the Governor having an original vote in common with the other members and a casting vote in the event of an equality of votes.

Ordinances which are enacted for the Colony alone are expressed to be "enacted by the Governor of the Gold Coast Colony thereof." Ordinances which are enacted for the whole of the Gold Coast are expressed to be "enacted by the Governor of the Gold Coast, with the advice and consent of the Legislative Council so far as the provisions hereof relate to the Colony."

This latter procedure is an innovation started at the Legislative Council held in March, 1935. Formerly a law which was to apply to the whole of the Gold Coast had to be drawn up in three enactments, one for the Colony which was "enacted by the Governor with the advice and consent of the Legislative Council" and the other two for Ashanti and the Northern Territories Protectorate, which were enacted by the Governor alone. This multiplication of enactments has now been obviated by the procedure indicated above.

The Governor possesses the power to veto any ordinance, and all ordinances are subject to the right of His Majesty to disallow them. On the Bill being presented to the Governor, after being passed by the Legislative Council, he may either assent, dissent, or reserve it for the signification of the Royal pleasure.

36

R. L. Buell, *The Native Problem in Africa*
2 vols. (Cambridge, Mass., 1928), 1:923–24, 926–27, 928

RAYMOND LESLIE BUELL (1896-1946), although not an Africanist by training or by profession, produced the most important American reference book on Africa of the 1920s, *The Native Problem in Africa.* Born in Chicago, where his father was a Protestant clergyman, Buell studied at Occidental College, the University of Grenoble, and Princeton. Although Buell held several academic appointments, his main activities were as an adviser on foreign affairs. He wrote *The Native Problem in Africa* for the Committee on International Research at Harvard after a sixteen-month tour of black Africa in 1925-26. He became research director of the Foreign Policy Association in 1927 and served as that organization's president from 1933 until 1939. He was an internationalist Republican who worked on Wendell Wilkie's presidential campaign in 1940 and ran unsuccessfully for Congress. At the end of his life he was foreign affairs adviser to *Time* and *Life* magazines and wrote a study of Liberia, which was published posthumously.

French as well as outside observers have frequently complained of the high degree of centralization which prevails in the French Government at home as well as abroad. All colonial legislation takes the form of a decree prepared by the Minister of Colonies and promulgated by the President of the Republic. While as a rule such decrees are drafted by the local government on the spot, the Minister of Colonies frequently consumes a long time in issuing decrees; and sometimes they are issued over the head of local authorities. Originally a tight control was similarly exercised over the local budget.

To overcome the difficulties of centralization and to remove economic barriers to labor recruiting, the French Government has attempted to increase the initiative of local authorities and to convert the Colonial Office into an organ of control, as it is in the British Empire, through grouping the various colonies into two federations: (1) Afrique Occidentale Française, commonly called "A.O.F.," and (2) Afrique Equatoriale Française, called "A.E.F.," the first of which will now be discussed. . . .

All departmental heads are completely subject to the Governor. A department head in a French colony cannot issue any orders, nor discipline, appoint or dismiss an official in his own name. The head of the Education Department cannot even grant scholarships in the schools on his own authority; all of these matters take the form of a "decision" or other action of the Lieutenant-Governor acting ordinarily on the advice of the department head concerned. Such a system unifies the administration but it frequently slows down the efficiency of departmental machinery and increases the number of wheels in the French administrative bureaucracy.

Except in Senegal, which has a Colonial Council, the Lieutenant-Governor of each colony is assisted by a Council of Administration of which he is president. It contains four government officials, two elected representatives of the Chambers of Commerce and Agriculture, and a number of natives who were at one time appointed by the Governor-General upon the advice of the Lieutenant-Governor. . . .

Each colony in the federation retains its own budget which is fed by the native head taxes and some local fees. All customs duties are now paid into the central government. These budgets do not, moreover, have to be submitted, as does the budget of the government-general for approval to the Minister of Colonies, but merely to the Governor-General at Dakar, which thus expedites administration and makes possible the re-allocation of expenditure to meet new needs.

37

Félix Eboué, "African Political Institutions, 1941"

in *African History: Texts and Readings,* ed. Robert O. Collins (New York, 1971), pp. 112–13. Translated by Nell E. Painter and Robert O. Collins

FÉLIX EBOUÉ (1884–1944), the pro-Allied governor-general of French Equatorial Africa during the Second World War, rose to the highest position ever attained by a black man in the French colonial bureaucracy. Born in French Guiana, on the northern shore of South America, he completed his secondary education in Bordeaux and graduated from the Ecole coloniale in Paris in 1908. He spent most of the next twenty-three years in Oubangi-Chari (now the Central African Empire), where he rose through the ranks of the colonial administration. After brief terms in Martinique and the French Sudan (now Mali), Eboué obtained his first command position as governor of Martinique. After a troubled administration, he was named lieutenant-governor of Chad, a clear demotion. His disgrace, however, was only temporary. Of all the heads of French African colonies, he was the first to rally to the cause of General de Gaulle, who wanted to continue the war on the side of the allies. After a series of colonial coups d'état, Eboué was named governor-general of the French Equatorial African federation. Between 1940 and 1944 he presided over the war effort without much concern for the welfare of his African charges, but did not live to see the Allied victory.

Starting from such a principle, we must first confirm or reconfirm their recognition, and in all cases, promote native political institutions. Let one [principle] be well understood: there is no question of considering political custom as something set or immutable as museum objects. It is very clear that custom changes and will change, and that we are not here to sterilize it by fixing it. But we must understand its profound meaning and consider it as essential as the tradition that shaped it and feelings that gave birth to it. This tradition is that of the motherland. To strip the native of these two motors of human life is to rob him without retribution. It would be about as insane as taking his land, vineyard, cattle, and soup pot from the French peasant in order to make an ordinary factory worker, charged with handling the products of an industrialized countryside.

Furthermore, if we do not reconfirm the bases of native political institutions, these bases will themselves disappear and will give way to an uncontrollable individualism. And how will we be able to act on this collection of individuals? When I see impatient administrators seize, unmake, condemn, and remake chiefs and thus sap the strength of a traditional institution, I think that institution, due to their faults, loses its efficiency along with its vital character. I could tell them this: the only means remaining to ward off the breakdown of natural command will be administration by native civil servants. Because the chief of a subdivision cannot directly watch each person he administers, he will have to use civil servants as intermediaries instead of the chiefs he will have lost. I leave it to each person to judge the best solution from his own experience. If an ambitious administrator pretends to do without chiefs and civil servants, at least to reduce them to the state of simple instruments in his hands—precise and punctual instruments—I am sure that he is fooling himself, but in any case, I am convinced that his successor would not have the same good fortune. The continuity of effort, whose prerequisite is the decisive superiority of a single administrator, would be compromised from the moment of his departure. He would have built his cathedrals on the sand.

I have just been speaking of chiefs. In truth, although native institutions are often monarchical, they are not always. The opposite is true. The nomadic tribes of the North, which live under a regime of organized anarchy, could be cited as an example. And even within a monarchical state, the chief does not represent the only political institution. His power is amended, attenuated, and shared by more than one principle and more than one institution. Nothing must be forgotten or rejected of all this. No constituted council will be omitted, no guardian ousted, and no religious taboo neglected on the pretext that it would be ridiculous, bothersome, or immoral. There is no question of denying or condemning what exists and what counts, but to lead it along the way to progress.

The institution of the chief, however, is most important, and will take the most care with his person. A preliminary question is posed here: Who should be chief? I will not answer as I did in Athens:

"The Best One." There is no best chief, there is a chief, and we have no choice. I have already spoken of the frequent mutations of the chiefs; they are deplorable and no less absurd. There is a chief designated by custom; the point is to recognize him. I use the term in the diplomatic sense. If we arbitrarily replace him, we divide the command into two parts, the official and the real; no one is fooled except us, and if we flatter ourselves for getting better results from the chief, we overlook, most of the time, that he himself obeys the real chief, and that we are dealing with dupes.

Chiefs are not interchangeable. When we depose them, public opinion does not; the chief preexists. The preexistence often remains unknown to us, and the most difficult thing for us is to discover the real chief. I want the governors and administrators henceforth to adhere to this tenet. Not only do I mean that power will no longer be given to a parvenu whose services must be repaid (are there not a hundred other ways to repay them?), but I want the legitimate chiefs to be searched out where our ignorance has let them hide and reestablished in their outward dignity. I know what will be said: that all that has disappeared, that it is too late, that poor incorrigibles will be found from whom nothing is to be had. I believe that this is not true; occult power subsists because it is traditional power. May it be discovered and brought out into the light of the day, may it be honored and educated. Results are certain to be forthcoming.

38

The fundamental principles of overseas Portugal

in *Emerging Nationalism in Portuguese Africa: Documents,* ed. and trans. Ronald H. Chilcote (Stanford, Calif., 1972), p. 18

THESE PRINCIPLES were devised by Antonio de Oliveira Salazar (1889-1970) during the early years of his rule as dictator of Portugal, from 1928 until 1968. Salazar drew them up in 1930 while holding the colonial portfolio. They were incorporated into the Colonial Act of 1930 and became part of the constitution in 1951.

The Constitution of Portugal (1951), Articles 133 to 136.

It is intrinsic in the Portuguese Nation to fulfill its historic mission of colonization in the lands of the Discoveries under their sovereignty and to diffuse among the populations inhabiting them the benefits of their civilization, as well as to exercise the moral influence enjoined on it by the Patronage of the East.

The Overseas Territories of Portugal shall be known as "provinces." Their politico-administrative organization shall be on lines best suited to their geographical situation and their social standards.

The Overseas Provinces, as an integral part of the Portuguese State, are united among themselves and with Metropolitan Portugal.

This unity between the Overseas Provinces and Metropolitan Portugal involves, in particular, the obligation to contribute in an adequate manner to the preservation of the integrity and the defense of the whole nation, and to the aims of national policy as defined, in the common interest, by the bodies in which sovereignty resides.

IN THE MINDS OF THE COLONIZERS, THE ECONOMIC BENEFITS WHICH COULD BE gained from African colonies were second in importance only to the question of political ownership. During the High Colonial Period, no European power ever proposed to abandon title to a territory, even though many colonies cost their metropolitan governments more than they produced. Rather than granting independence, imperial governments frequently ran colonies as a function of the value and nature of their exports.

In theory, even the poorest territories produced agricultural goods which could be exported to the mother country. In practice, however, the costs of production and transport often made such shipments uneconomic. Administrators in poor colonies (today's Fourth World) therefore relied on whatever revenue they could raise, frequently depending on the receipts from taxes on migratory laborers. Despite this distinction between colonies that raised most of their revenues from agricultural exports and those that relied on labor exports, the two groups tended to be classed as a single entity, the colony with a peasant economy. Within this broad category, then, a wide disparity arose between relatively rich peasant economies and poor ones.

This variety of agrarian economies emerges in the document in our collection dealing with peasant economies. Albert Sarraut, the most famous of the French colonial ministers in the 1920s, was undoubtedly thinking of better-off colonies when he wrote the defense of colonial economic practices which appears in Document 39. Geoffrey Gorer, the British anthropologist, saw the other side of the coin during his trip to West Africa in 1934, described in Document 40. It took an African, however, to experience the injustice of the entire system. Speaking in 1948, Nnamdi Azikiwe, the first president of Nigeria, recounted in (Document 41) a very revealing personal experience which occurred during the Second World War.

From a material point of view, the inhabitants of colonies and regions of colonies which relied on the export of minerals fared better than their counterparts in agricultural colonies. Colonial governments frequently in-

Chapter Six

Colonial
Economies

tervened directly in the management of European mines to assure minimum standards of health and nourishment for African as well as European miners. This was precisely the job done by M. A. B. Denton-Thompson in the Belgian copperbelt, covered by his reports for 1916 (Document 42). Needless to say, European officials could not put themselves into the shoes of their African charges. A better picture of life in the mines can be found in Document 43, the narrative of three Maniema Africans who worked in the copperbelt in the late twenties.

A third category of colonial economies is represented by the settlement colonies. Some of the latter relied on agricultural exports while others relied on minerals; what they both had in common was a permanently settled European population which either determined the policy of the treatment of Africans or had a large input into it. General J. C. Smuts' address to the South African Parliament in 1923 represents a relatively liberal settler point of view. As prime minister of a self-governing British dominion, Smuts, in Document 44, seems to have been genuinely concerned for the welfare of Africans in South African cities.

One might pose more difficult questions about the sincerity of the duke of Devonshire in his 1923 white paper, *Indians in Kenya* (Document 45). Although the Colonial Office was then resisting efforts by a handful of Kenya settlers to obtain self-government, the noble aims enunciated in the document seem more a rationale for barring advancement by Kenya's Indian community. The true situation of Africans in Kenya is better represented by excerpts from Norman Leys' *Kenya* (Document 46). The settlers were pushing Africans off the land with the active cooperation of the colonial administration.

39

Albert Sarraut, *La mise en valeur des colonies françaises*

(Paris, 1923), in *France and West Africa*, ed. John Hargreaves (London, 1969), pp. 226–27. Translated by Hargreaves

ALBERT SARRAUT (1872-1962) was one of the leading theoreticians and practitioners of French colonial economic development. Born in Bordeaux to a wealthy family, he studied law and entered politics as a young man. He won a seat in the National Assembly in 1902, serving continuously in that body and in the Senate for thirty-eight years. He obtained his first cabinet-level post in 1906 and then moved to the administrative post of governor-general of Indochina, which he held from 1911 to 1914 and from 1916 to 1919. On the basis of this experience he became colonial minister from

1920 to 1924 and again in 1932-33. He served in a number of other posts, including that of premier, which he held for a total of five months in the 1930s. During the war he was deported by the Germans but survived (his brother was killed by French fascists). After the war he played an honorary role in colonial organizations.

Economically, a colonial possession means to the home country simply a privileged market whence it will draw the raw materials it needs, dumping its own manufactures in return. Economic policy is reduced to the rudimentary procedures of gathering crops and bartering them. This is literally a policy of "exploitation" in the pejorative sense of the word, a policy of depletion and stagnation which gradually ruins the colonies, condemning them to anaemic weakness and breaking any spirit of creative initiative. In the lands subject to it, the crop-gatherers come simply to engross raw materials and natural produce; to get them more quickly they do not hesitate to destroy the plants that bear them. They cut down trees and do not replant, leaving the work of reproduction to nature. Nor do they think of conserving the fertility of the soil by rational and scientific land-use, of acclimatising and developing new crops, of creating and renewing new sources of wealth. They do not replace what they have taken away. They bleed but do not close the wound; if the wounded organism loses its vital forces, so much the worse. Moreover, by strictly imposing on its colonial "dependency" the exclusive consumption of its manufactured products, the metropolis prevents any efforts to use or manufacture local raw materials on the spot, and any contact with the rest of the world. The colony is forbidden to establish any industry, to improve itself by economic progress, to rise above the stage of producing raw materials, or to do business with neighbouring territories for its own enrichment across the customs barriers erected by the metropolitan power.

It's the same policy of exploitation and astriction towards the human being, whom the "pacte coloniale" exhausts and maintains in the status of an infant (for the word "tutelage" would be a euphemism). The native, yellow or black, is less a man than a tool, who is worth only as much as can be got out of him, and who is thrown away when he is broken. . . .

[But now] the old mercantile or imperialist concept of the early days is being purified, is swelling and soaring into the idea of human solidarity. Colonial France will organise, to her own advantage no doubt but also for the general advantage of the world, the exploitation of territories and resources which the native races of these backward territories have been unable to develop by themselves, with the result that the profit has been lost, not only to them but to the whole world."

40

Geoffrey Gorer, *Africa Dances*
(London, 1935; rpt. New York, 1962), pp. 105–7

GEOFFREY GORER (b. 1905) is a talented British journalist-turned-anthropologist whose descriptions of the colonial world are some of the best produced during the 1930s. Born in London, he attended a prestigious British public school and Cambridge University, later studying at the Sorbonne and the University of Berlin. After his first book, *The Revolutionary Ideas of the Marquis de Sade*, published in 1934, he undertook a series of travels which took him all over the world. Two of his books from this period, *Africa Dances* (1935) and *Bali and Angkor* (1936), resulted from these travels, which led him to a systematic study of anthropology in the United States under the tutelage of John Dollard, Ruth Benedict, and Margaret Mead. Since then he has written perceptive studies of people in the Himalayas, the United States, and Russia.

In principle the Negro does not object to the head-tax. Tribute from the conquered to the conqueror is not a foreign notion to them. It is noteworthy in this connection that in Dahomey and the Ivory Coast events are always dated "from the French conquest". This does not mean that it does not lie very heavy on them and cause them great anxiety; one man said to me "I can't sleep for thinking of the taxes; if I am put in prison what will happen to my children? If they let us alone we could get the money; but they force us to make roads and don't pay us; they don't give us any time to make up; what can I do?" But the idea of the head-tax doesn't shock them, though individual methods of assessment and collection may do so.

The speech quoted above also gives the general reaction to forced labour. The idea of slavery or peonage, under which a man and his

family belong to another and work for him, receiving in return
food and shelter, is quite in accordance with their outlook, but they
cannot understand and do resent intermittent unpaid work, which
often interferes with their agriculture and consequently their ability
to pay their taxes. It would probably suit the Negro mentality better if a man could do his whole labour service in one stretch, provided he was not taken outside his tribal district. It is this forcible
breaking up and destruction of the family and tribe which rouses
the Negro's keenest resentment and misery; in a manner of speaking they do not live as individuals, and to separate a man from the
environment in which he was born is to cause distress to the whole
group. This is the reason why the recruiting officer, whether he is
looking for soldiers or for labourers for another part of the country, is more feared and hated than the greatest bully and extor-
tioner. Most Negroes would prefer death to military service. . . .

. . . It is to escape conscription that thousands of families cross
the English frontiers every year.

There is no doubt that the Negroes of French West Africa are a
dispirited, miserable and resentful people, who can now only be
ruled by fear. It is not merely the colonial policy which has brought
them to this state, but the brutal and abusive manner in which the
French treat them on nearly every occasion, and the systematic
way in which they are cheated in every transaction, which the
cheaters quite erroneously believe their simplicity prevents them
from realizing. Actually it is their fear and their experience with the
results of complaints which keep them apparently quiet. The
following quotation from Andre Gide's *Voyage au Congo* (p. 113)
is unfortunately too typical. He is describing a conversation with a
trader. "He told me he had spent a long time in the Gold Coast and
when we asked him which country he preferred he replied: "In the
Gold Coast you can't do anything. Imagine, down there nearly
every nigger can read and write." . . . He couldn't hide his anger
against the English traders who are stupid enough to pay directly to
the Negro the market price of his goods, which 'spoils the business'.
He admitted cynically that when there was not sufficient profit on
the goods he made up for it by 'faking the weights' . . . He complained loudly against the administration 'which is destroying
business,' but only the upper branches of the administration; he
was full of praise for the sub-administrator of the district where he
was working: 'A nigger can go and complain if he likes: he'll soon
put him in his place for you.'" Similarly Albert Londres (*Terre*

d'Ebène, p. 150) mentions the weighing machine of a cotton buyer on which a man weighed seventy kilos before the market opened, and fifty kilos after. Any number of similar examples could be given. My reason for preferring to quote French books rather than give my own observations is I should think obvious; it is not for lack of material. Mention has already been made of the ludicrously low prices at which Negroes are forced to sell their provisions to Europeans and those working for them; in some regions indeed they are not allowed to name a price but should receive thankfully whatever is offered for their goods. The Negro cannot even always buy where he likes; in some districts seed must be bought from the government store. A further piece of chicane is the fines that public and private employers can inflict arbitrarily on their workpeople and deduct from their wages. The truck system is also extremely common. Paradoxically enough, it is the Negroes who are given the reputation of being dishonest.

41

Nnamdi Azikiwe, address delivered at the inauguration of the African Continental Bank, September 1, 1948

in *Zik* (Cambridge, 1961), pp. 211–14

NNAMDI AZIKIWE (b. 1904), one of the leading advocates of African independence, became the first president of Nigeria. His father was an Ibo who worked as a clerk for the colonial army, which took the family to northern Nigeria, where the future president was born. He attended school in southern Nigeria but had learned the languages of the three major regions of the country by the time he was seventeen. After three years as a government clerk in Lagos he went to the United States, where he studied and sometimes taught at Storer College, Howard University, and Lincoln University. He returned to Africa in 1934 to become editor of a newspaper in Accra, where he stayed for three years before moving on in 1937 to Lagos, where he founded a chain of six newspapers, a bank, and a political party, the National Council for Nigeria and the Cameroons. Between 1947 and 1960 he played a leading role in politics as a molder of opinion and as an influential member of various national and regional legislative bodies. When Nigeria became independent in 1960 he served for three years as governor-general and then for three years more as president. Driven from office in the first military coup of 1966, he agonized over the question of Biafran secession, opting for the central government in 1969.

You may wish to know why I founded the bank we are opening today. More than five years ago, I was invited by the British Council to visit war-time Britain in the company of seven other West African journalists. During my absence, my business as a newspaper publisher did not fare very well. On my return I decided to improve it by increasing the price of the *West African Pilot* from one penny to two pence. In the meantime, I made use of my personal resources and influence and the business was able to survive.

In the process of revitalizing my newspaper enterprise, I found myself on the short end of the bargain and my personal problems became involved and complicated. With the co-operation of some friends, I planned to acquire a rubber plantation in Benin in order to have an independent source of income, apart from my other enterprises. Since the owner required immediate cash settlement, I was obliged to seek the co-operation of a banking establishment. At that time, I was shareholder of the National Bank of Nigeria with whom I operated a personal account in addition to my business accounts. But the bulk of these accounts was handled by the Bank of British West Africa. I needed £400 to add to what savings I had effected and I was prepared to offer my building at 76 King George Avenue as a collateral. The Lagos Town Council had assessed its value at £1,450. I had valid title to the land on a leasehold from the Crown for a period of 99 years from 1938, and the property was not encumbered.

The manager of the expatriate bank treated me shoddily. He kept me standing in his office for some minutes and he was condescending in his attitude and demeanour. He did not make me feel that he was talking business with me. He left me under the impression that racial factors were at work, and he acted as if he was doing me a favour. After ascertaining my desires, he regretted that he could not render immediate assistance because he would have to contact London for orders, which would take some time. He advised me to make other arrangements if it was possible to do so.

Naturally, my pride was hurt and I was bitter. That a bank which had been used as a depository for my private and business funds for seven years should regard me as an extraneous factor made me ruminate on the fate of other less fortunate Africans who made use of the banking facilities made available by non-Nigerian business organizations. I felt that other things being equal, it was morally wrong for Europeans to establish banks in Nigeria and then make it difficult for Nigerians to use them to the mutual advantage of both parties. Then it dawned on me that political freedom was not enough; economic freedom must be won also.

I returned home from the bank crestfallen and I drafted a letter to the Manager, part of which read as follows:

. . . Since 1937, I and my business establishments have patronized your bank and our turn-over is respectable. The interest which you draw from us is out of proportion to the benefit we derive from your banking facilities. . . .

As long as business executives of your type are so prejudiced and unreasonable, so long will you find it impossible to have Africans of my type willing to co-operate with you, beyond the ordinary veneer of business relationship. The time will come when I, Nnamdi Azikiwe, will head a bank and face you on even terms so that you will realize that in banking, as well as in any other business activity, discretion and common sense are valuable assets in human relations. . . .

I assure you of my continued co-operation, from a business point of view, but you have made it clear to me that unless Africans establish their own banks in order to call off such bluffs, the economic exploitation of Africa will continue with impunity. I will yet own a bank of my own and I am not dreaming.

In the meantime, I acquired an interest in the Tinubu Properties Limited from a Swedish realtor. Because one of the objects of the company was "generally to act as bankers for customers and others", I changed the name of the company to Tinubu Bank Limited. Last year, we resolved to re-christen it the African Continental Bank Limited. After acquiring the business I spent four years working to organize it. In association with my parents and relatives I have been able to accumulate sufficient initial funds with which to open the doors of the bank to the public.

The background of this bank is a challenge that in running it as a business venture, we should not be in a hurry for immediate profits; rather, we should place a premium on service, integrity and efficiency. I am not a banker by profession but I have been able to attract employees who are experienced in the law and practice of banking; it is they and not I who will operate the business. I look forward to a bright future in this business venture, but under present-day conditions, I hope that no investor in this bank will expect to reap profit by way of dividend until after the bank has existed for at least ten years.

I do not expect smooth sailing in all the activities of the bank, but I have implicit faith that if the bank is run on an efficient basis, if the employees are competent and honest, and if our patrons are men and women whose word is their bond, the bank will succeed in being a blessing to Nigerian business entrepreneurs. This is a bold attempt to do for our people what others have denied them. There is scope for expansion in Nigerian banking. I pray that with the co-operation of older banking institutions, this pioneering venture will succeed. It is a most vital phase in our struggle for economic freedom.

42

M. A. B. Denton-Thompson, "Native Labour in the Katanga"

monthly and quarterly reports, January and April 1916, in the Public Record Office, London, FO 369/917

MERRICK ARNOLD BARDSLEY DENTON-THOMPSON (1888-1969) was the first British governmental official assigned to supervise the welfare of Zambian Africans (who were British charges) working in the copper mines in what was then the Belgian Congo. The son of an Anglican bishop, Thompson attended a British public school and Cambridge University. In 1911 he enlisted in the Southern Rhodesian civil service, transferring a year later to that of Northern Rhodesia, where he served as an administrative officer from 1912 until 1915. On the basis of his family, his education, and his performance, he received the desirable post of vice consul and superintendent of Rhodesian natives in the newly established (1910) town of Elisabethville (now Lubumbashi). After eight years in this joint appointment, he became a full member of the consular service of the Foreign Office, serving with distinction in Europe and South America until his retirement in 1948.

. . . those responsible for the administration of justice, although able and just, are in most cases unable to speak a native language, with the exception perhaps . . . of Swahili. They rely therefore principally upon native interpreters who speak French fluently, but have very little knowledge of the dialects of Northern Rhodesia and must frequently interpret with a view to the speedy ending of the case. . . .

The Katanga is the natural labour market for Rhodesian natives, and all methods hitherto employed to prevent them from crossing into this territory have largely failed. . . .

[Kambove] mine was inspected for the first time during January. . . . [Fifty Rhodesians are reported, but] a large number of Rhodesians appear in the books as voluntary Congo natives. It will be remembered that a similar state of affairs was found to be in existence at Lubumbashi in September last. Strict orders have again been issued to the Compound Managers by Messrs. Robert Williams & Co. that the greatest care should be exercised when engaging natives in order to insure that Rhodesians are classified as certified and thus have the benefit of the repatriation and deferred pay arrangements. . . . The present hospital arrangements are more unsatisfactory, the hospital itself being a very considerable distance from the compound and offices.

43

Three Africans from the Maniema District, Belgian Congo, on conditions in the Katanga copper mines, 1926–28

in Yogolelo Tambwe ya Kasimba, "Mission de recrutement des travailleurs de l'U.M.H.K. au Kivu-Maniema (1926–1928)," M.A. thesis, National University of Zaire, Lubumbashi Campus, pp. 88, 102, 105. Translated by Bruce Fetter

ALTHOUGH a large proportion of the Africans recruited by the Union minière du Haut-Katanga remained in the camps, few first-hand narratives have been collected describing camp life from the African point of view. During the academic year 1972–73, a Zairian undergraduate, Yogolelo Tambwe ya Kasimba, as part of an honors thesis collected several descriptions of life in the Elisabethville camps from workers who had been recruited by the short-lived Union minière Maniema mission in Orientale province. Until descriptions are collected from Africans who remained in the camps, those collected by Yogolelo will have to be taken as representative. Moreover, since most of the narratives were collected from men who left the camps before 1928, they provide a description uncolored by later changes in the mines.

The Maniema workers, having been transported five hundred miles from their homes to the copperbelt, were placed in the Lubumbashi preparation camp for acclimation.

The first description is that of the Bwana Muzuri Samilondo:

The head of that camp, who was called "Monsieur Sikamo," was a mean white man who often beat us. . . . We spent several weeks in that Lubumbashi camp passing our time at nothing but eating and medical examinations. Then they divided us into work teams and sent us to different camps. I personally was sent to Ruashi, where I worked on a team with a steam shovel.

Bwana Asani Rajabo described the work conditions at Ruashi:

The drill holes chosen to hold the explosives were dug by the African foreman with a borer. It was then necessary to insert the necessary number of charges before lighting the fuse; but since the workers often miscounted the charges, they sometimes set them off before everyone had left the scene and taken shelter. That explains why we had a number of accidents at Ruashi.

We had two work crews: on one week the first worked from 7 a.m. to 3 p.m., the second from 3 p.m. to 11 p.m.; the following week the morning crew worked at night and the evening crew in the morning. No, there was no rest period and we had nothing to eat on the job. Only those who worked [underground] at Kipushi received a roll called a "kampopo" before descending into the pit.

Bwana Lungumbu Saidi summed up their impressions of life at the Ruashi camp:

Life at the camp was pleasant; only the food did not suit us. . . . The people from Maniema died in large numbers, because they were not accustomed to maize flour. Yes, we lost many of our people at Ruashi, some died from work accidents, other, the majority, from diarrhea. The man who had diarrhea one day died in two or three days. All of us wanted only one thing: to terminate our contract and return to our country—we were so frightened by the number of people who died each day.

44

J. C. Smuts' address to the South African House of Assembly, February 6, 1923

in *South African Parties and Policies, 1910–1960: A Select Source Book,*
ed. D. W. Krüger (London, 1960), pp. 380–82

. . . a very great change has come over South Africa within our own lifetime. I remember as a young man in this part of the country when I grew up here, it was a very unusual thing to see a Black man in this part of South Africa. We had our towns, and villages, we had our White population and Coloured people, who lived either among the Whites or on the fringes of the towns and villages, but the Native, except in certain harbours like working on the Docks, was a most unusual sight in those days. That was not so long ago when I was a young man. What is the position today? A complete change has come over South Africa owing to the economic development of the country, and owing to forces entirely beyond human control there has been a great flux, there has been a great influx of Natives from other parts of South Africa into towns like this and to other towns, and in fact the most tremendous social and political phenomenon of our day and our generation has been just this—the pressure of the Natives on the larger industrial centres of South Africa. The Native population has increased by leaps and bounds.

But the provision for their reception has not been made correspondingly, and today we are up against one of the most difficult problems in this respect in South Africa. No special means have been established for the reception of these people. No doubt there are locations in many towns in South Africa, many villages have their small locations, but for the influx which has taken place in the large industrial centres all over South Africa we have been entirely unprepared. The result has been that the Natives have gone into the towns, they have mixed with the rest of the population, they have not been segregated in their own areas next door, they have freely mixed with the rest of the population, and, Sir, the most lamentable results have ensued in consequence. Some years ago we had a

Commission in this country which inquired into tuberculosis. The inquiry disclosed one of the most terrible conditions in South Africa, due very largely to this—due to this overcrowding of all sorts and conditions of people without any proper provision being made, without any sifting out, or any proper housing accommodation being provided.

We had another Commission, the Commission which inquired into assaults on women. That Commission made a similar report, showing that this lamentable situation which arose in South Africa was largely due to this intermixture of the population and the unwholesome conditions under which Native and White lived together. I need not paint the picture more than needs be; we know the effect of our neglect of dealing with this question has been that our White civilisation has been dragged down, that the Whites have suffered and the White civilisation in South Africa, which we should hold up, has been degraded by the conditions of the present system. The Native, on the other hand, has suffered to an appalling extent as a result of this neglect. The Native has come to our towns unprovided for—innocent, untutored people, who often fall into the hands of criminals and pick up diseases and vice.

The result of all this neglect of our duty to deal with the situation has been harmful in the extreme both to the White and the Native population. Now this is a matter which has become more urgent, but it is not one which is beyond solution. There are aspects of our great Native question which appear to be almost beyond solution— questions so large and of which we know so little and over which we have so little control that they seem to be beyond all human control. But this question is not such a one. Although the question is difficult, housing and the urban control of Natives is manageable even at this late hour—if we undertake the task with energy and good will; and if the country responds—as I have no doubt it will— we may remove one of the biggest blots which is today resting on our civilisation. I am sure we can do so, and I hope we shall.

In dealing with this question, which has been delayed to some extent because legal responsibility has been shifted from one authority to another, hon. members, when they look at the clauses of the Bill, will see the various authorities which are referred to. In the first place, without doubt, responsibility, both moral and legal, rests upon the towns, the urban authority or the municipalities. The Native populations in the towns form just as much the people as the Whites do, and are there for the economic life of the town, and there is no doubt that, in the first instance, the responsibility for their care, control and proper condition rests on the towns. The towns can under our Constitutional system come under the purview of the Provincial Councils—which is the second authority. Above all is the Union Parliament and Union Government. The South Africa Act lays down, as hon. members are aware, that Native affairs as a whole shall be a charge to the Union.

We have, therefore, all the constitutional authorities concerned and all in their degree responsible for dealing with this matter. Hon. members will see that the Bill says that wherever necessary proper conditions by way of locations or otherwise shall be made by the town, and where a town through culpable or prolonged neglect does not do its duty, the Union Government will step in, and at the town's expense, do what the town should have done. Hon. members will see that it is laid down with regard to the establishment of locations that in the first place there shall be established in the necessary places a location for each town.

Of course, in most of the towns of South Africa they have these locations already, and I do not assume that under this Bill it will be necessary, even in a small percentage of cases, to take any special action; and these local authorities will find that this Bill exerts no pressure whatever. But there are places where the Native populations have increased out of all bounds, and for these cases it is laid down that locations must be established, or existing accommodation for the reception of Natives must be increased. Everything should be done to see that the Natives who are taking part in the economic life of a place are properly received and housed there.

45

The Devonshire White Paper: Indians in Kenya

in *African History: Text and Readings*, ed. Robert O. Collins (New York, 1971), pp. 340–41

THE DEVONSHIRE WHITE PAPER: INDIANS IN KENYA (1923) was an official statement of British policy issued by the colonial secretary, the duke of

Devonshire, in regard to the rights of Africans, Asians, and Europeans in colonial Kenya. The colonial secretary issued it to clear up a long-standing controversy as to whether Asians should share the privileges granted to European settlers in the Kenya government and in the settlement of the Kenya highlands. In effect, the duke and the Colonial Office decided against the Indians, reaffirming their second-class citizenship. In order to make this decision more palatable, however, the British officials justified their action on the grounds that the welfare of Africans was more important than that of either of the immigrant groups. This justification proved a powerful weapon in the hands of the defenders of African rights when, a few years later, friends of the settlers in the British government attempted to grant full powers of self-government to the European settler community.

GENERAL STATEMENT OF POLICY

The general policy underlying any decision that may be taken on the questions at issue must first be determined. It is a matter for satisfaction that, however irreconcilable the views of the European and Indian communities in Kenya on many points may be, there is one point on which both are agreed, namely, the importance of safeguarding the interests of the African natives. The African population of Kenya is estimated at more than 2½ millions; and according to the census of 1921, the total numbers of Europeans, Indians and Arabs in Kenya (including officials) were 9,651, 22,822 and 10,102 respectively.

Primarily, Kenya is an African territory, and His Majesty's Government think it necessary definitely to record their considered opinion that the interests of the African natives must be paramount, and that if, and when, those interests and the interests of the immigrant races should conflict, the former should prevail. Obviously the interests of the other communities, European, Indian or Arab, must severally be safeguarded. Whatever the circumstances in which members of these communities have entered Kenya, there will be no drastic action or reversal of measures already introduced, such as may have been contemplated in some quarters, the result of which might be to destroy or impair the existing interests of those who have already settled in Kenya. But in the administration of Kenya His Majesty's Government regard themselves as exercising a trust, the object of which may be defined as the protection and advancement of the native races. It is not necessary to attempt to elaborate this position; the lines of development are as yet in certain directions undetermined, and many difficult problems arise which require time for their solution. But there can be no room for doubt that it is the mission of Great Britain to work continuously for the training and education of the Africans towards a higher intellectual moral and economic level than that which they had reached when the Crown assumed the responsibility for the administration of this territory. At present special consideration is being given to economic development in the native reserves, and within the limits imposed by the finances of the Colony all that is possible for the advancement and development of the Africans, both inside and outside the native reserves, will be done.

His Majesty's Government desire also to record that in their opinion the annexation of the East Africa Protectorate, which, with the exception of the mainland dominions of the Sultan of Zanzibar, has thus become a Colony, known as Kenya Colony, in no way derogates from this fundamental conception of the duty of the Government to the native races. As in the Uganda Protectorate, so in the Kenya Colony, the principle of trusteeship for the natives, no less than in the mandated territory of Tanganyika, is unassailable. This paramount duty of trusteeship will continue, as in the past, to be carried out under the Secretary of State for the Colonies by the agents of the imperial Government, and by them alone.

46

Norman Leys, *Kenya*
(London, 1925), pp. 177–78

NORMAN M. LEYS (1875-1944), a Scot by birth who lived for a time in the United States, studied medicine at the University of Glasgow, specializing in obstetrics. Unable to afford to buy a practice, Leys studied for a year at the Liverpool School of Tropical Medicine, from which he went in 1902 to the port of Chinde, in Portuguese East Africa. Entering the British colonial medical service, he went to Nyasaland (1904), to the East Africa Protectorate, later Kenya (1908), and back to Nyasaland (1913) before a lung disease later diagnosed as tuberculosis ended his career in 1918. Although his years in Africa cannot be traced in detail, it is clear that his attitudes toward race and colonialism evolved only gradually. As early as 1905 he considered writing to members of Parliament about affairs in Nyasaland (against the rules). But in 1908, while stationed at Nakuru, in the East Africa Protectorate, he accompanied a punitive expedition against the Kisii, an affair of which he was far less critical than the parliamentary undersecretary at the Colonial Office, Winston Churchill. In 1911-13 he exposed the violation of a treaty with the Masai, which amounted to confiscation of land wanted for European settlement, writing both to his old teacher, Gilbert Murray, and to the future Labour prime minister, Ramsay MacDonald. For his role in the Masai affair he was dismissed from the East Africa Protectorate, and spent the war years (except for a year when he nearly died of tuberculosis), in Nyasaland. While there, in 1915, he interviewed participants in the celebrated uprising led by John Chilembwe. About this time he began to contemplate the book that would be *Kenya*. In 1918 Leys retired on pension and bought a small country practice at Brailsford, a village near Derby. He wrote a 45-page "letter" to the secretary of state for the colonies, of which *Kenya* (published six years later) is really an extension; the letter was apparently ignored. He met Joseph H. Oldham (secretary of the International Missionary Council, one of the founders of the World Council of Churches, and an important influence in British colonial thinking and policy between the wars), and began a second career as publicist, agitator, and crusader for the reform of British colonial administration in Kenya. His works include *Kenya* (1925), *Last Chance in Kenya* (1931), and *The Colour Bar in East Africa* (1941).[*]

In point of fact the number of Africans dispossessed by the alienation is comparatively trifling, perhaps no more than 50,000. There really was room for colonisation. There really was more land than the Africans of Kenya could use. But that very land that was in excess of their needs is precisely the area which the Government has for twenty years by every means in its power been trying to make them work upon for the profit not of themselves but of European grantees. The whole situation is essentially absurd. The chief fact that impressed the authorities twenty years ago was the existence in East Africa of ten thousand square miles of first-class land, nearly empty of people and accordingly nearly useless to the world. They met that fact by the proposal to fill these empty spaces by European colonists. And now, after twenty years, the 7487 square miles of alienated land occupied by, and 335 of them are

[*] This biographical information was provided in a personal communication from John Cell of Duke University, editor of *By Kenya Possessed: The Correspondence of Norman Leys and J. H. Oldham, 1918-1926* (University of Chicago Press, 1976).

cultivated by, no more, and by now probably less, than 1893 Europeans. The real cultivators of the 335 square miles of alien land under cultivation are of course the fifty or sixty thousand African employees who work for wages, employed, most of them, in growing crops which they could and often do grow just as well at home.

The essential facts about the numbers of labourers in Kenya, available and actually at work, are these. In 1920 the chief Native Commissioner, as reported in the Daily Leader of Nairobi of February 27, made the following calculations in view of the working of the proposed Registration Ordinance. He believed there were 375,000 males in the country between the ages of 16 and 30. Of these a proportion are not really available, such as the Masai and the small cultivators and petty traders of the coast. Mr. Ainsworth's figure for labourers actually available was only 209,000, "less medically unfit." Those unfit in European countries for such work as labourers do in Kenya are 15 per cent to 20 per cent of the age groups 16 to 30. The proportion is certainly greater in Kenya—Dr. Philip of the Scottish Mission put it at 40 per cent for the Kikuyu. If we accept 20 per cent we get 167,000 as the number of able-bodied labourers actually available. To that figure an addition must be made to include those brought under "close administration" (as described in Chapter V) during the last four years. Exactitude is obviously impossible. To escape the least suggestion of partiality, let us take an outside figure, and suppose that 250,000, or two-thirds of the total population of suitable age, is the true figure of men available as wage-earners. Deducting nomads and Masai, that is a proportion at least as high as of those who, in European countries far healthier than Kenya, are found fit for some form of military service. It makes practically no allowances at all for the kinds of work in native agriculture that are always done and can only be done by able-bodied men.

AFRICAN PRIORITIES DURING THE HIGH COLONIAL PERIOD WERE QUITE DIF-
ferent from those of Europeans. The colonizers were most interested in
political control and economic exploitation, while their charges were concerned most with physical survival. Although many Africans' standard of living dropped as a result of decreased agricultural production, when their
labor was diverted from food production to export-oriented activities, few
actually starved. Those Africans who did relatively well in the colonial
system could therefore concentrate on secondary priorities.

Of these the most important was European education, which many
Africans recognized as a valuable tool for advancement in colonial society.
Curiously, Europeans established schools for reasons quite different from
those which brought Africans to attend them. South of the rain forest, most
schools were run by missionaries, who saw them as an effective agency—
along with hospitals—for winning souls. The discrepancy between European and African goals in education was a constant source of tension. As a
result, mission schools produced both the Europeans' closest associates and
their most violent opponents.

One of the plainest expositions of European educational goals appears in
Document 47, Martin Schlunk's report on German colonial schools, issued
just before the First World War. Nothing could demonstrate the implementation of German goals better than Document 48, an examination actually
administered to African schoolchildren in Togo in 1909.

By the 1920s European colonial governments had recognized the
necessity of spending colonial revenues to support the mission schools. In
Africa as in Europe, schools trained their charges for more than religious
vocation, and administrators hoped that the mission schools would produce
clerks, artisans, and patriotic citizens to aid in colonial development. The rationale for increased state support for the mission schools is well described in
Document 49, the 1925 report of the Advisory Committee on Native
Education in the British Tropical African Dependencies.

Those Africans who rejected the missions expressed their discontent in

Chapter Seven

The First Steps
in African
Modernization

a variety of ways. Some, like John Chavafambira, who is quoted in Document 50, returned to the religion of their ancestors, tolerating European dominance but protecting their personal integrity. Others, like the two young Watchtower adepts quoted in Documents 51 and 52, joined sects which brought together elements of both precolonial religion and evangelical Protestantism. (It ought to be added that syncretic religions seem to have appealed principally to Africans who were denied access to the best mission schools.)

Finally, a very few black Africans translated their discontent into political action. One such man, a Zimbabwean, James Mhaso, appears in Document 53. Such reactions were, however, rare: overt political activity attracted the attention of the colonial administration, which spared no effort in suppressing "troublemakers." Before the Second World War, African defenders of the colonial state were as common as political activists.

47

Martin Schlunk, "Das Schulwesen in den deutschen Schutzgebieten"

in *Abhandlungen des Hamburgischen Kolonialinstituts,* Vol. 18 (Hamburg, 1914), trans. in *Traditions of African Education,* ed. D. G. Scanlon (New York, 1964), pp. 42–43. Translated by Wallace Morgan

THROUGHOUT HIS long career, Martin Schlunk (1874–1958) was one of the leading German Protestant missionary authorities. Born in India to missionary parents, he served as head of a North German federation of Protestant Missions from 1902 until 1928. Just before the First World War the Colonial Institute asked him to compile the results of a questionnaire sent out in 1911 to all German schools in Africa. His article "The School System in the German Colonies" includes the results of this compilation. Between 1924 and 1946 he was chairman of the German Evangelical Mission Council and the Society for Mission Sciences. From 1928 until 1948 he held the chair in Mission Sciences at the University of Tübingen.

My justification for making these statements is as follows: The first statement takes it for granted that it is the duty of all the colonial schools to foster a feeling of loyalty on the part of the natives toward Germany and the German people. I say this in spite of the fact that we live in an age when many feel that it is the function of the teacher to fight all manifestations of patriotism and nationalism. We would not get far if we were to apply this humanistic nonsense to our natives in Africa. No, if Germany is to have colonies, and she must have them in order to live, every school must become an instrument of indoctrination of obedience for the German Reich and its rulers. But German language instruction is not absolutely essential here. It could help, but on the other hand, it could also have the opposite effect, since it would enable the natives to read all that undesirable literature which preaches internationalism instead of patriotism.

I am well aware of all the noble reasons given in favor of teaching German in our colonial schools. I agree that it should be taught there whenever possible. But it must never become the language of instruction.

It must be admitted that many of the natives in the German colonies have great gifts for learning languages. It would be no great difficulty to teach those gifted students to speak German well in six to seven years. But even if they are able to speak it after that time in the manner of parrots, what would we have gained? German would still be a foreign tongue for them.

It is a different matter when we speak of the high schools in our African colonies. The pupils of those schools stand as a special class between us and the rest of the natives. If these pupils learn to speak German well, as is the case in Togo, then I would be prepared to admit that there is some sense in it. Although I feel that there is some danger in teaching German, even in the high schools, I am aware that we must have some German-speaking natives in order to govern the country.

It is important that we do not expect too much from the teaching of the German language. I am convinced that we shall have grave racial problems in our colonies in a few decades. It is absurd to think that even German-speaking natives will then be on our side. They will remain children of their culture whether they have learned to speak German or not. On the contrary, those natives who have received an education from us will then become leaders of their people in the struggle against us. The only chance of averting this is to use the schools for character education. The only schools that can do that job satisfactorily are the theological seminaries of the various missions. It is true that they have to teach German, because none of the necessary books are as yet available in the native languages. But the students of these seminaries are specially selected and are taught really to understand German and not just to parrot it.

In sum, the native language must be the language of instruction in the elementary schools. The German language should be taught in the high schools as a foreign language.

48

A Togo School Examination, 1909

in Hans W. Debrunner, *A Church between Colonial Powers* (London, 1965), pp. 114–15. Translated by Dorothea M. Barton.

GERMAN CATHOLIC MISSIONARIES shared a number of assumptions about African education with their Protestant colleagues. The examination reproduced below was administered in November of 1909 by the Togo government to 55 pupils of both denominations.

Saturday, 20.xi.09.

10–10½ a.m. *Calligraphy*. A passage was written on the blackboard and the pupils had to copy it.

10½–11 a.m. *Spelling*. The chairman of the commission dictated a simple passage from a short story, with which none of them were acquainted.

11–12 a.m. *Geography*. The following questions had been set as a task:

(*a*) The large states of Europe and their capitals.

(*b*) What are the names of Germany's most important mountains?

(*c*) What are the names of the most important rivers in Germany and in what direction do they run?

The last question was intended to show whether the pupils could not only reproduce the names mechanically, but could also visualize a map.

3–4½ p.m. *An Essay*. The subject set was: 'What good things have the Europeans brought us?'

5½–6 p.m. *Reading.* In addition to passages known to the pupils, they had to read aloud an unfamiliar article from a little book, called "Drei Kaiserbuchlein", out of the bookshop of the North German Mission.

Monday, 22.xi.09

7½–9 a.m. *Oral Arithmetic.* The questions were asked by the teachers themselves.

10–11. *Written Arithmetic.* One question each was chosen from amongst those proposed by the school associations:

(1) Multiply 118.92 by 67¼ and then divide the number obtained by 3,964.

(2) In 1906 Togo exported copra worth 8,000 marks, in 1907 11,000 marks' worth. What was the increase per cent on the export of 1907?

(3) A labourer drinks brandy worth 0.25m a day. (*a*) how much does he pay for the brandy in a year? (*b*) How many days must he work for the brandy, if he earns 2m a day? (*c*) How many kgs of pork could he have bought with this sum, if pork costs 65 pfennige a kg?

From 11–12 and from 3–6 in the afternoon, *useful knowledge, grammar* and *translation* were examined.

Tuesday, 23.xi.09

7–8 a.m. *History.* The task set was:

The reign of emperor William I and the wars he had waged. Name those men who had specially supported his government.

From 8–11½ a.m., the examinations in translation were completed.

49

Education Policy in British Tropical Africa

(London, 1925), in *Traditions of African Education,* ed. D. G. Scanlon
(New York, 1964), pp. 92–95, 97–98

THE ADVISORY COMMITTEE on Native Education in the British Tropical
African Dependencies was created in 1923 by the duke of Devonshire,
while he was secretary of state for the colonies, to advise the Colonial Office
on educational policy in tropical regions of the British Empire. Up to this
time education in British Africa had been left largely in the hands of missions, but after the First World War these organizations came to realize that
they lacked the resources necessary to support adequate educational
systems. Although the missionaries did not want to give up their educational
role, they did hope that the Colonial Office would take over certain of the
administrative responsibilities. The Colonial Office welcomed this initiative
and appointed the Advisory Committee on Native Education in the British
Tropical African Dependencies as a semi-official policy board. That agency's
recommendations, published in 1925, are an important statement of the
British government's aims for African education.

As a result on the one hand of the economic development of the
British African Dependencies, which has placed larger revenues at
the disposal of the Administrations, and on the other hand of the
fuller recognition of the principle that the Controlling Power is
responsible as trustee for the moral advancement of the native
population, the Governments of these territories are taking an increasing interest and participation in native education, which up to
recent years has been largely left to the Mission Societies.

In view of the widely held opinion that the results of education in
Africa have not been altogether satisfactory, and with the object of
creating a well-defined educational policy, common to this group
of Dependencies—comprising an area of over 2½ million square
miles with a population of approximately 40 million—the Secretary
of State decided in 1923 to set up an Advisory Committee on
Education in British Tropical Africa.

The Committee feels that it has now reached a point at which it is
possible to formulate the broad principles which in its judgment

should form the basis of sound educational policy, and with the approval of His Majesty's Government, set forth these views to the local Governments, together with some indication of the methods by which they should be applied. . . .

The central difficulty in the problem lies in finding ways to improve what is sound in indigenous tradition. Education should strengthen the feeling of responsibility to the tribal community, and, at the same time, should strengthen will power; should make the conscience sensitive both to moral and intellectual truth; and should impart some power of discriminating between good and evil, between reality and superstition. Since contact with civilization—and even education itself—must necessarily tend to weaken tribal authority and the sanctions of existing beliefs, and in view of the all-prevailing belief in the supernatural which affects the whole life of the African it is essential that what is good in the old beliefs and sanctions should be strengthened and what is defective should be replaced. The greatest importance must therefore be attached to religious teaching and moral instruction. Both in schools and in training colleges they should be accorded an equal standing with secular subjects. Such teaching must be related to the conditions of life and to the daily experience of the pupils. It should find expression in habits of self-discipline and loyalty to the community. With such safeguards, contact with civilization need not be injurious, or the introduction of new religious ideas have a disruptive influence antagonistic to constituted secular authority. History shows that devotion to some spiritual ideal is the deepest source of inspiration in the discharge of public duty. Such influences should permeate the whole life of the school. One such influence is the discipline of work. Field games and social recreations and intercourse are influences at least as important as classroom instruction. The formation of habits of industry, of truthfulness, of manliness, of readiness for social service and of disciplined cooperation, is the foundation of character. With wise adaptation to local conditions such agencies as the Boy Scouts and Girl Guide Movements can be effectively utilised provided that good Scout Masters are available. The most effective means of training character in these ways is the residential school in which the personal example and influence of the teachers and of the older pupils—entrusted with responsibility and disciplinary powers as monitors—can create a social life and tradition in which standards of judgment are formed and right attitudes acquired almost unconsciously through imbibing the spirit and atmosphere of the school. . . .

The Native Teaching Staff should be adquate in numbers, in qualifications, and in character, and should include women. The key to a sound system of education lies in the training of teachers, and this matter should receive primary consideration. The principles of education laid down in this memorandum must be given full and effective expression in institutions for the training of teachers of all grades, if those principles are to permeate and vitalize the whole educational system. The training of teachers for village schools should be carried out under rural conditions, or at least with opportunities of periodical access to such conditions, where those who are being trained are in direct contact with the environment in which their work has to be done. This purpose can often best be served by the institutions of normal classes under competent direction in intermediate or middle rural schools. Teachers for village schools should, when possible, be selected from pupils belonging to the tribe and district who are familiar with its language, traditions and customs. The institution of such classes in secondary and intermediate schools should be supplemented by the establishment of separate institutions for the training of teachers and by vacation courses, and teachers' conferences.

50

Statement of a Zimbabwean non-believer, 1937

in Wulf Sachs, *Black Anger: The Mind of an African Negro Revealed by Psychoanalysis* (London, 1947; rpt. New York, 1968), pp. 106–8

JOHN CHAVAFAMBIRA was born in the Manyika District of Southern Rhodesia shortly after the turn of the century. In the early 1920s he migrated to South Africa, where he worked as a servant for Europeans and as a healer for Africans. While living in Johannesburg, he met the psychoanalyst Wulf Sachs, who recorded Chavafambira's biography. The bracketed interpolations are those of Sachs.

. . . John went on to talk about religion.

"We used to talk a lot about Christians. Even now we do. We don't think a lot of Christians. We don't believe in Jesus. We used to pray in olden times to our native god, Mwari, and to the *midzimu*, for rain. It always helped. Now we pray to Jesus and rain never comes. We have no corn, no land, nothing. We all hate the Christians; they talk, talk, and nothing comes to us from it. I am only waiting to go home and learn how to pray to our god and will never pray to Jesus, and won't be a Christian any more. I became a Christian when I was quite small. I was still stupid. My mother was a Christian and also my second father, and all the children were baptized. My children were not baptized and never will be. My father also does not believe any more in Christianity. He became a native doctor. The Christian priests are even so bad [he probably meant stupid] that they are against native doctors and native medicines. When a missionary comes to our houses at home, they chase him away. Nobody wants to talk to them. In the kraals nobody wants to be a Christian any more. Why should they be? [And here he became rather agitated.] The white people came to our country, it is the natives' country [he was emphatic about it], took everything away from us—the land, the cattle—and made us work. We cannot move without a pass, have to pay taxes; and they have given us Jesus. We don't want him. I read in the Bible that the Jews also refused to have Jesus, and believe in God. We are also the same; I won't send my children to church, but I will send them to school to learn native and English."

One day, he said, a strange man came and joined the circle. He was a silent, taciturn man, who listened to their talk but said nothing. He came often, although he was not a patient. He eventually broke his silence with a bitter attack upon Christianity, remarking, at the end, that the missionaries were no longer popular among the kraal-folk, who were turning away from the churches.

"That is true," a chorus of voices attested, though the majority of those present were Christians belonging to various denominations.

"I am also a Christian," the stranger said. "I belong to the Apostolic Church. But my *midzimu* are angry with me because I don't kill any goats to them, and the minister talks of hell where I will go if I remain a heathen. I want so much to know what is this heaven and this hell."

"Yes, and they also tell us that *lobola** is a sin," someone put in. "To have more than one wife is a sin. How can one marry without *lobola*? And how can one wife work the land?"

They say if you make a sin you go to hell," the stranger interrupted again. "I would like to know what it is, hell." His face was stubborn and dull. Fear of hell seemed to have drained all life out of him.

Tentatively, someone tried to explain. But he failed. For the conception of hell is utterly foreign to the African mind. When people die, they become *midzimu*, and continue to live in the places where they lived in the flesh. They actually continue to live, only in a different way, and are in constant and intimate contact with the living. The dead and the living form a chain that must not be broken. There is no division of the worlds between them; the idea of hell, of "the other world," is utterly incomprehensible to them.

"And why do they want us not to talk to our *midzimu*? You are a *nganga*,"† they said to John; "why don't you ask them?" "When I go to church," another said, "it is the Catholic Church. I look at all the statues. I like to look at them and think they might be my *midzimu*."

"Yes, that is right," John remarked. "The same happens to me in my church. I pray, I think of my *midzimu*, and the faces change even if I don't close my eyes. The woman with the child turns into my mother, Nesta."

John sat silently pondering this thought, till Maggie broke in loudly: "Well, I don't want any other *midzimu*, and I don't like the priests, I won't be a Christian."

But John loved the statue of Christ. He even referred to him as the Great Healer. Was he perhaps, he wondered, the great-great-great-grandfather of all the *ngangas*? He knew that Christ was born in Africa, and wished that he could have proved that Christ was a real African, black as all Africans. But he knew from the Bible that Christ was a Jew, and he had not seen a black Jew.

* bridewealth—B. F.
† healer—B. F.

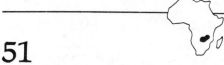

51
The testimony of Mulakasa, September 18, 1925

in F. L. Brown, "Legal proceedings including summaries of evidence in the Mwanaleza case, 1925," Rhodes House, Oxford University MSS Afr. s. 1066, pp. 9–13

MULAKASA (born ca. 1895) was one of the earliest followers of Mwana Lesa, the Malawian evangelist and witch-hunter who ordered the execution of more than seventy "witches" before his arrest by colonial authorities. Mwana Lesa (his real name was Tomo Nyirenda) had originally studied at a Scottish Presbyterian mission in Nyasaland before becoming acquainted with the teachings of Jehovah's Witnesses. In April 1925, a few months after his baptism into the sect, he began preaching among the Lala people, who were politically decentralized and economically distressed. Mulakasa, a man of about thirty, was one of Mwana Lesa's early converts and became an elder in the movement. The following excerpt is from Mwana Lesa's trial, which was held in September and October 1925.

Tomo Nyendwa (sic) came to Musakanya village during March 1925: he was accompanied by four young men, 2 of Chimese villages and 2 of Chupamwanda villages (these are villages of Chief Mulungwe). Tom baptised everyone he found in the villages, men, women and little children. He told us not to commit adultery, not to refuse food to our neighbour and to cease witchcraft. He said we must be baptised so that our hearts should be changed and that then the Americans would come and give us much wealth. . . .

Tomo had a number of women followers. At the end of the day he would give each Elitata, Dikoni or Preacher a woman with whom he might sleep for the night but the man was forbidden to have connections with the woman as if he did so he would die in the morning. At first we had a different woman each night this was merely to keep us warm and we had no connections. We told Tom that this was not a good custom and he agreed that if one of us wanted to marry a woman we could do so if we told him. He would then gather the Elitatas, deacons and preachers together and celebrate the marriage with hymns and prayers. . . .

At Chondoka village Tom had said that he was able to detect witches. Mafumbi asked Tom to find and get rid of all the witches in his country as they were the cause of his (Mafumbi) being ill in his legs and eyes. . . .

[The witches were drowned or starved.] My job was with the witches, who were confined in the huts. If any had sufficient goods to ransom himself I would tell Tom and then Tom would collect the goods and I would release the witch. Also I had to take people with disputes to Tomo: he would settle the affair: award compensation and receive part of the compensation himself. People from all over the country brought their affairs to Tomo and he settled them as if it were at the Boma.

52

The testimony of Chifwalo, a sixteen-year-old preacher in Mwana Lesa's movement, October 1925

in F. L. Brown, "Legal proceedings including summaries of evidence in the Mwanaleza case, 1925," Rhodes House, Oxford University MSS Afr. s. 1066, pp. 63, 66–67

CHIFWALO was another of Mwana Lesa's followers who testified at the trial. More typical of the movement than Mulakasa, he was only sixteen when he became a preacher for Mwana Lesa.

Tomo used to say he was an aeroplane and a roof and that he would kill anyone who opposed him. The song he used to sing when finding witches was "The Ndeke is roaring" (the aeroplane is roaring). I know what an aeroplane is. It is a thing made by white men that flies and kills people. He said he was a roof because it meant he had strength. (The interpreter explains that if I were to go out and kill three lions I should be quite reasonable in saying I was a roof so this apparently is a native metaphor for power or strength.) . . .

When Tomo taught us Teachers he used to make us in the early night time take fire and go and make a fire out in the bush and watch by it till the evening star set for God Coming. He told us we should see God Coming through the trees in the middle of a shining light that he would be—but that we must not be afraid or run away or we should die. When God came all the dead would rise and all would live happily. The Black man in their part and the white man in theirs. He told us we were "Christians" when he baptised us. Our "Church" was coming. The Watch Tower was the house of the "Church."

53

Excerpts from Southern Rhodesian Criminal Investigation Division Reports, 1929–30

in T. O. Ranger, *The African Voice in Southern Rhodesia* (Evanston, 1970), pp. 153–54, 158–59

THE TWO EXCERPTS which follow are taken from Southern Rhodesian Criminal Investigation Division reports of meetings organized by the Industrial and Commercial Workers Union of Africa. The I.C.U., founded in South Africa by a Malawian, was the most effective representative of African rights in that part of the continent between the wars. The first excerpt is taken from remarks made by James Mhaso, a supporter of the I.C.U., at a meeting held in Bulawayo on June 29, 1929. The remarks in the second excerpt, from a meeting held in the same city on January 11, 1930, were made by Solomon, an African policeman employed by municipal authorities.

James Mhaso: "You will all understand that a man who is hungry will never be quiet. . . . We want the Government to understand that the native is starving. . . . We ask the Government to give us sufficient pay, but we do not want the same pay as Europeans. We will be obedient but we must complain. We criticize the Government because there should be proper pay for married men. We have a lot of taxes; we pay rent at the location (urban housing compound), and also go to the Beer Hall; and we will do that until we die. This is a trap made by the Government. If you brew beer today, and are found in possession of it, you are arrested. It is the same beer as the Government makes in the beer halls. . . . When I heard the Police were stopping beer outside, I thought the Government were going to do something good instead of giving us a Beer Hall.

If the white people did not believe in uplifting the native they should have left us in darkness. We are workers suffering. You must all understand that. Your perspiration is counted for nothing. Everything is worked by natives. You are digging gold out of the earth and are making holes in mines. That is the work of natives, working with pick and shovel. All roads are made by natives but if you walk there you are arrested. Natives sweep the pavements but are not allowed to walk on them. All big houses are built by natives. You must all understand that. One day the road will tell you that it was made by natives.

We were all made by God and God has given us minds to think. We have been give talents but we do nothing with them. The ministers were sent here by God to help us but they do not do so. Why did the ministers tell us that God said that if we want life we must dig in the ground? A minister can buy a motor car but if a native buys a motor car they think it is wrong. The ministers do not want the natives educated today. . . .

Solomon: You remember Masabalala who was detained by the CID (in Port Elizabeth, South Africa in 1920). He created such a disturbance that he cost the Government £40,000 and seventy lives were lost. When he got here he was not allowed to see his family and was made to report to the (Southern Rhodesian) CID every four hours. I told him to leave my room because I was disgusted. You must think for yourself. . . . I was born in Rhodesia and am a servant of the Government and I challenge any of you to come against it. I was in Johannesburg when two Europeans were shot for making misleading statements, they were shot for going against the British flag. . . . Don't follow agitators unless you have studied things for yourselves.

ALTHOUGH FEW BLACK AFRICANS POSSESSED THAT COMBINATION OF administrative skill and self-confidence necessary to organize a modern nationalist movement, the phenomenon did appear among light-skinned Africans at either end of the continent. The spread of nationalism to colonial Africa was, as Karl Deutsch has so ably demonstrated, part of a worldwide process associated with improvements in transportation and communications and the desire of organized populations to gain control of their political destiny and economic resources. The slowness with which nationalist movements developed in Africa is not so much the result of the difficulty of transmitting nationalist ideas, which were readily available in the corpus of nineteenth-century European thought, as to the difficulty encountered by nationalist leaders in trying to organize a solid following within their own societies.

Three countries alone possessed the prerequisites—organized leadership and a politically active mass—for nationalist movements in Africa before the Second World War: Egypt, Tunisia, and white South Africa. In all three cases, the nationalist victory was not won until after the war. Nonetheless, the three nationalist movements served as beacons for later nationalist movements on the continent.

In prewar Egypt there were nationalist leaders and popular followings, but the two seldom got together for political purposes. One might well argue that the Egyptians were better organized politically in the 1920s than they were at any time before the military coup d'état of 1952. Hundreds of thousands of Egyptian peasants had been moved out of their homes during the First World War to aid the British in their war against the Turks. These displacements produced in the immediate postwar period a discontented populace which was eager to demand the end of British rule. They found their spokesman in Sa'd Zaghlul, creator of the Wafd party (see Document 54). Zaghlul succeeded in winning formal independence from the British, but died before a modern Egyptian state could be created. In his absence the political party which he founded degenerated into an elitist instrument, protecting the privileges of the wealthy alone.

Chapter Eight

Nationalist Movements Before the Second World War

The next spokesman who attracted widespread support was Hassan al-Banna, founder of the Muslim Brethren. His organization achieved great popularity, but it lacked direction, presenting a hodgepodge of social promises, Islamic theology, and chauvinism, as Document 55 indicates. The real mobilizer of the Egyptian state was Gamal Abdel Nasser, who came to power after the Second World War had given a boost to non-Western nationalism. Document 56 shows, however, that his vision of a modern Egypt came to him while he was still a teenager in the 1930s. Document 57 demonstrates the style he adopted after gaining power.

Tunisians, although more urbanized and thus more easily organized than the Egyptians, faced a more difficult struggle for independence. The country was legally a protectorate in which the bey was "advised" by the French administration, but in fact the French had encouraged the development of a substantial European settler community. The settlers, of course, vociferously opposed the exercise of political power by Tunisians other than the docile beys and their court. The first demands for modern political rights therefore came not from the bey but from Western-educated Tunisians who opposed his regime. As Document 58 shows, this group in 1919 had only a tiny political base, being limited by its concern for better treatment for the Tunisian elite rather than for the population as a whole.

The next generation of Tunisian political activists had more generous ideas and a broader base of support. The Depression had forced many Tunisian farmers off their land and many city dwellers out of their jobs. These groups formed a discontented multitude to which Habib Bourguiba and the Neo-Destour appealed (Document 59).

Afrikaner nationalists in South Africa are not usually regarded as similar to the North African nationalists, but they nonetheless have a good deal in common. Like the Egyptians, they were subject to a relatively liberal colonial regime in which they received considerable formal representation. Afrikaners, in the same way as their North African counterparts, felt that real power rested in the hands of foreigners. Their target, however, was not a group of foreign-born administrators, but the English-speaking section of the white South African population.

Afrikaner nationalist leadership came from a small secret organization, the Broederbond, founded in 1919 (see Document 62). By the 1930s the Broederbond had amassed considerable political power, a situation which led to its denunciation by the Afrikaner prime minister, J. B. M. Hertzog (Document 60). By the late thirties the Broederbond had thrown its support to a rump of Hertzog's old Nationalist party, which espoused many of the racist and corporatist ideas of the Nazis in Germany (Document 61). Needless to say, not all that is ugly in South Africa today can be traced to the Broederbond. Documents 63 and 64 show the antidemocratic trends which were present in the dominant United party on the eve of the Second World War.

Black Africans also longed for independence, but their goal seemed much further away. Their most eloquent statements regarded the ironies of colonization. One of the most moving is the poem of Léopold Senghor contained in Document 65.

54

Sa'd Zaghlul, *Collected Speeches*

(Cairo, 1924), p. 27, in Albert Hourani, *Arabic Thought in the Liberal Age 1798–1939* (London, 1962), p. 221

SA'D ZAGHLUL (1857–1927) became the leader of Egyptian opposition to the continuation of British rule in Egypt after the First World War. Born to a family of well-to-do farmers, he studied first at the Islamic Al Azhar University, where he was influenced by the ideas of Jamal ad-din al-Afghani, and then at the French School of Law in Cairo. He first rose to prominence as son-in-law of Mustafa Fahmy, a powerful collaborationist of the British regime. In 1906 Lord Cromer chose Zaghlul to serve as the first Egyptian to head a ministry (education), but in 1913 he broke with the British and began to rally Egyptian support as speaker of the Legislative Assembly and unofficial leader of the opposition. After the war he was one of the organizers of the Wafd (delegation) sent by Egyptian nationalists first to London and then to the Paris peace conference. Jailed and exiled between 1921 and 1923, he nonetheless became the prime minister of the new constitutional monarchy, and head of the Wafd political party, positions which he held until his death in 1927.

They ask us, "Where is your programme?" And we answer, we are not a party, we are a delegation empowered by the nation and expressing its will about a matter which it has assigned to us: this matter is complete independence, and we strive to this end alone. . . . As for internal questions—should education be compulsory, should it be free, or should interest be paid on the Debt, should cotton be sown on a third or half of the cultivable area—these are matters which I leave to men who know more of them than I do. But so far as independence is concerned, we are a nation and not a party. Anyone who says we are a party demanding independence is a criminal, for this implies that there are other parties which do not want independence. The whole nation wants independence, we are the spokesmen of the nation in demanding it, we are the trustees of the nation.

55

Hassan al-Banna, "Towards the Light"

(Cairo, 1936), in Robert G. Landen, *The Emergence of the Modern Middle East: Selected Readings* (New York, 1970), pp. 261–64. Translated by Landen

HASSAN AL-BANNA (1906–1949) was the founder of the Muslim Brotherhood in Egypt. The son of a pious watchmaker in the Nile Delta, al-Banna displayed his commitment to orthodox Islam at an early age. After receiving teacher training in Arabic, he moved to the Suez Canal Zone, where he perfected his ideas for an organization to promote greater Islamic practice in the lives of Egyptians. After a transfer to Cairo in 1933, he become increasingly active in politics, supporting Palestinian Arabs and criticizing the Wafd government. His movement was officially outlawed in December 1948, and he was assassinated two months later, but it still holds the loyalty of a sizable number of Egyptians.

The following are the chapter headings for a reform based upon the true spirit of Islam (according to its very conservative and puritanical exponent):

I. In the political, judicial, and administrative fields:

    1st. To prohibit political parties and to direct the forces of the nation toward the formation of a united front;

    2nd. To reform the law in such a way that it will be entirely in accordance with Islamic legal practice;

    3rd. To build up the army, to increase the number of youth groups; to instill in youth the spirit of holy struggle, faith, and self-sacrifice;

    4th. To strengthen the ties among Islamic countries and more particularly among Arab countries which is a necessary step toward serious examination of the question of the defunct "Caliphate";

5th. To propagate an Islamic spirit within the civil administration so that all officials will understand the need for applying the teachings of Islam. . . .

10th. To train and to use the "Azharis," that is to say, the graduates of Al-Azhar University [the most important Muslim university in Cairo], for military and civil roles;

II. In the fields of social and every day practical life: . . . .

3rd. To root out clandestine or public prostitution and to consider fornication as a reprehensible crime the authors of which should be punished;

4th. To prohibit all games of chance (gaming, lotteries, races, golf);

5th. To stop the use of alcohol and intoxicants—these obliterate the painful consequences of people's evil deeds;

6th. To stop attacks on modesty, to educate women, to provide quality education for female teachers, school pupils, students, and doctors; . . . .

27th. To combat foreign customs (in the realm of vocabulary, customs, dress, nursing) and to Egyptianize all of these (one finds these customs among the well-to-do members of society); . . . .

III. The economic field:

3rd. To facilitate and to increase the number of economic enterprises and to employ the jobless there, to employ for the nation's benefit the skills possessed by the foreigners in these enterprises;

4th. To protect workers against monopoly companies, to require these companies to obey the law, the public should, share in all profits. . . .

56

Gamal Abdel Nasser to a friend, 1935

in Anthony Nutting, *Nasser* (London, 1972), p. 7. Translated by Nutting

GAMAL ABDEL NASSER (1918-1970) was the leading exponent of Egyptian nationalism and head of the Egyptian state from 1954 until his death. Nasser's family came from Upper Egypt, where his father worked for the post office. After displaying discontent with the Wafd regime while still a teenager, he entered the military academy at Cairo. He showed great heroism in the war of Israeli independence, but became disillusioned with King Farouk's government after the Arab defeat. In 1949 he was one of the founders of the group of army officers that in 1952 overthrew the monarchy. Two years later he became prime minister, and in 1956 he was elected president of Egypt. During his sixteen years in power he sought to mobilize the Egyptian people for the development of the country but was ultimately diverted from local affairs because of his involvement in pan-Arab and Third World activities.

Egypt . . . is in a state of hopeless despair. Who can remove this feeling? The Egyptian Government is based on corruption and favours. . . . Who can cry halt to the imperialists? There are men in Egypt with dignity who do not want to be allowed to die like dogs. But where is . . . the man to rebuild the country so that the weak and humiliated Egyptian people can rise again and live as free and independent men? Where is dignity? Where is nationalism? . . . the nation sleeps like men in a cave. Who can awaken these miserable creatures who do not even know who they are?

57

Gamal Abdel Nasser, speech to the Armed Forces Exhibition at Cairo, September 27, 1955

in J. C. Hurewitz, *Diplomacy in the Near and Middle East*, 2 vols. (New York, 1956), 2:402–5. Translation by the U.S. State Department

When I speak to you now, my brothers, I speak to all the men of the armed forces; I speak to all the men of the fatherland; I speak to Egypt—Egypt which revolted on July 23, 1952—Egypt which placed its faith in the goals of this Revolution; Egypt which was determined to achieve these goals—Egypt which finally threw off the occupation and threw off slavery. When I speak to you today, I speak to all Egypt.

My brothers, this is my feeling when I look at the battlefield, and I see the men of the armed forces on guard along the frontiers; when I look at the frontiers of Egypt and see the men of the armed forces standing staunch and firm and faithful, exerting every effort for the safety of this country and its sons.

The fifth goal of your Revolution was to set up a strong national army. From the beginning of the Revolution you have all exerted every effort to achieve this goal and we have worked with you with all our might and with every means at our disposal. We have worked with you to achieve this goal because to achieve it means liberty; to achieve it means glory; to achieve it means dignity.

My brothers, we met the greatest obstacles—we met many difficulties in achieving our aim. We did everything we could to set up military factories; we did everything we could to provide the army with the heavy armaments it needed; and we did everything we could so that Egypt's army might be a strong national army.

Yes, my brothers, we did a lot.

But there were the greatest difficulties in our way. We believed that if we wanted to create such an army for Egypt we had to preserve our freedom. We believed that if we wanted to achieve this strong national army for Egypt, we had to become free in our internal and our foreign policies.

My brothers, we will never agree that this army be formed at the expense of this country's freedom, or at the expense of this country's glory, or at the expense of this country's dignity. We have always been determined that the formation of this strong national army should go hand in hand with true liberty and with real glory.

We have proclaimed Egypt's policy on many occasions. We declared that Egypt after the Revolution of July 23 would go forward with its independent policy; it would go forward having rid itself of imperialism; it would go forward having rid itself of domination; and it would go forward having rid itself of foreign influence. These were our hopes and these were your hopes. We did everything we could to preserve these hopes. We did everything we could, my brothers, to preserve these goals—and we were confronted by many obstacles.

You know that heavy weapons are controlled by the big powers. You know that the big powers have never agreed to supply our army with heavy weapons except with conditions and except with stipulations. You know that we refused these conditions and these stipulations because we are jealous of our true freedom and we are jealous of our independent policy. We are anxious that Egypt have a strong independent policy so that we may make of Egypt a new independent personality which will really rid itself of imperialism, will really rid itself of occupation, will really rid itself of foreign domination in all its aspects. We have been making progress along this path.

Today, my brothers, we hear an outcry from London, we hear an outcry from Washington about the arming of Egypt's troops. But I would like to tell you that throughout the last three years we have tried to get heavy weapons for the army by every means, not for aggressive purposes, not to attack, not to make war, but for defense, for security, for peace.

We wanted to strengthen our army so as to provide security for ourselves, to provide security for our nation, to provide security for our "Arabism." We wanted to get weapons for the army so that we could always feel secure, safe, and tranquil. We never intended to strengthen our army for aggressive purposes. We never intended to strengthen the army for wars. But the army which is the defender and protector of our homeland must always stand prepared to defend the borders and the country's honor. Such is our purpose and this is our goal. We have always declared this throughout the last three years. We do not want arms for aggression. We want arms so that we can be tranquil, so that we feel at peace and not threatened.

Today, my brothers, I sense an outcry here and I sense an outcry there. I sense these outcries now that we have been able to obtain for the army the weapons of which it is in need, without conditions and without restrictions, so as to achieve the goal which this Revolution undertook—that Egypt should have a strong national army to defend its true independence and protect its true freedom.

On this occasion I would like to tell you, my brothers, the story of the arming of our troops. When the Revolution took place we went to each of the states, we went to every quarter to get weapons for the army. We went to Britain; we went to France; we went to America; we went to the rest of the states to get weapons for the army in the interest of peace and defense. What did we get? We got only demands. They wanted to arm the troops after we had signed a document or after we had signed a pact. We declared that even though we had wanted and had decided to arm our troops, we would never sign a document. We were arming our troops in the interest of our freedom, of our independent personality, of our Revolution, of the glory of our country, of Egypt's dignity. We declared that we would not arm our troops at the expense of our freedom.

We requested arms but what was the result? The result, my brothers, is a long and bitter story. I remember now, I remember as I talk to you that we sometimes humiliated ourselves but we never abandoned our principles. We humiliated ourselves when we requested arms—we begged for arms—but at the same time we were determined to hold to our principles and we were determined to preserve our high ideals. And what was the result? Never, my brothers, could we achieve our goal, the greatest goal for which this Revolution was undertaken, the creation of a strong national army.

France always bargained with us. She bargained with us over North Africa. She says to us, "We will give you arms on the condition that you should not criticize our position in North Africa, and on condition that you relinquish your 'Arabism,' that you relinquish your humanitarianism and on condition that you should keep silent and close your eyes when you see the massacres in North Africa."

We said to her, "How can we relinquish our 'Arabism'? How can we give up our humanitarianism? We never can."

France's arms offer to us was always like a sword above our necks. We were always being threatened, my brothers, with the cutting off of arms. We were always being threatened, my brothers, with the supply of arms to Israel and the cutting off of arms for Egypt. This is the story of France and now I'll tell you the story of America.

From the time of the Revolution we asked for arms and we were promised arms. And what was the result?

The promise was a promise circumscribed with conditions. We would get arms if we signed a mutual security pact. We would get arms if we would sign some form of alliance. We refused to sign a mutual security pact. We refused to sign any form of alliance. And, my brothers, we could never get a single weapon from America.

What was the story of England? England told us that she was ready to supply us arms. We accepted gratefully. What was the result? England provided us with a quantity of arms which was not sufficient to achieve the goals of this Revolution.

What was the result of all this, my brothers? The army opposing us is obtaining arms from various parts of the world. Israel's army has been able to obtain arms from England, France, Belgium, Canada, Italy and from various other states. It can always find someone to supply it arms, while we read in the foreign press—in the British, American or French newspapers—that Israel's army can defeat all the Arab armies combined. It was only last month, my brothers, that I read many articles in that sense, that the Israeli army could defeat Egypt, that the Israeli army could beat the Arabs, that the Israeli army was superior in armament, that the Israeli army was superior in equipment.

This is what they have said in their press and I said to them, since you feel like this why do you prevent us from obtaining arms? I asked them this, and what was the result? France complained about our feelings towards North Africa, and prevented us from obtaining arms.

When we saw this, when we saw this domination, when we saw this influence which was being used against us, we decided to ask all the states of the world to supply us arms without conditions. I told them these arms would not be used for aggression, that they would be used for defense, that we had no aggressive intent, that our intentions were peaceful, that we wanted to have a strong independent army to defend our country and help it to achieve its free and independent goals, that we want to have a strong army not for aggression but for defense.

I said this, my brothers, in the name of Egypt to America, to England, to France, to Russia, to Czechoslovakia and to the rest of the states and I waited for their answers. I waited, and what was the result? I got answers from some of them that I could get arms with conditions. I refused, for I have already told you that although we are ready to humiliate ourselves by asking for arms, we will never abandon our principles.

We received a reply from Czechoslovakia saying that she was prepared to supply arms in accordance with our needs and those of Egypt's army on a commercial basis, the transaction to be considered like any other commercial transaction. We agreed and last week Egypt signed a commercial agreement with Czechoslovakia to supply us arms. This agreement permits Egypt to pay in Egyptian products such as cotton and rice. This offer we gratefully accepted. In this way, my brothers, we achieve one of the goals of the Revolution, the formation of a strong national army.

Today, my brothers, as I talk to you I sense the outcry raised here and there—an outcry in London, an outcry in Washington. These outcries seek to continue to control us, to continue to influence us.

We will fight to destroy this control. We will fight to destroy this influence. We will fight to achieve the goals of the Revolution and we will fight to create a strong national army able to achieve the greatest goals of the Revolution, able to obtain peace. Yes, my brothers, peace—that peace which we proclaimed at Bandung, the peace which we have proclaimed on many occasions.

This army which we create is for the sake of peace. We create it so that we can be secure in our lot, we create it so that Egypt will not be a state of refugees. We create it against aggression, we create it against any territorial designs against our nation's soil.

When I hear someone say that this opens the way for Russian influence or foreign influence in Egypt or the Middle East, I think of the remote past and I say that this commercial agreement without conditions does not open the way for Russian or foreign influence, but, my brothers, it means the eradication of the foreign influence which so long oppressed and dominated us.

My brothers, when we are able to equip our army with the necessary arms without conditions or restrictions, we destroy foreign control—that control which I have felt and which you have felt in the guise of equipping our army and in the guise of providing it with arms. Those who talk to us about foreign influence know that they themselves have no intention of seeing foreign influence wiped out.

We intend to destroy foreign influence. Egypt—independent Egypt, revolutionary Egypt, strong Egypt—will never allow foreign influence in her land. They know we will never accept their influence, and their control. They know that Egypt after the Revolution of July 23 has determined to destroy forever foreign influence, foreign oppression and foreign control and to go forward as a free independent power with her own foreign policy, motivated by her own interests and not by the interest of any of the foreign camps.

They know this when they talk of influence for they think that it is their influence which has come to an end in this country—that it is their influence which has gone away forever.

Today we are a free and independent nation. We will fight for our liberty and we will fight for our independence and may God be with us all.

58

The Nine Demands of the Destour Party, 1919

in 'Allal al-Fasi, *The Independence Movements in Arab North Africa* (New York, 1954), p. 56. Translated by Hazem Zaki Nuseibah

THE NINE DEMANDS formed the platform promulgated in 1919 by Tunisia's first modern political party, the Destour. Reflecting the concerns of a small French-speaking elite, the platform calls for limited self-government within the French Empire.

1. The establishment of a legislative assembly, consisting of Tunisian and French delegates to be elected by universal suffrage,

with powers to prepare its own agenda and also with extensive powers of supervision over fiscal matters.

2. The establishment of a government responsible to this assembly.

3. Separation of the legislative, judicial, and executive branches of government.

4. The appointment of Tunisians to all government posts if they possess qualifications equal to French candidates.

5. Equal salaries for French and Tunisian employees.

6. The establishment of elected municipal councils.

7. Compulsory education.

8. Eligibility of Tunisians to purchase of lands administered as state domains.

9. Freedom of the press, of meetings, and of association.

59

The platform of the Qism al-Jabal Conference, May 12–13, 1933, adopted by the Neo-Destour party, 1936

in 'Allal al-Fasi, *The Independence Movements in Arab North Africa* (New York, 1954), p. 65. Translated by Hazem Zaki Nuseibah

BY THE TIME of the Depression, the moderate projects of the Destour had proved inadequate to improve the life of ordinary Tunisians. A new generation of educated Tunisians, led by Habib Bourguiba, who later became the nation's first president, advocated more active opposition to the French administration. They arrived at the following, more radical, platform at the Qism al-Jabal Conference on May 12-13, 1933.

Destour leaders refused to accept the program or the leadership of the younger generation. Bourguiba and his friends then founded their own organization, the Neo-Destour, which adopted the Qism al-Jabal platform as its own in 1936.

1. A Tunisian parliament elected by universal suffrage, competent to draw up its own agenda and in possession of full legislative powers.

2. A government responsible before parliament.

3. Separation of legislative, judicial, and executive branches of government.

4. The extension of the jurisdiction of the Tunisian judiciary over all residents of Tunisia.

5. Civil rights and freedoms for all citizens without exception.

6. Compulsory education for all.

7. Safeguarding the economic life of the country.

8. The initiation of all necessary measures for uplifting the country from the moral and material degeneration into which it has relapsed so that it may occupy a worthy place among the self-governing civilized nations.

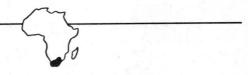

60
General Hertzog's denunciation of the Broederbond
Cape Times, November 8, 1935

GENERAL JAMES BARRY MUNNIK HERTZOG (1866-1942), who earned his title in the Boer War, was the first prime minister of South Africa elected by a political party that appealed uniquely to Afrikaners. Like Smuts, he was born in a small town in the Cape Colony, from which he went to the small city of Stellenbosch and then to Europe to study law. Like Smuts, he served in the judiciary of a Boer republic (the Orange Free State) before his service in the Boer War. An early associate of Smuts and Botha, he became minister of justice (1910-12) in the first cabinet of the Union of South Africa, but resigned from the government to protest what he considered excessive Anglophilia. In 1914 he led the formation of the Nationalist party, which in alliance with the Labour party won the election of 1924. Hertzog served as prime minister from 1924 until 1939, a period during which South Africa was buffeted by a number of conflicting forces. As head of the government he played a leading role in finding a local solution for the problems caused by the migration of large numbers of blacks and poor whites to South African cities. Where the former were concerned, he took a hard line, spearheading efforts between 1929 and 1936 to deprive Cape Africans of their place on the common voter rolls. In other matters, however, he was not a reactionary: he pioneered the creation of a government-owned steel industry and championed the rights of Afrikaans-speaking Coloured people. As far as European parties were concerned, he walked a fine line, opposing both Afrikaner chauvinists and British imperialists. Disagreeing with the declaration of war against Germany in 1939, he resigned from office and aligned himself with his former enemies on the Afrikaans right. The latter outmaneuvered him and won the support of a majority of the Afrikaans electorate.

General Hertzog then referred to a "secret society," Die Afrikaner Broederbond, which, he said, was established in 1918 with the laudable task of promoting and safeguarding the cultural interests of Afrikaans-speaking Afrikanerdom and with the definite provision in its constitution that party politics were to be excluded.

But in the long run, said General Hertzog, the bond was converted from a cultural to a party political organization.

In August, 1932, the chairman of the executive council, who is the highest authority of the bond, said with the general approval of the congress:

"I consider that national culture and national welfare cannot unfold fully if the people of South Africa do not also constitutionally sever all foreign ties.

"After the cultural and economic needs the Afrikaner Broederbond will have to devote its attention to the constitutional need of our people.

"Added to that the objective must be an entirely independent genuine Afrikaans form of government for South Africa, a form of government which, through its embodiment in our own personal head of State, bone of our bone and flesh of our flesh, will insure and cement us to irresistible unity and strength."

"On January 16, 1934," said General Hertzog, "a circular letter was issued by the executive council of the bond and signed by the chairman, Professor J. C. van Rooy, and the general secretary, Mr. I. M. Lombard. It was directed to all members of the bond and reads as follows:

"'Our test for brotherhood and Afrikanership does not lie in a political direction but in aspiring after the ideal of a never-ending existence of a separate Afrikaans nation with its own culture.

"'It has been made sufficiently clear that what we expect of members is that they should have as their object the Afrikaansing (versfrikaansing) of South Africa in all aspects of its life.

"'Brothers, your executive council cannot tell you to promote party political fusion or union, or to fight it, but we can appeal to every brother to choose in the party political sphere that which according to conviction is most helpful for the bond's object and the bond's ideals.

"'Let us focus our attention on the fact that the primary consideration is whether Afrikanerdom will reach its ultimate destiny of bossism (baasskap) in South Africa. Brothers, our solution for South Africa's ailments is not that one party or another shall obtain the whiphand but that the Afrikaner Broederbond shall govern South Africa.' "

General Hertzog said that to become a member of the bond a person must be Afrikaans-speaking; his home language must be Afrikaans; he must subscribe to the ideal of a never-ending existence of a separate Afrikaans nation with its own culture as stated by Professor van Rooy, Mr. Du Plessis and others on various occasions. . . .

"Neither the one nor the other will ever succeed in a policy of domination, and when the Potchefstroom fanaticism is out once again to incite Afrikaans-speaking Afrikanerdom, my own people, whether [sic] South Africa has not suffered sufficiently from Afrikaner strife and dissension; I want to ask you whether our language and our freedom are of so little value and significance to us that we should once again stake them in a gamble from pure racial animosity and fanaticism."

General Hertzog said that the Broederbond had been converted into a secret purified National Party that was occupying itself with secret propaganda work, for the promotion of the interests of the purified brothers and of the purified National Party.

The bond had been put at the disposal of the purified National Party in ever-increasing measure since 1932, and its doors have been thrown wide to all who could pass as leading or prominent purified Nationalists, but the wider the doors of the bond were opened for the purified party the tighter they were closed on the United Party, so that since 1932 not a single leading political person taking an active part in politics and belonging to the United Party had been taken up by the bond. . . .

"It is," said General Hertzog, "to the purified National brothers to whom must be ascribed the fact that the bond has been misused in various ways for the purposes and objects for which it was never intended, and which have shocked the feelings of right and justice of those among the brothers who do not belong to the purified National Party to such an extent that some of them were obliged to take refuge in active protest. . . .

"Of this secret Broederbond, which has as its ideal dissension among the Afrikaner nation through the exclusion of the English section from the Government of the land Dr. Malan has been a member and brother since coalition [1933].

61

Manifesto of the Purified Nationalist party
Cape Times, April 5, 1938

THIS WAS AN ENGLISH translation of the platform used by the Purified Nationalist party as the basis of its campaign in the South African elections of 1938. Despite strong anti-British sentiment among many Afrikaner voters, the party was soundly defeated by the United party, led by Smuts and Hertzog.

IV. IMMIGRATION AND THE JEWISH QUESTION.

While the Party welcomes in general the immigration of suitable and assimilable European elements, it will with an eye to South Africa's special problems, take steps to put a stop to any further immigration of Jews, to combat the practice of changing names, to exercise stricter control over naturalization, and to institute a professional permit system for unnaturalized foreigners along the lines existing in England and France and other countries.

Further, it will take all possible steps to equip South Africa's original Afrikaans- and English-speaking elements to earn a livelihood in every possible walk of life and to protect them from unfair competition.

V. COLOUR PROBLEMS.

(A) The Party aims at revision of our existing native legislation, with the object of abolishing the native franchise for House of Assembly and Cape Provincial Council, prohibiting the flocking of surplus natives into our urban areas, effectively to bring about their removal from those areas, and to make residential segregation in such areas effective.

(B) The Party will put a stop to the present wholesale buying of land by the State for natives, and leave the acquiring of land by the native more to his own initiative, and in conformity with his real needs.

(C) The Party further aims at the logical application of the segregation principle in regard to all non-Europeans, as being in the best interests of Europeans and non-Europeans, and therefore undertakes to introduce legislation for—(1) separate residential areas, separate trade unions, and as far as is practical also separate places of work, for Europeans and non-Europeans; (2) restriction of employment in certain directions to European labour only and/or in accordance with a determined, just and equitable quota for Europeans and non-Europeans; (3) separate representation for enfranchised Cape coloureds in our legislative bodies; (4) the application of the Immorality Act (1927) to all non-Europeans and the prohibiting of mixed marriages and employment of Europeans by non-Europeans.

VI. GENERAL ECONOMIC REFORM.

(A) The party promises an immediate and thorough inquiry into the rise of the cost of living.

(B) In order at all times to safeguard the legitimate interests of the producers, distributors, employees and consumers respectively, and further to protect all classes of persons from exploitation of any nature, the party promises to establish a central economic council, with instructions to advise the Government from time to time in regard to price fixing, producers', distributors', and sellers' organizations, systematic economic development, and other necessary measures.

62
L. J. du Plessis's description of the Broederbond
Johannesburg Star, October 12, 1948

Secret "Broederbond" that Aims to Rule the Union

Once Well-Intentioned Movement Now in Sight of "Baasskap"
by L. J. du Plessis, a former Secretary of the Broederbond

Preliminary talks on the formation of an Afrikaans organization to propagate the Afrikaans language and bring together serious-minded young Afrikaners in Johannesburg and along the Reef, were held in my family home in 1918. It was finally called the Afrikaner Broederbond and every member was expected to carry a button with the letters A.B. on it.

It was nothing more than a semi-religious organization, meetings being held in the parsonages of the Jeppe and Irene congregations as well as in the Irene church hall, where the Rev. Wm. Nicol was minister.

The idea originated in the mind of Mr. H. J. Klopper, present M. P. for Vredefort. Like other movements this one flourished for a while and then appeared to die. It was during one of these lowtide periods that I was for a time its secretary. I think I am correct in saying that the Bond really progressed when large numbers of teachers joined it, including Mr. I. Lombard and Mr. Greybe. The latter has been chairman of the Transvaalse Onderwysers Vereniging for more than twenty years.

The last meeting I attended was round about 1922 in the Carlton Hotel when it was decided by majority vote, that the Bond would go underground. What happened since I can only surmise when hearing of prominent members like Bosman becoming manager of Volkskas and Professor L. J. du Plessis chairman; Erasmus secretary of the Transvaalse Onderwysers Vereniging; Diederichs chief organizer of the Reddingsdaadbond; Albert Hertzog "protector" of the mine workers; Rev. Wm. Nicol, Moderator of the Dutch Reformed Church for three consecutive synods; Klopper chief of the Afrikaanse Taal en Kultuur Vereniging; and last, but not least, Dr. Verwoerd, editor in chief of Die Transvaler.

It is not necessary for me to go into detail on the activities of all these organizations. Every enlightened observer in South Africa must realize that there is a central body co-ordinating the activities so as to ensure the one aim of segregating all Afrikaans-speaking persons from the rest of the population and making them the exclusive and privileged element in South Africa. The conclusive evidence is there that it is not only colour apartheid but also race apartheid that is the ultimate aim of the Bond.

The following few examples will illustrate: The Afrikaans youth has been deliberately segregated by means of separate organizations like the Voortrekker movement in place of the Boy Scouts and Noodhelp Liga in place of the Red Cross, the Volkspele—games for the youth made so exclusive that only Afrikaans-speaking persons can ever feel at home there.

There are, however, two organizations of which I have personal experience and knowledge and of which I would like to give more information—the Afrikaans Taal en Kultuur Vereniging, and the Afrikaans churches.

I have no hesitation in saying that the former, the so-called cultural organization for railwaymen, was created by that fervent Afrikaner, H. J. Klopper, with the specified object of instilling in the minds of the thousands of unskilled railway workers and their families his brand of Afrikanerhood.

That was, of course, also the object in organizing the 1938 Ossewatrek—by the Afrikaanse Taal en Kultuurvereniging—which culminated at the Voortrekker monument under construction. This was shortly after the 1938 general elections and the Nationalists openly boasted that if the elections had been held after the trek the results would have been very different.

During one of the Afrikaanse Taal en Kultuur Vereniging congresses, a senior railway official, a foundation member of the Bond, addressed the congress and said, inter alia, that members should be encouraged and helped financially to have large families, because that was the only way Afrikanerdom could be strengthened. Finally, as recently as September 8 last, the Minister of Transport used the following words when addressing another congress of the Afrikaanse Tall en Kutuurvereniging:—

"As a result of the symbolic Ossewatrek of ten years ago the Afrikaanse Taal en Kultuur Vereniging laid the foundation of cooperation and unity, and under that mighty unity the Afrikander had to-day succeeded in gaining control (baasskap) in South Africa." . . .

Can anyone blame me for regarding anything touched by the Broederbond with suspicion? I have the desperate feeling of one who sees the guilty escape for lack of evidence.

There is no doubt in my mind that the supposedly strained relations between the HNP and the O.B. are all sham. I would not be in the least surprised if Dr. Malan and Dr. van Rensburg often sit round the same conference table. I am even reluctantly compelled to believe the same of Mr. Havenga. I believe, however, that he is the one man who can raise the curtain of secrecy over the Broederbond.

63

Book banning by the United party
Cape Times, June 23, 1938

THE FOLLOWING two reports from the *Cape Times* in 1938 indicate the limits of South African democracy under the United party of Smuts and Hertzog. The *Cape Times*, then an advocate of liberalism and loyalty to the British Empire, was generally critical of government proposals to restrict freedom of the press.

Big List of Banned Publications . . .

In explaining the underlying principles on which books or periodicals are banned in South Africa, the Minister of the Interior, Mr. Richard Stuttaford, told me that the Film Censorship Board, of which Mr. Harry N. Venn is the Chairman, makes the recommendations.

The Department of the Interior than asks the Department of Customs and Excise to prevent the books in question from coming into the country.

The authorities act generally on certain well defined principles, it was stated. Books or periodicals in which sex plays too conspicuous a part are not being allowed in to the country, while purely sensational literature calculated to harm the child mind, or to create an undesirable social or moral outlook in the youth of South Africa is similarly banned to a large extent.

Native Population

The authorities are being guided in their decisions by the fact of the various elements of the native population which it is claimed may achieve an undesirable social or moral outlook were they to be introduced to pictures of naked women or to frank discussions of sex relations.

64
Newspaper censorship by the United party
Cape Times, November 4, 1938

The Cape Times, November 4, 1938
Control of Union Newspapers
U.P. Congress Asks for Legislation

Bloemfontein, Thursday . . . .

When the Free State Congress of the United Party resumed tonight all Ministers had left on their return to Pretoria. Nineteen branches of the Party had presented motions calling for legislation to control newspapers.

Among these were suggestions that the Government should legislate to make it compulsory for newspapers to correct "deliberate false statements" by the publication of special admissions of guilt, and that persons using insulting or abusive language at public meeting or in the Press, or by way of posters, be punished.

Ultimately the following resolution was adopted unanimously: "The Government is requested to pass legislation authorizing the prosecution of persons or newspapers who supply or publish irresponsible or false information, together with persons or parties who circulate libellous posters."

Harmful Propaganda

A resolution was passed unanimously requesting the Government to take immediate steps to put a stop to the continuous influx of harmful propaganda matter in the form of printed leaflets, booklets and other forms of literature, all of which were being imported from overseas and distributed among the citizens irrespective of race, creed or colour.

Particular reference was made to Communist propaganda by Europeans among natives.

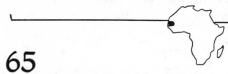

65

Léopold Sédar Senghor, "To the Senegalese Sharpshooters, Dead for France"

(Tours, 1938), in *Black Poets in French*, ed. Marie Collins (New York, 1972), pp. 111–15. Translated by Collins

LÉOPOLD SÉDAR SENGHOR (1906–) is a Senegalese statesman and one of the greatest living French-language poets. Born in the coastal town of Joal, he earned early recognition for his literary gifts and was sent to Paris for his university education. He taught in French high schools from 1935 to 1944 and achieved the coveted *agrégation* (the highest state certification) in French literature. After the war he entered politics and from 1946 to 1959 sat in the French National Assembly, representing Senegal. Since that country's independence in 1960, he has been its president.

To the Senegalese Sharpshooters
Dead for France

Here is the Sun
That makes virgins' breasts bold
That makes old people on green benches smile
That would wake the dead under a maternal earth
I hear the noise of cannon—is it from Irun?[1]
They're putting flowers on graves and warming up the Unknown
    Soldier.
You my dark brothers, no one names you.
They promise five hundred thousand of your children to the glory
    of the future dead, thanked in advance the future dark dead

Die Schwarze schande![2]

Listen to me Senegalese Sharpshooters, in the loneliness of black
    earth and death
In your eyeless earless loneliness, more than in my somber skin in
    the heart of the country
Without even the warmth of your comrades lying against you as
    once in the trench once in village palavers

Listen to me, Sharpshooters with black skin, even though earless
and eyeless in your triple enclosure of night.

We have not rented mourners, not even the tears of your former
wives
—They remember only your great flashes of anger, preferring the
ardor of the living.
The laments of mourners are too light
Too quickly dried the cheeks of your wives, like the Fouta water-
falls in dry season
The warmest tears too clear and too quickly drunk in the corners of
forgetful mouths.

We bring you, listen to us, we who would spell your names in the
months when you were dying
We, in these days of fear without memory, bring you the friendship
of your peer companions.
Ah! that I might one day with a voice the color of glowing embers,
that I might sing
The friendship of comrades fervent as entrails and delicate, strong
as tendons.
Listen to us, Dead stretched out in the water of the depths of the
Northern and Eastern plains.
Receive this red soil, under the summer sun this soil red from the
blood of white victims
Receive the salute of your black comrades, Senegalese Sharp-
shooters
DEAD FOR THE REPUBLIC!

    [1] City in Spain, a scene of action during the Spanish Civil War.
    [2] "Black disgrace," the expression is used in German to describe an unspeakable
abomination, *viz.* "black hole of Calcutta" in English.

THE DECOLONIZATION OF AFRICA WAS A MIRROR IMAGE OF THE ORIGINAL European scramble. Although plans for independence had been discussed for a long time, the arrangements for the independence of tropical Africa were completed in the five years between 1957 and 1962. After that time, only the oldest white settlements in southern Africa remained, and most of them became independent after new struggles in the 1970s.

The preconditions for the rush to independence, described in chapter nine, were established in the 1940s and early fifties. Foremost, of course, was the Second World War, which destroyed the notion of colonial invulnerability. After the war, the triumphant Allies found themselves constrained to obey the international legal system which they had formerly manipulated to the disadvantage of their colonial charges. Only such states as South Africa, where the ruling groups were determined to hold on irrespective of consistency or fairness, did not succumb to the logic of decolonization and the rhetoric of self-government.

Other settler regimes yielded after political insurrections, as chapter ten shows. In the case of Kenya, where settlers had never constituted more than 1 percent of the population, the British government put down a major African uprising and then decided that the costs had been too great and abandoned the country. The French, who constituted 10 percent of the population of Algeria, put up a tougher fight, but once again the metropolitan electorate decided not to continue the struggle necessary to maintain colonial rule over an unwilling majority.

The selections included in chapters nine and ten, in addition to their political significance, also contain sketches of personality types which

Unit Three

Toward Independence

became important in post-independence Africa. We find political militants, intellectuals, politicians, and even the colonial police who are the spiritual ancestors of the military men who rule so many countries in Africa today. All too often, their comportment in the last days of colonial rule foreshadowed how they would behave when they achieved power.

THE SECOND WORLD WAR BROUGHT ABOUT FUNDAMENTAL CHANGES IN WORLD politics which made possible the independence of the colonies of Africa. The effect of the war on Africa was less direct than on the Middle East or Southeast Asia, where territories obtained their independence during or immediately after the war, but the advancements in Asia served as precedents for similar ones in Africa. There, however, progress was less immediate: after an initial enthusiasm for African rights during the war, colonial authorities lost steam, and granted colonial autonomy only after political pressure mounted in the 1950s.

Allied enthusiasm for African political development during the war was in part a function of their close call at the hands of the Axis. In May and June of 1940 the Belgians and French surrendered, leaving the colonies of the former effectively without a metropolitan authority and those of the latter under the orders of the pro-German government at Vichy. Had it not been for the heroic initiative of two men, Governor-General Pierre Ryckmans of the Belgian Congo and Governor Félix Eboué of Chad, the whole of French-speaking Africa might have become a potential Axis base. As it was, the Belgian Congo and the French Equatorial Africa federation both joined the Allied cause by the end of 1940, and the Axis were unable to get a foothold in black Africa.

As Document 66, the letter of November 9, 1940, from the British Colonial secretary to the British foreign secretary indicates, the British government had not made any provisions in Africa for such a sweeping Axis victory in Europe. Thus, if anti-Fascist elements in French Africa had not acted, the continent might well have been lost.

The closeness of the call had two effects: on a short-term basis, the loyal colonial administrations put all of their energies into the war effort, extracting every available ounce of material from the colonies. Once the tide had turned in 1944, they began to propose liberalizations in the colonial system, partly out of gratitude and partly out of guilt over the coercion they had used on Africans to promote the war effort. Document 67, the recommendations

Chapter Nine

Decolonization

adopted by the Brazzaville Conference of February 1944, called for such reforms as the abolition of forced labor, political representation in the metropolitan parliament, and improved educational facilities.

Although many of these reforms were abandoned or substantially delayed when the war was over, the wartime liberalism was perpetuated by changes in international law. In the immediate postwar period the most important development was the establishment of the United Nations as an effective agency to regulate international relations. Unlike the League of Nations, the UN included (until 1949, at least) all of the most important powers of the world. Given this mandate, it played an especially active role in colonial affairs, pushing territories under its jurisdiction toward independence and encouraging colonial powers to do the same. The difference between the League and the UN shows up with great clarity in documents 68 and 69, the colonial sections of the respective organizations' constitutions. Where Article 22 of the League Covenant calls for "tutelage" for "peoples not yet able to stand by themselves under the strenuous conditions of the modern world," Article 73 of the UN Charter urges its trustees "to develop self-government" and "to ensure, with due respect for the culture of the peoples concerned, their political, economic, social, and educational advancement."

Like the League, however, the UN lacked the power to interfere in the internal affairs of its member nations. Thus, independent nations frequently ignored the international organization's injunctions. This was particularly striking in the case of South Africa, when Afrikaner nationalists—and the Broederbond—came to power in 1948. General Smuts had been a longtime supporter of the League and had a great respect for international institutions. His successor, D. F. Malan, was concerned primarily with an internal agenda: the advancement of Afrikaners and the maintenance of white supremacy.

As Documents 70 and 71 indicate, Smuts was trapped when the nationalists introduced their policy of apartheid—complete separation of the races in South Africa. As a politician responsible to the white electorate, he could not oppose segregation; his main criticism of the nationalists was that the existing reserves were not large enough to hold the entire black population. Malan's reply ignored Smuts' logic: the blacks would be independent within their own territories. Little did it concern him that the lands allotted to the blacks, who accounted for 80 percent of the country's population, amounted to only 12 percent of the country's land. The nationalists were in power and were prepared to ignore reasons just as they were prepared to ignore international organizations. They had succeeded in gaining control of the sovereign state and could do as they pleased. The justification for their policies contained in the political program which they announced for the 1952 elections (Document 72) made it clear that they intended to rule the country on behalf of their constituents without compromise.

Thus, blacks in South Africa learned that there were limits to the justice which they could expect from European colonizers. There as in other parts of the continent they began to take the law into their own hands.

66

Secretary of State for the Colonies, Lord Lloyd, to Secretary of State for Foreign Affairs, Lord Halifax, November 9, 1940

Public Record Office, London, FO 371/24282

GEORGE AMBROSE LLOYD (1879–1941), first Baron Lloyd of Dolobran, a British statesman and colonial official, had the unenviable task of serving as secretary of state for the colonies in Churchill's original war cabinet. He was born to a wealthy family and attended Eton, then Cambridge University, from which he graduated in 1900. Elected to Parliament as a Conservative in 1910, he began his overseas career as a member of the Arab Bureau in 1916. Between 1918 and 1929 he served as governor of Bombay and then as high commissioner for Egypt, for which he was named to the House of Lords. During the 1930s, he published a two-volume account of his career in Egypt and served for three years as chairman of the British Council, an agency which introduces British culture to foreign visitors. His term under Churchill called for superhuman efforts at impossible jobs; in June of 1940, he flew to Bordeaux to try to keep the French in the war; thereafter he was responsible for coordinating the colonial war effort.

I asked the Chiefs of Staff at the end of July to prepare a comprehensive review of the strategical situation in Africa as a whole. I pointed out that the situation created in that continent by the capitulation of the French was entirely novel and had never been envisaged in any plans drawn up for the defence of our African possessions. I caused my Department at the same time to provide them with a paper setting out some of the political and economic considerations which I felt ought to be taken into account. The Chiefs of Staff referred the problem to the Joint Planning Sub-Committee who gave it some preliminary examination during August. This Sub-Committee reached the conclusion that the main issues were covered in a paper on the future strategy of the Chiefs of Staff, and I agreed in those circumstances that the consideration of the African appreciation should be deferred until I had seen the wider document. This paper, when it appeared, did not contain any comprehensive analysis of the African problem.

I then raised the matter with the Prime Minister and tentatively suggested to him the formation of a ministerial committee to deal with African problems rather on the lines of the Middle East Committee, of which Eden, Amery and I are members. The Prime Minister demurred to this, and suggested that the Middle East Committee might extend its scope to cover African questions.

Since then, I have had several long telegrams from Mitchell, the Deputy Chairman of the East African Governors Conference, urging the importance of getting out a proper strategical plan for the whole of Africa South of the Sudan and the Sahara. There has also been Lord Hailey's telegram.

Every symptom in fact today increasingly suggests the necessity of our being prepared with plans for any emergency happening in Africa, and in this connection I need not remind you of the rumours of military preparations in Dakar for an offensive to recover the de Gaulle colonies. I am very doubtful if we are prepared to meet such an eventuality if it occurred.

67

Recommendations adopted by the Brazzaville Conference

République française, Ministère des Colonies, *Conférence africaine française, Brazzaville 30 janvier 1944–8 février* (Paris, 1945), in *France and West Africa*, ed. John Hargreaves (London, 1969), pp. 235–40. Translated by Hargreaves

THE CONFERENCE convened by General De Gaulle at Brazzaville in January 1944 raised hopes for greater political rights among the educated elites in the French colonial empire. By this time the French African colonies had passed into Gaullist hands, and the Allies were preparing for the invasion of France. Thus, it was a combination of wartime liberalism and military self-interest which led French officials to promise substantial reforms of the French colonial system. Most of these reforms, however, were rejected by French voters in 1946.

PART I. POLITICAL ORGANISATION OF THE FRENCH EMPIRE.
INTERNAL POLITICAL ORGANISATION OF THE COLONIES.

The French African conference at Brazzaville, before approaching this part of the general programme proposed for examination, deemed it necessary to lay down the following principles:

The purposes of the civilising work which France has accomplished in her colonies exclude any idea of autonomy, any possibility of evolution outside the French imperial bloc; the eventual establishment—at however remote a date—of "self-governments" in the colonies must be ruled out.

A. *Political Organisation of the French Empire*

The general programme of the Conference summed up this problem thus:

"It is desirable that France's political power should be exercised with rigour and precision in all the lands of her empire. It is also desirable that the colonies should enjoy great administrative and economic liberty. It is equally desirable that the colonial peoples should experience this liberty themselves and their sphere of responsibility should be gradually established and increased so that they shall become associated with the conduct of public business in their countries."

The Conference, after discussion in its session of 6 Feburary 1944, adopted the following recommendations. . . .

1. It is desirable and indeed essential that the colonies be represented in the future assembly which will be charged with drafting the new French constitution. . . .
2. It is essential that the representation of the colonies within the central power in the Metropolis should be assured on a broader and much more effective basis than in the past. . . .
4. In any case the new organism which will be created, colonial Parliament or—preferably—Federal Assembly, must strengthen and guarantee the unbreakable political unity of the French world and at the same time respect the identity and local liberties of each of the territories making up the group France-Colonies (or, if the term may be introduced despite the objections which it may raise, the French Federation). . . .

B. *Internal Political Organisation of the Colonies*

. . . It is indispensable to create means of political expression which will allow the heads of the colonies—to whom we wish to allow the broadest possible scope for initiative in internal administration—to base themselves both on the European side and on the native side on a well-balanced and legitimated representative system.

We therefore recommend the suppression of the present consultative bodies and their replacement, in the first place, by district and regional councils composed of native notables; these will utilise, whenever this seems possible, the support of existing traditional institutions: in the second place, by representative Assemblies composed partly of Europeans and partly of natives. The manner of nomination must be by election, and the method should be by universal suffrage, wherever and whenever this is recognised as possible. Failing this, nomination would be made by co-option. In exceptional cases a small number of European [and] native members, well known for their special capabilities or for services rendered, might be nominated by the Governor.

The functions of district and regional councils should be consultative; those of the Assemblies should be deliberative as regards the voting of the budget and the approval of new services, consultative in all matters arising from the Governor's powers of legislation and the making of regulations. In addition administrative councils, composed wholly of officials, should assist the Governor, purely in the application of regulations.

Part II. Social Questions.

A. *Constituent Elements of Colonial Society*
[General Programme:]

"Respect for native life, and its progress, will be the basis of our whole colonial policy, and we must submit absolutely to the obligations which are implied. The natives will not be interchangeable, nor subject to eviction, nor to arbitrary demands for forced labour. Colonies are essentially places where Europeans and natives live together. While subordinating our policy to developing the life of the local races, we must also provide European activity with its just place.

Before anything else, the Conference must then define the role of the European in the colony. Only after solving this problem will it have the means to approach the others. . . ."

B. *Organisation of Native Society. Traditional Institutions. Formation of Cadres.*

In this part of its study the Conference had to accept the existence of two elements in native society:
—on the one hand, the masses, still faithful to customary institutions
—on the other, an elite which has grown up in contact with us.

The problem thus consists in seeking the surest method of making the native mass evolve in the direction of an even closer assimilation to the principles which constitute the common basis of French civilisation, and in particular of leading it closer towards political responsibility. At the same time it is fitting to give the native elite the earliest possible opportunities of proving its capacities in face of the harsh realities of responsibility and command. After discussion in committee and in plenary session on 3 February 1944 the Conference adopted the following recommendation:

Traditional political institutions must be maintained, not as ends in themselves, but as means of allowing immediately the maximum vigour of expression in regional and municipal life. The administration must watch and control the working of this accession by the natives to political responsibility. . . .

C. *Social and Family Customs*

Native justice. . . . The progressive suppression of the ordinary penalties of the *Indigénat* must be guaranteed as soon as the war ends.

D. *Education*

. . . Recommendations

i. The education of the African natives must reach and permeate the masses, teaching them how to live better, and at the same time culminate in a reliable and speedy selection of elites.

ii. The same importance as is attached to the education of boys must be given to the education of girls; this must advance in step so as to avoid an imbalance fatal to society and to the native family.

iii. Instruction must be given in French, the use in teaching of local spoken dialects being absolutely forbidden, in private as well as public schools.

iv. The instruction of the masses can only be successfully undertaken if schools are established in all villages which can provide an enrollment of fifty pupils, boys and girls. The necessary condition of this is the training of native teachers of both sexes in normal schools, which must be established as quickly as possible. . . .

E. *Labour Code*

. . . Recommendations

Although the war effort demands the temporary maintenance of present labour laws, the conference is unanimous in affirming the absolute superiority of freedom of labour; local authorities will be allowed a maximum of five years in which to re-establish this.

The re-establishment of a free labour market cannot take place without a marked improvement in the moral and material condition of the worker, shown in an increase in wages, in the organisation of apprenticeships and the development of vocational training combined with education in responsibility. . . .

With the aim of giving African Labour the place of honour it deserves, we further recommend:

i. The institution of one year's compulsory labour service between the ages of 20 and 21 for natives recognised as suitable, if not called up for military service. These natives would be employed solely on works of public importance. Natives who can prove that they have worked for eighteen months with a private employer will be exempt.

ii. The creation of savings books which would assure the native of a pension after 15 or 20 years at work. This measure should be extended to all categories of native labour.

iii. The regular observation of a weekly rest-day.

iv. The limit of a day's work to be fixed at eight hours. . . .

ECONOMIC QUESTIONS.

. . . Recommendations

The object of our colonial policy must be the development of the productive potential of the overseas territories and the growth of their wealth so as to assure the Africans of a better life by raising their purchasing power and improving the standards of living. . . .

The industrialisation of the colonial territories should be encouraged. It will have to take place by stages, with prudence and method, within the strict limits imposed by the general plan for production. To this end it will be placed, as regards previous authorisation and control of profits, under control of the public power. With this reservation, it will in general be carried out by private initiative.

The Administration will assist such initiatives
—by bearing the cost of pilot factories whose importance it has recognised during their experimental period
—by supporting industries which are vital for the country but appear to be unremunerative
—by creating centres of research and experiment, available to industrialists. . . .
The Conference recommends the despatch of a mission to Russia to study the system of collective farming.

68

The Mandate System: the League of Nations Covenant, 1919

TWO ARTICLES of the League of Nations Covenant (1919) reflect the legal and political solutions to the problem of dealing with non-white colonies after the First World War. Article 22, which was drafted primarily by General J. C. Smuts, reallocated the former German and Turkish colonies to members of the Allies under League of Nations supervision. The League mandates were thus a force for more humane colonization but not for independence. Article 23, which deals with colonies under Allied control, had little effect on anyone.

Article 22.

To those colonies and territories which as a consequence of the late war have ceased to be under the sovereignty of the States which formerly governed them and which are inhabited by peoples not yet able to stand by themselves under the strenuous conditions of the modern world, there should be applied the principle that the well-being and development of such peoples form a sacred trust of civilisation and that securities for the performance of this trust should be embodied in this Covenant.

The best method of giving practical effect to this principle is that the tutelage of such peoples should be entrusted to advanced nations who by reason of their resources, their experience or their geographical position can best undertake this responsibility, and who are willing to accept it, and that this tutelage should be exercised by them as Mandatories on behalf of the League.

The character of the mandate must differ according to the stage of the development of the people, the geographical situation of the territory, its economic conditions and other similar circumstances.

Certain communities formerly belonging to the Turkish Empire have reached a stage of development where their existence as independent nations can be provisionally recognised subject to the rendering of administrative advice and assistance by a Mandatory until such time as they are able to stand alone. The wishes of these communities must be a principal consideration in the selection of the Mandatory.

Other peoples, especially those of Central Africa, are at such a stage that the Mandatory must be responsible for the administration of the territory under conditions which will guarantee freedom of conscience and religion, subject only to the maintenance of public order and morals, the prohibition of abuses such as the slave trade, the arms traffic and the liquor traffic, and the prevention of the establishment of fortifications or military and naval bases and of military training of the natives for other than police purposes and the defence of territory, and will also secure equal opportunities for the trade and commerce of other Members of the League.

There are territories, such as South-West Africa and certain of the South Pacific Islands, which, owing to the sparseness of their population, or their small size, or their remoteness from the centres of civilisation, or their geographical contiguity to the territory of the Mandatory, and other circumstances, can be best administered under the laws of the Mandatory as integral portions of its territory, subject to the safeguards above mentioned in the interests of the indigenous population.

In every case of mandate, the Mandatory shall render to the Council an annual report in reference to the territory committed to its charge.

The degree of authority, control, or administration to be exercised by the Mandatory shall, if not previously agreed upon by the Members of the League, be explicitly defined in each case by the Council.

A permanent Commission shall be constituted to receive and examine the annual reports of the Mandatories and to advise the Council on all matters relating to the observance of the mandates.

Article 23.

Subject to and in accordance with the provisions of international conventions existing or hereafter to be agreed upon, the Members of the League:

(a) will endeavour to secure and maintain fair and humane conditions of labour for men, women, and children, both in their own countries and in all countries to which their commercial and industrial relations extend, and for that purpose will establish and maintain the necessary international organisations;

(b) undertake to secure just treatment of the native inhabitants of territories under their control;

(c) will entrust the League with the general supervision over the execution of agreements with regard to the traffic in women and children, and the traffic in opium and other dangerous drugs;

(d) will entrust the League with the general supervision of the trade in arms and ammunition with the countries in which the control of this traffic is necessary in the common interest;

(e) will make provision to secure and maintain freedom of communications and of transit and equitable treatment for the commerce of all Members of the League. In this connection, the special necessities of the regions devastated during the war of 1914–1918 shall be borne in mind;

(f) will endeavour to take steps in matters of international concern for the prevention and control of disease.

69

Colonies and Trust Territories: the United Nations Charter, 1945

LIKE THE RECOMMENDATIONS of the Brazzaville Conference, the United Nations Charter (June 26, 1945) reflects the liberalism which prevailed among the Allies at the end of the Second World War. The very order of presentation is reversed; where the League Covenant speaks first of the mandates and then of colonies in general, the UN Charter in Article 73 speaks first of the progress of all colonies toward self-government, then of the disposition of former enemy colonies.

Declaration Regarding Non-self-governing Territories

Article 73

Members of the United Nations which have or assume responsibilities for the administration of territories whose peoples have not yet attained a full measure of self-government recognize the principle that the interests of the inhabitants of the obligation to promote to the utmost, within the system of international peace and security established by the present Charter, the well-being of the inhabitants of these territories, and, to this end:

a. to ensure, with due respect for the culture of the peoples concerned, their political, economic, social, and educational advancement, their just treatment, and their protection against abuses;

b. to develop self-government, to take due account of the political aspirations of the peoples, and to assist them in the progressive development of their free political institutions, according to the particular circumstances of each territory and its peoples and their varying stages of advancement;

c. to further international peace and security;

d. to promote constructive measures of development, to encourage research, and to cooperate with one another and, when and where appropriate, with specialized international bodies with a view to the practical achievement of the social, economic, and scientific purposes set forth in this Article; and

e. to transmit regularly to the Secretary-General for information purposes, subject to such limitation as security and constitutional considerations may require, statistical and other information of a technical nature relating to economic, social, and educational conditions in the territories for which they are respectively responsible other than those territories to which Chapters XII and XIII apply.

Article 74

Members of the United Nations also agree that their policy in respect of the territories to which this Chapter applies, no less than in respect of their metropolitan areas, must be based on the general principle of good-neighborliness, due account being taken of the interests and well-being of the rest of the world, in social, economic, and commercial matters.

Chapter XII
International Trusteeship System

Article 75

The United Nations shall establish under its authority an international trusteeship system for the administration and supervision of such territories as may be placed thereunder by subsequent individual agreements. These territories are hereinafter referred to as trust territories.

Article 76

The basic objectives of the trusteeship system, in accordance with the Purposes of the United Nations laid down in Article 1 of the present Charter, shall be:

a. to further international peace and security;
b. to promote the political, economic, social, and educational advancement of the inhabitants of the trust territories, and their progressive development towards self-government or independence as may be appropriate to the particular circumstances of each territory and its peoples and the freely expressed wishes of the peoples concerned, and as may be provided by the terms of each trusteeship agreement;

c. to encourage respect for human rights and for fundamental freedoms for all without distinction as to race, sex, language, or religion, and to encourage recognition of the interdependence of the peoples of the world; and

d. to ensure equal treatment in social, economic, and commercial matters for all Members of the United Nations and their nationals, and also equal treatment for the latter in the administration of justice, without prejudice to the attainment of the foregoing objectives and subject to the provisions of Article 80.

Article 77

1. The trusteeship system apply to such territories in the following categories as may be placed thereunder by means of trusteeship agreements:

a. territories now held under mandate;

b. territories which may be detached from enemy states as a result of the Second World War; and

c. territories voluntarily placed under the system by states responsible for their administration.

2. It will be a matter for subsequent agreement as to which territories in the foregoing categories will be brought under the trusteeship system and upon what terms.

Article 78

The trusteeship system shall not apply to territories which have become Members of the United Nations, relationship among which shall be based on respect for the principle of sovereign equality.

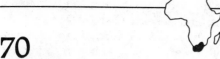

70

General J. C. Smuts, Leader of the Opposition, in the South African House of Assembly, August 16, 1948

in *South African Parties and Policies, 1910–1960: A Select Source Book,*
ed. D. W. Krüger (London, 1960), pp. 411–12

Well, sir, this country is faced with two practical issues in regard to this question of Native policy. The Government must decide, the country has to decide between these issues. The first is this: We may say that the Native reserves are destined to be and are to be, according to the policy of this country, the only home of the Native people of this country. That is a clear-cut policy. That we can understand. Send them to the reserves. The reserves must be their home and that is a solution of the Native question. I do not know whether that is the policy of the Government. I should like to know because it is a very important matter.

That is one of the alternatives before us, namely, the reserves, but if you adopt that solution you are up against vast difficulties. The first difficulty is this, that you must have the land; you must have the soil; you must have the ground to accommodate and absorb the Native people of South Africa. According to the Fagan Report, at present the reserves which are already congested, which are already over-populated, accommodate only about 40 per cent of the Native people. Well, if we have to place the Native people, 100 per cent of them, on reserves, one can see what a land question arises before the country. We will have to double, we will have to treble the Native reserves of this country, and the practical question arises at once where is this land to come from? We do not know. All I know is that it is impossible even to carry out the mere modicum of expropriation which is involved in the Hertzog* scheme, the Hertzog scheme of segregation. As the Minister of Native Affairs will find out more and more, we are up against an insoluble proposition even to carry out the Hertzog scheme.

* Albert Herzog, son of the late prime minister.—B. F.

Whether you go to the Transvaal or to Natal, or anywhere else, you find the farmers of this country, the landowners of this country say: "Are we going to sell the land of our fathers? We shall not." Everywhere you are up against this stalemate in regard to this question; and therefore the policy of segregating and congregating our Native population as a whole in the Native reserves, is a policy which it is impossible to carry out in this country. If that is the apartheid which is contemplated then I have no difficulty at all in saying that it is an impossible policy, and it is not an honest policy because they know that it cannot be carried out.

And supposing that it were possible to carry it out what would happen? Supposing that we were to congregate our Native population in the reserves, and give them a fair chance and do our fair duty towards them, what is the industrial future of this country going to be? When industries start in the locations, in the reserves, and not as heretofore in our White areas, huge industries developing in the Native reserves based on cheap Native labour, what is going to happen to White South Africa, to White industrial South Africa? If this is the interpretation of apartheid—the segregation policy, the reserve policy, then you are up against something which is not only impossible, but which would be a deadly blow struck at the future of White South Africa.

71

Prime Minister D. F. Malan's response to Smuts, August 16, 1948

in *South African Parties and Policies, 1910–1960: A Select Source Book,* ed. D. W. Krüger (London, 1960), pp. 416–17

DANIEL FRANÇOIS MALAN (1874–1959), the first leader of the modern National party to become prime minister of South Africa, presided over the implementation of systematic *apartheid* in his country. Born in the rural Cape Colony, not far from the birthplace of his lifetime rival, J. C. Smuts, Malan attended the University of Stellenbosch and went on to Holland for a doctor of divinity degree, which he received from the University of Utrecht in 1905. For the next ten years he served as a pastor in the rural Cape Province, also demonstrating skill as a writer. In 1915 he became the first editor of *Die Burger,* organ of General Hertzog's party in Cape Town. Elected to Parliament as a Nationalist, he became minister of the interior in Hertzog's first government in 1924. Disagreeing with Hertzog on how Afrikaners should get along with English-speakers and non-whites, he left the Hertzog government in 1933 to form his own party, the Purified Nationalists. In the course of the next fifteen years, Malan's party overwhelmed all Afrikaner opposition and won the election of 1948. Malan's government was responsible for most of the *apartheid* legislation that exists today. During his term of office, from 1948 to 1954, he tightened racial segregation, attacked the courts, and laid the foundations of a police state. Like many Afrikaner nationalists, he was concerned with bringing his people to equality with South Africa's English-speakers as much as in assuring white supremacy.

If you want to know what the positive side of our policy is, let me put it this way just briefly. In the first place, if we are going to take away anything from the Natives—and it is our intention to take away the representation which they enjoy in this House at the moment—then we want to give them something else which in our opinion is better for them, in other words, to call into being institutions for them in their own reserves, and to promote and further develop institutions of their own which will enable them to have a large measure of self-government and which will enable them at the same time to retain their own national character.

With regard to those who do not live in the reserves, just as little as the Europeans are allowed to live or to continue to live in the reserves without permits—Europeans can only live in the reserves under permit and they have no say in the Bunga¹ and in the other self-governing institutions in those territories—just so little should the Native who lives in the European area be given any greater privileges than that. And is there any injustice in that? Why should the Native not be here under permit; why should he have a certain amount of say in European institutions? Why should that not be withheld from him?

Furthermore, as far as the Coloureds are concerned, we do not want to deprive the Coloureds of representation in this House. We want to give the Coloured representation in this House, but through a better system than we have at present and that is to give them representation just as the Natives have it now. The Coloureds have no territories of their own. The Native has his own territory and his own national home.

A further measure which is essential is that we want apartheid as far as our educational institutions are concerned, more particularly in our universities. An intolerable state of affairs has arisen here in the past few years in our university institutions, a state of affairs which gives rise to friction, to an unpleasant relationship between Europeans and non-Europeans. If you want confirmation of that, you need only go to the universities and there you will discover what the position is. For that reason all the universities, as far as I know, except the Witwatersrand University, have broken away from Nusas[2] which was the strongest organisation amongst all the universities. That organisation has been banned from the universities. We do not want to withhold higher education from the non-Europeans, and we will take every possible step to give both the Natives and the Coloureds universities—and sufficient university-training as soon as we can, but in their own spheres; in other words, in separate institutions. I do not want to enlarge on this matter. There will be sufficient opportunity to discuss these matters further at a later stage.

I want to avail myself now of this opportunity to launch an attack in connection with the general attitude of the Opposition. There is one question in regard to which I want to approach them, not because it does us any harm but because it harms South Africa generally, in the international sphere as well, and that is the fact that they are continually bringing South Africa in discredit abroad, and particularly in connection with the change of Government which has taken place here.

[1] General Council of the Transkei.
[2] National Union of South African Students.

72

The program of the National party of South Africa, 1952

in *South African Parties and Policies, 1910–1960: A Select Source Book,* ed. D. W. Krüger (London, 1960), pp. 97–98

THIS IS the official program of the National party, taken from that organization's constitution of 1952. It represents the party's policy toward English-speakers and non-whites in the final years of D. F. Malan's prime ministership.

VI. Equal Language Rights and Co-operation between the European Races

15. The party desires to foster a spirit of mutual trust and cooperation between the European races. It will thus ensure that equal language rights for the English- and Afrikaans-speaking section of the population are observed in practice and maintained in every way in all spheres of South African national life where the State is concerned or is able to exert influence. The principle of bilingualism will therefore be applied faithfully, not only in the various departments of the Civil Service, but also in all parts of the Provincial Administration and in all public administrative bodies in State or State-aided institutions.

VII. Relations with the Non-European Races

16. As a basic principle of its attitude towards Natives and Coloureds the party recognises that both are permanent parts of the country's population, under the Christian trusteeship of the European races. It is strongly opposed to every attempt which might lead to the mixing of European and non-European blood, and strives to cultivate a spirit of goodwill and mutual trust between Europeans and non-Europeans, as being in the best interests of South Africa.

In accordance with this principle it desires to give the non-European races the opportunity to develop themselves, each race in its own field, in both the material and spiritual spheres, in keeping with their natural gifts and abilities. Furthermore the party assures them fair and just treatment under the law and in the administration of the country.

It also declares itself in favour of the territorial and political segregation of the Native, and of separation between Europeans and non-Europeans in general and in the residential and—as far as is practicable—in the industrial spheres. In addition it wishes to protect all groups of the population against Asiatic immigration and competition, among other means by preventing further encroachment on their means of livelihood and by an effective scheme of Asiatic segregation and repatriation.

CHANGES IN INTERNATIONAL LAW PRECIPITATED BY THE SECOND WORLD WAR affected political developments outside of the narrow jurisdiction of the United Nations. One domain particularly important for the liberation of Africa was the matter of the legal recognition of political regimes. Between 1900 and 1930 there had been a fair degree of consensus over which was the legitimate government over most territories in the world. Beginning in the 1930s, however, the liberal democracies and the League of Nations had refused to recognize Axis conquests. During the war, moreover, the Allies had taken the liberty of recognizing governments in exile (De Gaulle's Free French, for example) which had no legal standing in their own country. Thus, the notion arose that different nations might recognize regimes competing for the same territory.

Implicitly, these diplomatic acts facilitated the task of revolutionaries. Regimes which could not obtain approval by the entire United Nations might hope to gain recognition by some of its member nations. Thus, the Russians or Arabs might support the independence of a colony against the wishes of the colonizing power, threatening but in practice seldom according political recognition.

The diplomatic weapon, however, was not necessary to obtain the independence of most of colonial Africa. The precedents set in Asia in the 1940s demonstrated the potential costs of holding onto a colony against the will of its population. One might even say that the invention of the Molotov cocktail made it possible for small groups of poorly equipped insurgents to cause great damage to an intransigent regime. Thus, relatively small outbreaks of violence rather than full-scale war were all that was needed to dislodge the British from West Africa and the French from Tunisia and Morocco.

In white settler colonies, however, the colonizers were determined to hang on to their territories. This determination provoked anticolonial wars which proved costly and difficult but which the Africans ultimately won. The case studies of Kenya and Algeria show colonialism at its ugliest and some of

Chapter Ten

Revolutionary Change

the atrocities which were in fact committed by both sides in their struggle for the land.

In Kenya, the Movement of Unity, more commonly known as Mau Mau, pitted the members of only one ethnic group, the Kikuyu, against the British administration and settler community. As Document 73 shows, the Kikuyu had been politically active since the 1920s, with an educated elite which could present their grievances to the English-speaking world. It was not the elite, however, that led the Kikuyu revolt. It was, rather, the disinherited young men of Kikuyuland who had shouldered the greatest proportion of the colonial burden. Document 74 describes the conditions which led to the creation of the Movement of Unity. Document 75 describes the British repression of it. Despite the British military victory, the colonizers ultimately decided to withdraw from the country, leaving it in the hands of the basically Kikuyu elite.

The French did not abandon Algeria nearly so easily. The territory had been treated as part of Metropolitan France for nearly a hundred years, and in 1954 one million of its ten million inhabitants were French. The other nine million inhabitants had been relatively inactive during the independence struggles of the neighboring Moroccans and Tunisians, but they were nonetheless dissatisfied with French rule. Document 76 contains the initial appeal to arms launched by the National Liberation Front. Although the French sent their best forces to Algeria and even overthrew the Fourth Republic over the government's inability to win the war, the Algerians continued to fight. Increasingly desperate, French officials employed increasingly brutal means to put down the rebellion, as Documents 77 and 78 attest. Despite all these measures, the Algerians refused to give up and the French ultimately had to come to terms with them. In May 1962 the French and Algerians signed a series of agreements (Document 79) putting an end to the war and recognizing Algerian independence.

Thus the wheel of time had come full circle. The French had legally recognized Algerian independence; international law was now on the side of the Algerians as it had formerly been on the side of the European colonizers. The former colonial subjects had finally mastered colonial law.

73

Parmenas Githendu Mockerie, *An African Speaks for His People*

(London, 1934), in *The Africa Reader: Independent Africa*, ed. Wilfred Cartey and Martin Kilson (New York, 1970), pp. 99–103

PARMENAS GITHENDU MOCKERIE (b. 1910) was one of the first Kenyans to present the case for African rights to the British reading public. Trained as a teacher at mission schools, he taught in schools for the Kikuyu while he was still a teenager. The early thirties were the high point of his career: he was selected to attend a teacher refresher course at Makerere College in Uganda in 1931 and then went to London with Jomo Kenyatta to testify before the British parliamentary commission investigating East Africa. Before leaving England he published *An African Speaks for His People* with the support of Leonard and Virginia Woolf.

The population of Kenya (according to recent estimates) consists of 3,000,000 Africans, 45,000 Indians, 12,000 Arabs, 17,000 Europeans; and the area of the country is approximately 225,000 square miles. Politically, the European community is organized through the activity of the European landholders, who have district associations which combine to form the Settler's Convention of Associations, whose body is represented on the Kenya Legislature by eleven elected European members. The Indian community is represented by five and the Arab by two members. The African community has no direct representation on this official body although its direct taxation to the central government is greater than that contributed by the non-Africans.

The laws of the country, most of which affect Africans, have caused them to form organizations for furthering the interests of the African community. There are two chief societies, namely, the Kikuyu Central Association, representing the Kikuyu tribe, and the Kavirondo Taxpayers' Association, organized by the Kavirondo tribe. The idea of forming African societies originated with Mr. Harry Thuku, a Kikuyu man, who in 1921 formed a society known as the East African Association. The object of the Association was to organize African men and women to protest against the reduction of wages which was introduced in 1921 by the Convention of Associations. The rate of wages was and is ten shillings a month of thirty working days of nine hours each. The proposed reduction was thirty-three and one-third percent, that is, a laborer who earned fourpence a day would only be given two pence half-penny for working on the European plantations for nine hours. The British government of Kenya during this time had passed legislation to subject all Kenya Africans over sixteen years of age to the Kipande, a system which restricted them from moving from one place to another unless they carried pass permits on their persons, and which authorized all employers of African workers to enter their wages on the permit. This system is a great hardship to the African people, and rouses anger when the holder of the permit is treated as a criminal if he forgets to carry it on his person.

The reduction in wages produced a decline in the supply of labor on the plantations, so official pressure was thought necessary to help the farmers to secure it. Forced labor was exercised through African chiefs, whose positions as civil servants were endangered if they failed to induce the requisite number of men and women to work on European plantations.

Harry Thuku, who was the leader of the East African Association, was arrested on March 15, 1922. The East African Association declared the first strike of Nairobi workers in the history of Kenya. Men and women demonstrators marched to the Nairobi police line, where their leader was confined. The demonstration was merely a protest against his arrest, and was quite harmless, because anyone who knows that the weapons of Africans are such things as sticks, would not contemplate that the demonstration could stand up against the defense force of Kenya with machine guns and rifles. Anyhow, the demonstration grew in size and instead of being dispersed peacefully, the police force was ordered to shoot down the demonstrators. The massacre was so intense that the official report admitted that twenty-five men and women were killed on the spot, but the leaders of the demonstration collected over two hundred names of persons who received bullets and died at their homes, and in addition there were many who, although they escaped death, suffered from permanent injury because they were afraid to go to hospitals to get bullets extracted; the only two hospitals in Nairobi are controlled by the government.

Mr. Harry Thuku and his two right-hand men were deported for nine years without trial. His Association was broken up when all its leaders were arrested and imprisoned. The African workers from Uganda and Tanganyika who were members of the Association discontinued their membership, and also the Kavirondo, who had been represented in the Association, were advised by the missionaries working among them to disaffiliate from the Association. The Kavirondo therefore formed their own society, the Kavirondo Taxpayers' Association, with the assistance of a British missionary. This association was formed to prevent the Kavirondo from joining the East African Association, which was supposed to contain some elements of revolution, but it stands for the principles for which Mr. Harry Thuku was deported. The Kikuyu tribe, having found that the East African Association had been deserted, formed its own organization, the Kikuyu Central Association, which has now a membership of fifteen thousand.

The Africans of Kenya have been handicapped in organizing their own societies, owing to the restrictions imposed upon them by the government. They are not allowed freedom to speak in public or freedom to hold meetings. Naturally, Africans are discontented because they find that European and Indian associations are free to hold meetings and collect funds for furthering the interests of their own organizations without interference by the government. This discrimination between races arises out of the idea that Africans are insensible to what is right and what is wrong, and must have special laws made for them. Under the Native Authority Ordinance almost any kind of restrictive rule can be made by the administration.

The Kenya Somali community, having realized the weight of restrictions laid on Africans, have requested the government to classify them with the foreign communities such as the Arab and Indian so as to exempt them from any sort of law that affects Africans. If the Somali had seen Africans enjoying the same rights of liberty as the white man and the Indian, there would be no necessity for them to request the government to classify them with the Indian community, as they are natives of Africa. The denial of freedom of association to Africans when they have no representation on the legislature of the country cannot be quietly accepted by them. The British government have pledged themselves to guard the interests of Africans in British colonies: this should mean efforts to improve their status and education. But when we come to the application of the pledge, we find it based on abstract theory.

It has been argued that the African people can be ruled through chiefs nominated by the government. This system can hardly be satisfactory to a community which had deposed the autocracy of hereditary chiefs before European colonization. The only place in East Africa where a system of hereditary chiefs was found intact during the advent of the white man was Uganda, where the common people were still under the yoke of despotic chiefs, whereas in Kenya the people had deposed them and established tribal democracy. Uganda still has hereditary kings, who nominate district chiefs, and the common people have no say in the chieftainship; but in Kenya the government nominates the chiefs, instead of allowing the African people the right of electing their own chiefs. Thus the government has introduced a foreign idea which has robbed the people of their form of democracy. Chiefs who are nominated by European officials cannot win the confidence of the people over whom they are imposed. African political associations in East Africa, having found that the government creates reactionary chiefs without the consent of the people concerned, constantly request the government to restore the right of the people to elect their chiefs. When a chief is appointed by the government, and his administration is corrupt, the people of that district are placed in an unhappy position. They cannot take legal action against him, because of fear of reprisals, and they realize that the chief would be supported by the courts in which he himself acts as judge.

Apart from the restrictions on freedom of association, the African people suffer badly from the Native Authority Ordinance, whereby a District Administrator can issue orders in his district which he executes because he acts both as administrator and as judge. It is hard for an African to find justice.

74

R. Mugo Gatheru, *Child of Two Worlds: A Kikuyu's Story*
(New York, 1964), pp. 90–97

MUGO GATHERU (b. 1925) is a talented member of the generation of young Kikuyus who grew up at the time that the Movement of Unity (Mau Mau) was fermenting. Born to a squatter family living on a European farm, Gatheru attended medical training school in Nairobi and would have continued his education in Kenya if he had not gotten in trouble with European authorities for protesting against the treatment of Africans. After a year in India, he went to the United States in 1950, where he spent the next eight years, which coincided with the Kenya emergency. He then went to England to study law and finally returned to Kenya at the time of independence. His autobiography, *Child of Two Worlds*, is one of the best descriptions we have of growing up in colonial Kenya.

The Kipande system was officially introduced in Kenya in 1921. Every male African above sixteen years of age had to be registered, finger-printed, and issued with a registration certificate—Kipande. Kipande was different from the passport, the birth certificate, the identity cards in Britain, or social security numbers in the United States of America.

In Kenya a policeman could stop an African on the road or in the street and demand that he produce his Kipande—regardless of whether the African concerned was as wise as Socrates, as holy as St. Francis, or as piratical as Sir Francis Drake.

Kipande was also used to prevent the African labourer escaping distasteful employment or from unjust employers who had power to have him arrested and then fined, imprisoned, or both. When Kenyatta took over the leadership of the Kenya African Union from James Gichuru he announced publicly that the Africans had carried "Vipande" (plural for Kipande) long enough and that they should burn them if the Kenya Government refused to repeal the ordinance which had instituted the system. The alternative, Kenyatta explained, was for the Kenya Government to issue

Vipande to all the races of Kenya—the Europeans, the Asians, and the Africans. The Africans, at that time, were seriously prepared to take action, illegal if necessary, to abolish Vipande whether the Government liked it or not. Mass meetings were held all over Kenya at which a lot of money was collected to buy wood for a big fire at the centre of Nairobi city on which all the Africans would burn their Vipande. This was to be an historic fire!

Quickly and wisely the Kenya Government promised the African leaders that the Kipande system would be repealed forthwith and that a system of identity cards for all the races in Kenya would replace it.

The Africans welcomed the government promise and in 1950 the Kipande system was abolished. But the scars of Kipande remained. In the thirty years of its existence Kipande caused great humiliation and hardship and was a constant grievance among my people. It cannot be said that the British Government knew nothing of this: when sending Kenyatta to England on various occasions from 1929 onwards the Africans instructed him to speak not only about the thorny problems of land but also to protest about Kipande.

A well-known missionary, and one of the few well-wishers of the Kenya Africans among the Europeans there, complained in a letter to the London Times of June 1938 that not less than 50,000 Africans in Kenya had been jailed since 1920 for failure to produce Vipande—an average of 5000 Africans per year!

When the Kenya Government announced officially in 1948 that the Kipande system would be abolished the Kenya settlers, as was expected, resisted strongly. The instrument which they had used so long in keeping the African labourers in a state of serfdom was now being lifted. They accused the Government of yielding to "African agitators" and "irresponsible demagogues"! The settlers did not stop to ask themselves what would be the effect of the frustrated anger of the Kenya Africans. They did not understand that no human being, of whatever nationality, can keep on indefinitely without breaking through such frustration. After all, the Kenya Africans had carried their Vipande on their persons from 1921 to 1950, and yet the Kipande was only one of innumerable grievances.

The Europeans and the Asians were free from having Vipande. The psychological effect of the Kipande system was equal to that of an African calling a European "Bwana" instead of "Mr.", or of a European calling a seventy-year-old African "boy", or referring to "natives" without a capital "N", or "native locations" in the city instead of "African sections."

The Africans were constantly worried by these passes. I remember full well that, whenever my father mislaid his Kipande he was as much worried and unhappy as if he had been an important government official accused of accepting a vicuna coat from a private citizen!

There were also numerous other passes which were equally insulting, and principally the so-called "The Red-Book" issued by the Labour Exchange and which every African domestic servant was required to carry. In the Red-Book the character of the African concerned, the amount of pay he was receiving, and the cause of dismissal were to be recorded.

I remember well one afternoon when I was walking with Muchaba who had been my chief aide during my *irua* or circumcision ceremony. We were in Pangani, one of the sections of Nairobi, when we heard a voice far away call "Simama" or "Halt!" We did not pay too much attention since we were discussing family matters. Suddenly, we heard another voice shouting loudly: "You! Stop there!" We looked back and saw two policemen hurrying towards us. We suddenly had butterflies in our stomachs. We stopped and waited for them and, as they were approaching us, I whispered to Muchaba:

"Do you have your Kipande with you?"

"No, I don't have it," he replied.

"I don't have mine either."

"We'll catch hell now," Muchaba said.

The two policemen came up to us.

"Why didn't you stop at once when we called you?" the first one asked.

And the second one, sarcastically:

"Who do you think you are?" even before we had a chance to reply.

"At first we didn't know you were calling to us, sirs," Muchaba said. "We are very sorry."

"No, you look like law breakers, like most of the Kikuyu," one policeman said.

"Show us your Kipande quickly!" the second one demanded. "I don't have mine, I have just forgotten it," Muchaba replied.

"Where?"

"Where I work," Muchaba said.

"Where and for whom do you work?" asked the policeman. "I work for a European lady just near the Fair View Hotel."

"What do you do?"

"I am a cook," Muchaba replied.

"Do you have any other pass as an identification?" asked the policeman.

"No. But I can give you my employer's address and the telephone number if you like," Muchaba said.

"Idiot!" shouted the policeman. "How stupid can you get? Do you expect us to make telephone calls for all criminals we arrest without their Vipande? We are not your telephone operators."

"What can I do then?" asked Muchaba.

"Carry your Kipande with you," replied the policeman. "Incidentally, who is this fellow here with his arms folded like a great bwana. Do you have your Kipande?" They turned to me.

"No, I don't have it. I have never had a formal Kipande," I said.

"What!" they both exclaimed thunderously.

"When I joined the Medical Department in 1945 the Senior Medical Officer went with me to the Labour Exchange to obtain my Kipande but I found out that the copies of the formal Kipande were exhausted. I was given an emergency certificate and told to get a formal Kipande later on," I explained.

"Are you still in the Medical Department?" they asked.

"No, I am working for the Kenya African Union as an assistant editor," I said.

"Where do you live?" they asked.

"Kaloleni," I replied.

"Just because you are working for that trouble-making KAU you think you don't have to carry Kipande?"

"No, that is not the reason. I just forgot my emergency certificate. I don't think that KAU is trouble making. We fight for the rights of everyone in Kenya, including the police," I said.

They looked at each other, confused.

"Do you have any other papers as identification?" they asked.

"I have some papers with the letter-heading of the Kenya African Union."

"We are not interested in letter-heads. We want official documents. Any fool can produce letter-heads."

This comedy finally ended and they decided to take us to the police station.

We walked in front of them and they followed us. As we were walking I tried to get a handkerchief from my pocket to blow my nose. One policeman thought that I was insulting him by putting my hands in my pocket like a big bwana and hit me on my shoulder with his truncheon. He hit me hard. I tried to explain to him that my nose was running but I saw he was ready to hit me again, and so I kept quiet. Muchaba said nothing.

As we approached the police station I heard somebody calling: "Hey you, that's Mr. Mathu's man. What did he do?"

Muchaba and I were afraid to look back in case we should be hit again. The two policemen answered the call and then suddenly told us to stop. We turned round and saw two other policemen coming towards us. I recognized one of them. He was my classmate at Kambui Primary School and he knew both Muchaba and I full well. We were relieved and happy! The four policemen conferred together and the one who knew us explained to his colleagues that we must have been telling the truth, and that we should not be arrested. Two of them agreed but the third still wanted to go to the police station.

At last they let us go but by then Muchaba was very late in returning to his work. His employer was very, very angry, as her dinner was late. Muchaba had not telephoned and she had no idea where to find him.

I advised Muchaba to take a taxi but there was none in sight. It was getting too late. Finally he took a bus and, when he arrived at his employer's home, he found her waiting near the gate holding a pen.

"Bring your Red-Book right away. You have no job now. You are entirely unreliable, a lazy, untrustworthy African. I hate you bloody niggers," she said.

Muchaba had no chance to explain anything. He was told to pack up his belongings and leave at once. He had some heavy luggage and couldn't move it all at once and so he took it bit by bit to the nearest street. Finally he took a taxi and came to my place. I took a chance and let him stay with me for the night! If the police had knocked me up in the night and found him with me, both of us would have been in trouble.

That evening, as he had never learnt to read or write English, Muchaba asked me to tell him what had been written in his Red-Book. I know Muchaba very well to be a sensitive and intelligent man and was sickened to read: "He is quick in his work; he likes sweet things and may steal sugar if he has a chance; sometimes his thinking is like that of an eleven-year-old child." When Muchaba heard this he was so angry that he burnt the book. I cannot blame him for this but it put him in serious difficulty as no one would give him another job unless he produced the book, even this one with its permanent defamatory record. It was more than a month before the Labour Exchange agreed to issue Muchaba with a new book (I can only liken the process to that when one loses a passport), and then he was able to get another job working as a cook for a wealthy Indian businessman.

Muchaba's story can also illustrate the considerable licence allowed by their superiors to the ordinary police force, at that time largely illiterate, which in itself contributed to the atmosphere of European superiority and power which sapped the resistance of the unorganized African population.

In the evenings the police could knock on the door of any African in the African locations and demand to know how many people were sleeping there, how many had Kipande, and proof of where they were working. This could have happened to any African rooming place, and almost always the police called about eleven o'clock or midnight.

In some cases, a man and his wife might be sleeping peacefully but they had to open the door quickly. Police would then ask the man to produce Kipande and to say where he was working. They would search everywhere with their flash-lights and, if they were satisfied, would leave the place without even saying sorry to the couple they had awakened.

I remember full well when the police knocked up one of my uncles at about 12:45 a.m. When three policemen entered the room my uncle and his wife were trying to fix their pyjamas. One of the policemen shouted:

"How many people do you have in this room, eh?"

"Only my wife and myself, sir."

"How many people do you usually accommodate?" the second policeman demanded.

"None at all except my wife."

"My wife, my wife," the third policeman shouted. "How do we know she isn't just a prostitute from Manjengo, eh?"

"No! No! You have it all wrong. This is my own legal wife and if you insist on disagreeing with me please take me to the police station," Uncle protested vehemently. His pride and dignity were badly shaken. Utterly hurt.

The three policemen left. They had caused great upset and inconvenience to my uncle and his wife but he had no remedy. He could not sue the Police Department which could always say "They did this in the course of their duty to uproot undesirable natives," and excuse invariably accepted by their superiors.

I would illustrate the general attitude of their superiors to the police by quoting from The Report of the Committee on Police Terms of Service, 1942, which among other things says:

"The evidence submitted to us indicates that, in general, the illiterate African makes a better policeman than a literate African. The latter is less amenable to discipline and is reluctant to undertake the menial tasks which sometimes fall to the lot of ordinary constables. That being so, it seems to us that the policy of recruiting literates should be pursued with great caution, and that no special inducements by way of salary are necessary. In fact, we venture to go so far as to recommend the abolition of literacy allowance for new entrants."

75

Josiah Mwangi Kariuki, *'Mau Mau' Detainee*
(Baltimore, 1964), pp. 52–54, 55–59

JOSIAH MWANGI KARIUKI (1929-75) was a courageous Kenyan who opposed both the settler administration and corrupt postcolonial politicians and finally paid for his principles with his life. Like Mugo Gatheru, he was born to a family of squatters on a European farm in the Rift Valley. His education was fitful: he studied at three secondary schools and took correspondence courses to round out his training. Upon his return to Kenya from school in

Uganda in 1952 he joined the Movement of Unity. A year later he was arrested by British authorities and spent a total of seven years in detention camps. His book *'Mau Mau' Detainee* describes his experiences in the movement and in colonial prisons. Between 1961 and 1963 he served as private secretary to Jomo Kenyatta, who became the first president of Kenya. Between 1963 and 1975 he served in the Kenya Parliament and became a rallying point for opposition to the entrenched political leadership. In 1975 he was assassinated by unknown assailants.

I was very surprised to see banana stems as to the best of my knowledge there were no banana plantations in this part of the Rift Valley Province but Kanyoi told me that they had been cut in Kabatini Forest from the *shamba* of a man called Kaburu Chege who was known to me and who had lived there in the forest for many years. It was clear to me that this was where the oath would be given. Kanyoi had been behaving strangely throughout the evening and in some ways I think I had begun much earlier to guess what was about to happen. I was told to move over to a place where three other people who were all known to me were standing. We were to take the oath together. We were then ordered to remove our shoes and our watches and other metal things we had with us. Kanyoi pointed at me and told the people that I was a student from school who seemed to have a sincere wish to help the country and had been very active in persuading people to join the Kenya African Union. He believe that I was, therefore, the right sort of person to be given the Oath of Unity, *Ndemwa Ithatu,* as I was likely to be just as active in serving this movement as I had been in K.A.U. The other three who were in my group were hit about a little but because of Kanyoi's remarks about me the people said "Do not beat the student," and I was left alone. We passed through the arch seven times in single file and then stood silently in a line facing the oath administrator, whose name was Biniathi, waiting for the next part of the ceremony.

Biniathi held the lungs of a goat in his right hand and another piece of goat's meat in his left. We bowed towards the ground as he circled our heads seven times with the meat, counting aloud in Kikuyu. He then gave each of us in turn the lungs and told us to bite them. Next he ordered us to repeat slowly after him the following sentence:

I speak the truth and vow before God
And before this movement,
The movement of Unity,
The Unity which is put to the test
The Unity that is mocked with the name of "Mau Mau",
That I shall go forward to fight for the land,
The lands of Kirinyaga that we cultivated,
The lands which were taken by the Europeans
And if I fail to do this
May this oath kill me,
May this seven kill me,
May this meat kill me.

I speak the truth that I shall be working together
With the forces of the movement of Unity
And I shall help it with any contribution for which I am asked,
I am going to pay sixty-two shillings and fifty cents and a ram for
   the movement
If I do not have them now I shall pay in the future.
And if I fail to do this
May this oath kill me,
May this seven kill me,
May this meat kill me.

I was given a box on the ears for failing to repeat one sentence correctly. It was delivered by the administrator's assistant, who was standing beside him holding a gourd full of the blood of the goat used for the ceremony. Biniathi anointed each of us on the forehead with the blood, saying that he did this to remind us that we were now fighting for our land and to warn us never to think of selling our country.

After this Biniathi came to each of us individually and made three tiny scratches on our left wrists. This was the meaning of *Ndemwa Ithatu* (the three cuts) and it also explained Kanyoi's earlier search for a *Mukuha*. He then brought the other piece of meat to our wrists so that a few drops of our blood went on to it. Next he gave us in turn the meat to bite and while we were doing this he said, "The act of eating this meat with the blood of each one of you on it shows that you are now united one to the other and with us." This was the end of the ceremony and all four of us then went over to sit down with Kanyoi who wrote out our names and asked us to give him the five shillings special oathing fee, which we all did. We then went to wait among the other people in the maize and our shoes and watches were returned to us.

My emotions during the ceremony had been a mixture of fear and elation. Afterwards in the maize I felt exalted with a new spirit of power and strength. All my previous life seemed empty and meaningless. Even my education, of which I was so proud, appeared trivial beside this splendid and terrible force that had been given me. I had been born again and I sensed once more the feeling of opportunity and adventure that I had had on the first day my mother started teaching me to read and write. The other three in the maize were all silent and were clearly undergoing the same spiritual rebirth as myself. . . .

In the evening we all went to another house where some people had been skinning a goat. We sat down and Biniathi then told us to take all our clothes off except our trousers, and we stood patiently waiting to be called by him. I was called second after Kanyoi and there was no disobeying the summons.

I took off my trousers and squatted facing Biniathi. He told me to take the thorax of the goat which had been skinned, to put my penis through a hole that had been made in it, and to hold the rest of it in my left hand in front of me. Before me on the ground there were two small wooden stakes between which the thorax (ngata) of the goat was suspended and fastened. By my right hand on the floor of the hut were seven small sticks each about four inches long. Biniathi told me to take the sticks one at a time, to put them into the ngata, and slowly rub them in it while repeating after him these seven vows, one for each stick. (After each promise I was to bite the meat and throw the stick on to the ground on my left side.)

1. I speak the truth and vow before our God
    And by this *Batuni* oath of our movement
    Which is called the movement of fighting
    That if I am called on to kill for our soil
    If I am called on to shed my blood for it
    I shall obey and I shall never surrender
    And if I fail to go
    May this oath kill me,
    May this he-goat kill me,
    May this seven kill me,
    May this meat kill me.

2. I speak the truth and vow before our God
   And before our people of Africa
   That I shall never betray our country
   That I shall never betray anybody of this movement to the
      enemy
   Whether the enemy be European or African
   And if I do this
   May this oath kill me, etc.

3. I speak the truth and vow before our God
   That if I am called during the night or the day
   To go to burn the store of a European who is our enemy
   I shall go forth without fear and I shall never surrender
   And if I fail to do this
   May this oath kill me, etc.

4. I speak the truth and vow before our God
   That if I am called to go to fight the enemy
   Or to kill the enemy—I shall go
   Even if the enemy be my father or mother, my brother or sister
   And if I refuse
   May this oath kill me, etc.

5. I speak the truth and vow before our God
   That if the people of the movement come to me by day or night
   And if they ask me to hide them
   I shall do so and I shall help them
   And if I fail to do this
   May this oath kill me, etc.

6. I speak the truth and vow before our God
   That I shall never take away the woman of another man
   That I shall never walk with prostitutes
   That I shall never steal anything belonging to another person in
      the movement
   Nor shall I hate any other member for his actions
   And if I do any of these things
   May this oath kill me, etc.

7. I speak the truth and vow before our God
   And by this *Batuni* oath of our movement
   That I shall never sell my country for money or any other thing
   That I shall abide until my death by all the promises that I have
      made this day

That I shall never disclose our secrets to our enemy
Nor shall I disclose them to anybody who does not belong to the
  movement
And if I transgress against any of the vows that I have thus con-
  sciously made
I shall agree to any punishment that the movement shall decide
  to give me
And if I fail to do these things
May this oath kill me, etc.

When I had said all these things I removed the thorax and laid it
on the ground, put on my trousers and went to another part of the
hut where I paid to Kanyoi six shillings and fifty cents, which was
the oathing fee. Thus it was that I took the second or *Batuni* oath.
This word seems to be derived from the English "platoon" and the
oath itself was taken by all those who were likely to be called on to
give active service to the movement.

The second oath was much stronger than the first and left my
mind full of strange and excited feelings. My initiation was not
complete and I had become a true Kikuyu with no doubts where I
stood in the revolt of my tribe. Complete secrecy had again been
enjoined on us as even some of those administering the first oath
had not yet taken the *Batuni*. . . .

The *Muma wa Thenge* (the he-goat oath) is a prominent feature
of our social life, an integral part of the ceremonies uniting partners
in marriages, in the exchange or sale of land (before the Europeans
came, when land was plentiful, the sale of land was almost
unknown), or in transactions involving cattle or goats. The warriors also took an oath, known as *Muma wa Aanake* (the oath of
the warriors) to bind them before going on a raid. The purpose of
all these oaths was to give those participating a feeling of mutual
respect, unity, and shared love, to strength their relationship, to
keep away any bad feelings, and to prevent any disputes. Most important of all, groups bound together by this ceremony would
never invoke sorcery against each other. The fear of being killed by
sorcery was prevalent among our people. The *muma* (oath)
removed that fear and created a new and special relationship between the families and clans involved. Envy, hate, and enmity
would be unknown between them.

The Oath of Unity (given the mysterious and sinister name of

"Mau Mau" by a cunning propaganda machine) had the same background. It was intended to unite not only the Kikuyu, Embu, and Meru but all the other Kenya tribes. These might not give their oaths in the same way, but every tribe in Kenya had an oath for bringing together and solemnizing certain transactions. It is not really surprising that the movement should have started first among the Kikuyu. They more than any other tribe felt the despair brought by pressing economic poverty; they more than any other tribe by their proximity to the forcing house of Nairobi were subject to urban pressures and the great increase in understanding and frustration brought by education; they more than any other tribe daily saw the lands that had been taken from them producing rich fruits for Europeans.

76

Proclamation of the National Liberation Front, November 1, 1954

in Michael K. Clark, *Algeria in Turmoil* (New York, 1959), pp. 112–13. Translated by Clark

THIS DOCUMENT is the Algerian equivalent of the American declaration of independence. Issued by the newly formed National Liberation Front, it announced the goals of the Algerian revolutionary movement. As in the American case, it took the colonizing power over seven years of bloody warfare to recognize the former colony's independence.

To the Algerian People!
To the militants of the National Cause!

After decades of struggle, the National Movement has reached its final phase of fulfillment. At home, the people are united behind the watchwords of independence and action. Abroad, the atmosphere is favorable, especially with the diplomatic support of our Arab and Moslem brothers.

Our National Movement, prostrated by years of immobility and routine, badly directed, was disintegrating little by little. Faced with this situation, a youthful group, gathering about it the majority of wholesome and resolute elements, judged that the moment had come to take the National Movement out of the impasse into which it had been forced by the conflicts of persons and of influence and to launch it into the true revolutionary struggle at the side of the Moroccan and Tunisian brothers.

We are independent of the two factions that are vying for power. Our movement gives to compatriots of every social position, to all the purely Algerian parties and movements, the possibility of joining in the liberation struggle.

GOAL. National independence through: 1) the restoration of the Algerian state, sovereign, democratic, and social, within the framework of the principles of Islam; 2) the preservation of all fundamental freedoms, without distinction of race or religion.

INTERNAL OBJECTIVE: Political house-cleaning through the destruction of the last vestiges of corruption and reformism.

EXTERNAL OBJECTIVES: 1) The internationalization of the Algerian problem; 2) The pursuit of North African unity in its national Arabo-Islamic context; 3) The assertion, through United Nations channels, of our active sympathy toward all nations that may support our liberating action.

MEANS OF STRUGGLE: Struggle by every means until our goal is attained. Exertion at home and abroad through political and direct action, with a view to making the Algerian problem a reality for the entire world. The struggle will be long, but the outcome is certain.

To limit the bloodshed, we propose an honorable platform for discussion with the French authorities:

1. The opening of negotiations with the authorized spokesmen of the Algerian people, on the basis of a recognition of Algerian sovereignty, one and indivisible.
2. The inception of an atmosphere of confidence brought about by freeing all those who are detained, by annulling all measures of exception, and by ending all legal action against the combatant forces.
3. The recognition of Algerian nationhood by an official declaration abrogating all edicts, decrees, and laws by virtue of which Algeria was "French soil."

In return for which:

1. French cultural and economic interests will be respected, as well as persons and families.
2. All French citizens desiring to remain in Algeria will be allowed to opt for their original nationality, in which case they will be considered as foreigners, or for Algerian nationality, in which case they will be considered as Algerians, equal both as to rights and as to duties.
3. The ties between France and Algeria will be the object of agreement between the two Powers on the basis of equality and mutual respect.

Algerians: The F. L. N. is your front; its victory is your victory. For our part, strong in your support, we shall give the best of ourselves to the Fatherland.

77

Frantz Fanon, *Les damnés de la terre*

(Paris, 1961); Eng. trans. *The Wretched of the Earth* (New York, 1966), pp. 203–6. Translated by Constance Farrington

FRANTZ FANON (1925-61) has become the patron saint of Third World liberation movements. Born on the Caribbean island of Martinique, Fanon volunteered for the Free French army during the Second World War. He entered medical school in France in 1945 and became a psychiatrist in 1950. From that time onward he divided his time between the physical and the spiritual. In 1952 he published his first book on the psychology of colonialism, *Black Skin, White Masks*. In 1953 he became head of the psychiatric department of a government hospital in Algeria, where he observed the beginning of the Algerian revolution. Between 1954 and 1956, he maintained his government job while secretly aiding the National Liberation Front. He then resigned in order to devote himself full-time to publicizing the revolution. While working for the NLF in Tunis, he became convinced that the Algerian war was only part of a larger colonial struggle, a view which he presented in his most famous book, *The Wretched of the Earth*, published shortly before his death. In the last year of his life, Fanon served as ambassador of the Provisional Government of Algeria to Ghana, where he became disillusioned with the veniality of postcolonial politicians.

COLONIAL WAR AND MENTAL DISORDERS

But the war goes on; and we will have to bind up for years to come the many, sometimes ineffaceable, wounds that the colonialist onslaught has inflicted on our people.

That imperialism which today is fighting against a true liberation of mankind leaves in its wake here and there tinctures of decay which we must search out and mercilessly expel from our land and our spirits.

We shall deal here with the problem of mental disorders which arise from the war of national liberation which the Algerian people are carrying on.

Perhaps these notes on psychiatry will be found ill-timed and singularly out of place in such a book; but we can do nothing about that.

We cannot be held responsible that in this war psychiatric phenomena entailing disorders affecting behavior and thought have taken or importance where those who carry out the "pacification" are concerned, or that these same disorders are notable among the "pacified" population. The truth is that colonialism in its essence was already taking on the aspect of a fertile purveyor for psychiatric hospitals. We have since 1954 in various scientific works drawn the attention of both French and international psychiatrists to the difficulties that arise when seeking to "cure" a native properly, that is to say, when seeking to make him thoroughly a part of a social background of the colonial type.

Because it is a systematic negation of the other person and a furious determination to deny the other person all attributes of humanity, colonialism forces the people it dominates to ask themselves the question constantly: "In reality, who am I?"

The defensive attitudes created by this violent bringing together of the colonized man and the colonial system form themselves into a structure which then reveals the colonized personality. This "sensitivity" is easily understood if we simply study and are alive to the number and day spent amidst the colonial regime. It must in any case be remembered that a colonized people is not only simply a dominated people. Under the German occupation the French remained men; under the French occupation, the Germans remained men. In Algeria there is not simply the domination but the decision to the letter not to occupy anything more than the sum total of the land. The Algerians, the veiled women, the palm trees and the camels make up the landscape, the natural background to the human presence of the French.

Hostile nature, obstinate and fundamentally rebellious, is in fact represented in the colonies by the bush, by mosquitoes, natives, and fever, and colonization is a success when all this indocile nature has finally been tamed. Railways across the bush, the draining of swamps and a native population which is non-existent politically and economically are in fact one and the same thing.

In the period of colonization when it is not contested by armed resistance, when the sum total of harmful nervous stimuli overstep a certain threshold, the defensive attitudes of the natives give way and they then find themselves crowding the mental hospitals. There is thus during this calm period of successful colonization a regular and important mental pathology which is the direct product of oppression.

Today the war of national liberation which has been carried on by the Algerian people for the last seven years has become a favorable breeding ground for mental disorders, because so far as the Algerians are concerned it is a total war. We shall mention here some Algerian cases which have been attended by us and who seem to us to be particularly eloquent. We need hardly say that we are not concerned with producing a scientific work. We avoid all arguments over semiology, nosology, or therapeutics. The few technical terms used serve merely as references. We must, however, insist on two points. Firstly, as a general rule, clinical psychiatry classifies the different disturbances shown by our patients under the heading "reactionary psychoses." In doing this, prominence is given to the event which has given rise to the disorder, although in some cases mention is made of the previous history of the case (the psychological, affective, and biological condition of the patient) and of the type of background from whence he comes. It seems to us that in the cases here chosen the events giving rise to the disorder are chiefly the bloodthirsty and pitiless atmosphere, the generalization of inhuman practices, and the firm impression that people have of being caught up in a veritable Apocalypse.

Case No. 2 of Series A is a typical reactionary psychosis, but

Case Nos. 1, 2, 4, and 5 of Series B give evidence of a much more widely spread causality although we cannot really speak of one particular event giving rise to the disorders. These are reactionary psychoses, if we want to use a ready-made label; but here we must give particular priority to the war: a war which in whole and in part is a colonial war. After the great world wars, there is no lack of publications on the mental pathology of soldiers taking part in action and civilians who are victims of evacuations and bombardments. The hitherto unemphasized characteristics of certain psychiatric descriptions here given confirm, if confirmation were necessary, that this colonial war is singular even in the pathology that it gives rise to.

Another idea which is strongly held needs in our opinion to be re-examined; this is the notion of the relative harmlessness of these reactional disorders. It is true that others have described, but always as exceptional cases, certain secondary psychoses, that is to say cases where the whole of the personality is disrupted definitively. It seems to us that here the rule is rather the frequent malignancy of these pathological processes. These are disorders which persist for months on end, making a mass attack against the ego, and practically always leaving as their sequel a weakness which is almost visible to the naked eye. According to all available evidence, the future of such patients is mortgaged. An example will best illustrate our point of view.

In one of the African countries which have been independent for several years we had occasion to receive a visit from a patriot who had been in the resistance. This man in his thirties came to ask us for advice and help, for around a certain date each year he suffered from prolonged insomnia, accompanied by anxiety and suicidal obsessions. The critical date was that when on instructions from his organization he had placed a bomb somewhere. Ten people had been killed as a result.

This militant, who never for a single moment thought of repudiating his past action, realized very clearly the manner in which he himself had to pay the price of national independence. It is borderline cases such as his which raise the question of responsibility within the revolutionary framework.

78

Text of the legal complaint by Djamila Boupacha, May 1960

in Simone de Beauvoir and Gisèle Halimi, *Djamila Boupacha* (Paris, 1962), Eng. trans. *Djamila Boupacha* (New York, 1962), pp. 191–93. Translated by Peter Green

DJAMILA BOUPACHA was born in the city of Algiers in 1938. She was a sympathizer of the National Liberation Front and was suspected by French authorities of planting a bomb, which had been defused before it could explode, at the University of Algiers in September of 1959. Arrested by French authorities in February 1960, she, her brother-in-law, and seventy-year-old father were subjected to torture, and she confessed to the accusation. After her ordeal, she filed a civil suit against French authorities and attracted a wide following in France.

During the night of 10/11th February, 1960, a party of about fifty *gardes mobiles, harkis* and police inspectors drove up to my parent's house at Dely Ibrahim, Algiers, in jeeps and army trucks, and dismounted there. One of them was Captain D—, on secondment to the El Biar Centre. I was resident at my parent's house at the time. I was savagely beaten up there before even being taken away. My brother-in-law Abdelli Ahmed, who was present that evening, suffered a similar ordeal, as did my father Abdelaziz Boupacha, who is seventy years old.

All three of us were removed to the Classification Centre [*Centre de Tri*] at El Biar. There I received a second beating up, so violent that I was knocked off my feet and collapsed. It was then that certain military personnel, including a captain in the paratroops, kicked my ribs in. I still suffer from a costal displacement on my left side.

After four or five days I was transferred to Hussein Dey. This, I had been told, was where I would get a taste of the "third degree." I found out what this implied—firstly, torture by electricity. (Since the electrodes would not stay in place when affixed to my nipples, one of my torturers fastened them on with Scotch tape.) I received similar electrical burns on my legs, face, anus, and vagina. This electrical torture was interspersed with cigarette-burns, blows, and the "bath treatment": I was trussed up and hung over a bath on a stick, and submerged till I nearly choked.

A few days later I was given the most appalling torture of all, the so-called "bottle treatment." First they tied me up in a special posture, and then they rammed the neck of a bottle into my vagina. I screamed and fainted. I was unconscious, to the best of my knowledge, for two days.

During the earlier part of my time in El Biar, I was brought into the presence of my brother-in-law Abdelli Ahmed, who also bore the most frightful marks of the beatings and tortures he had undergone. Nor was my father spared, despite his great age.

On 15th May, 1960, I was formally committed and charged with attempted wilful murder and consorting with malefactors. When brought before the examining magistrate I repeated the confession that had been forcibly extracted from me, under torture, by my inquisitors. I was then, and am still, severely shocked and shaken by my terrible ordeal. To my own sufferings must be added my father's experience—a most frightful shock for an old man—of seeing his twenty-year-old daughter still disfigured by the tortures she had endured.

My father is at present interned in the camp at Beni-Messous, but earlier his condition gave rise to such anxiety that he had to spend nearly a week in the Maillot Hospital.

My brother-in-law is under detention in the Civil Prison, Algiers, and his case is being dealt with separately from mine. Yet they are intimately linked: we were arrested on the same day, and the "malefactors" we stand accused of "consorting with" are the same men on the run. The reason for this separation is obvious. My brother-in-law and I are each a witness to the fact of the other's torture, and the authorities well might fear that if we were brought into a public courtroom together, we should testify to our common experience.

Though I chose Maître Gisèle Halimi of the Paris Bar as my defending counsel several weeks ago, it is only today that she has been able to come and see me, since her visitor's permit for Algiers was (with singular restrictiveness) made valid for three days, only, i.e. *from 16th to 19th May, 1960.*

The facts adduced above constitute the crime of wrongful detention of the person, with aggravating circumstances as under, *in that the aforesaid wrongful detention was prolonged for over a month, and accompanied by "physical torture."* These crimes are covered, and penalized, by Articles 341, 342, and 344 *in fine* of the new Penal Code. In the circumstances, *Monsieur le Juge d'Instruction,* I have the honour to lodge with you an indictment in respect of the aforesaid crimes, and hereby constitute myself plaintiff in the civil suit arising therefrom. [*Signed*) Boupacha. Detainee [No. 1134] in Algiers Prison. Algiers, 17th May, 1960.

79

The Evian Agreements, May 1962

in David C. Gordon, *The Passing of French Algeria* (London, 1966), p. 78. Translated by Gordon

THE EVIAN AGREEMENTS were the political documents which finally brought the Algerian War to an end. They represent the realization of the aims announced by the NLF's first proclamation so many years earlier.

Culture: While Algeria is to retain French cultural institutions it is not bound to them indefinitely. Some radio broadcasts and official texts are to be made available in French and the European population will be able to conduct administrative business in French. French schools can be established in Algeria (following the French system); periodicals and newspapers will enjoy mutual free passage between Algeria and France; provisions will be made for the study of the culture of each nation in the other's territory; Algerian higher education, with French aid, will be modelled on the French system.

Citizenship: Europeans (who can prove regular residence) will have three years to opt for Algerian citizenship or to be considered foreigners; the converse is true for Algerians in France. In the interim each will enjoy civil rights in the other's country, but not political rights. Europeans will be given representation in the Algerian parliament in proportion to their numbers, but only in a single college in which each delegate will vote as a separate individual. An "Association de Sauvegarde" will function to represent the interests of the European community but will play no political role. Provisions are made to set up a Court of Guarantees for Europeans who feel discriminated against.

Economics: Algeria will remain in the franc zone but is free to establish protective tariffs and to negotiate its own proper relationship to the Common Market. The Algerian Government is allowed to nationalize land and property provided this is done without discriminating between European and Moslem and that compensation is offered. France will contribute to the compensation of dispossessed Europeans. (The nationalization of oil is not precluded by any article.) Capital can be withdrawn from Algeria provided this is not seriously harmful to Algeria's economy. French Sahara development schemes will continue to operate with profits shared between the two countries. France will provide technical assistance, training, and personnel to the best of her ability, wherever needed.

Military: French air bases and installations in Amguel, In Ekker, Colombe-Béchar, and Reggane will be maintained by France (for five years, and flight to them is assured). The airfields in Bône and Boufarik will be kept for the same period and the Mers el Kebir naval base is leased by France for fifteen years.

Boldface numerals refer to document numbers

Index